THE DISTRIBUTED CLASSROOM

Learning in Large-Scale Environments
Justin Reich and Nichole Pinkard

Writers in the Secret Garden: Fanfiction, Youth, and New Forms of Mentoring, Cecilia Aragon and Katie Davis, 2019

Peer Pedagogies on Digital Platforms: Learning with Minecraft Let's Plays on YouTube, Michael Dezuanni, 2020

A Manifesto for Teaching Online, Siân Bayne, Peter Evans, Rory Ewins, Jeremy Knox, James Lamb, Hamish Macleod, Clara O'Shea, Jen Ross, Phil Sheail, and Christine Sinclair, 2020

The Distributed Classroom, David A. Joyner and Charles Isbell, 2021

THE DISTRIBUTED CLASSROOM

DAVID A. JOYNER AND CHARLES ISBELL

THE MIT PRESS   CAMBRIDGE, MASSACHUSETTS   LONDON, ENGLAND

The MIT Press would like to thank the anonymous peer reviewers who provided comments on drafts of this book. The generous work of academic experts is essential for establishing the authority and quality of our publications. We acknowledge with gratitude the contributions of these otherwise uncredited readers.

This book was set in ITC Stone and Avenir by New Best-set Typesetters Ltd. Printed and bound in the United States of America.

Library of Congress Cataloging-in-Publication Data

Names: Joyner, David, author. | Isbell, Charles, author.
Title: The distributed classroom / David A. Joyner and Charles Isbell.
Description: Cambridge, Massachusetts : The MIT Press, 2021. |
    Series: Learning in large-scale environments | Includes
    bibliographical references and index.
Identifiers: LCCN 2020053035 | ISBN 9780262046053 (hardcover)
Subjects: LCSH: Education, Higher—Effect of technological
    innovations on. | Internet in higher education. | Web-based
    instruction. | Blended learning. | Open learning.
Classification: LCC LB2395.7 .J69 2021 | DDC 378.1/7344678—dc23
LC record available at https://lccn.loc.gov/2020053035

10   9   8   7   6   5   4   3   2   1

CONTENTS

SERIES FOREWORD

Learning across the life span is more important than ever, and with the wealth of resources and communities available online, there has never been a better time to be a learner. Learners of all ages—in formal and informal settings—are turning to online tools to help them develop new skills and knowledge, for work, school, and leisure. The field of large-scale learning engages in the study of networked environments with many, many learners and few experts to guide them.

Large-scale learning environments are incredibly diverse: massive open online courses (MOOCs), intelligent tutoring systems, open learning courseware, learning games, citizen science communities, collaborative programming communities, community tutorial systems, social learning networks, and countless informal communities of learners on platforms such as Reddit, YouTube, and fanfiction sites. These systems either depend upon the direct participation of large numbers of learners in a single instance, or they are enriched by continuous improvement based on analyzing data generated by many learners over time. They share a common purpose—to increase human potential—and a common infrastructure of data and computation to enable learning at scale.

Technologies for large-scale learning are sometimes built deliberately, as in the case of MOOC platforms, and they are sometimes adapted from technologies originally developed for other purposes, as in the case of video-sharing sites. In some cases, they are used by individual learners around the world, and in other cases, large-scale learning environments are embedded within more traditional and small-scale educational systems such as classrooms and schools. They can be used to foster human capacity and create new opportunities, but they can also be used to teach and spread hateful ideologies. With a capacious enough definition of learning, large-scale learning technologies are implicated in nearly every part of the human experience in the networked world, from schooling to professional learning to politics to health care and beyond.

The Learning in Large-Scale Environments series from the MIT Press seeks to investigate, critique, and explain these large-scale environments and the various ways they are hybridized with residential learning space. Just as large-scale learning environments are diverse, our series includes books with a diverse set of methodological and theoretical perspectives, ranging from learning science to computer science to sociocultural research traditions. The series examines large-scale learning environments at multiple levels, including technological underpinnings, policy consequences, social contexts and relationships, learning frameworks, and the experiences of educators and learners who use them. Our hope is that researchers will find valuable contributions to the scholarly literature and that educators and policy makers will find useful insights as they consider how best to support the learning needs of students of all ages around the world.

Justin Reich
Nichole Pinkard
Series Editors, Learning in Large-Scale Environments

PREFACE ON COVID-19

Over the last year, we have seen an unprecedented rapid shift to remote, online, and hybrid learning driven by the COVID-19 pandemic. Schools and universities around the world have had to quickly figure out how to teach online.

Much has already been made of this emergency change. Skeptics of remote learning have urged the community to treat this as a temporary shift, noting the numerous perceived weaknesses of online education.[1] Advocates have looked at this as an opportunity to speed up the shift to more remote options, noting its benefits to cost, access, and scale.[2] Students have spoken up as well: many have regarded the online experience as so inferior as to be worth lawsuits seeking the return of tuition dollars.[3] While some students have reflected positively on the transition,[4] the overall impression from students, parents, and teachers has been largely negative; the push to remain remote, partially or completely, throughout fall 2020 and into spring 2021 came largely from health concerns, not faith in online learning.

During the early part of the pandemic (at least in the United States), this emergency shift was been toward exclusively remote education: all students were online, all classes were online, and there was no in-person experience. One complete experience was replaced with another. In some ways, this simplifies the transition: classes are replaced one-to-one with remote analogues. While the world of online education is new to many faculty and students, it is not entirely new on its own: distance learning has existed for over a century, and modern technology has moved it more into the mainstream than ever before, with most colleges offering some online classes and programs in a typical distance-learning model. Under this model, the assumption from the outset is that all students are remote. This is how we in Georgia Tech's College of Computing run our online Master of Science in Computer Science (OMSCS) program. Launched in 2014 under the leadership of then Dean Zvi Galil,[5] we have grown to over eleven thousand students from all around the world, and none of them are required to come to campus. In addition to serving as the college's current Dean (Charles) and the program's executive director (David), we teach six classes between us, totaling over three thousand students each semester.

So for all the complexity involved in navigating new and unfamiliar platforms and technologies, there was also some simplicity in this transition: entirely in-person courses were transitioned to entirely remote courses. The two structures could be considered alternatives. There are design decisions to be made within each, of course, such as whether an online course should be synchronous or asynchronous, but the distinction between in-person and remote is clear.

As the pandemic dragged on, however, the situation became more complex. As colleges were planning for fall 2020 and beyond, they began facing decisions about remaining all online or pursuing a hybrid model. Under a hybrid model, there would once again be an in-person experience, but with heavy restrictions. Class sizes would be limited. Large classes might progress in small mini-sections, with each student spending a fraction as much time in the classroom. Some students and instructors might be unable to return to campus due to visa issues or medical conditions, requiring their own remote access. The threat of another sudden emergency shift would loom over course designs. Some classes would be offered online. Some students would attend online classes. Some students might exclusively attend online classes, while still others participate on campus. The number of combinations and permutations of the multitude of variables was mind-boggling, and it was difficult to give any individual teacher good advice on how to handle their unique class situation.

At the core of this difficulty, though, was the desire to bring back the in-person experience as much as possible. If the online experience was believed to be universally equivalent to the in-person experience, then students, teachers, and administrators would likely not hesitate to remain online for the foreseeable future. But there is a belief that the classroom experience is superior, and we would argue that belief hangs on that word choice: *classroom*. There are dynamics and experiences and interactions that occur in person that do not automatically translate to online learning because of the lack of a "classroom." This criticism is not specific to remote learning either; the same objection is lodged at large lecture halls, again for lacking interactions we would more commonly attach to classrooms: conversation among peers, communication with teachers, personalized input on one's work, and peripheral participation with a social learning community. There is an old adage that "distance education starts in the third row" which reflects this tension: students who are not sitting up front and actively engaged may as well be distance learners.

For years, this issue has plagued large core classes and upper-level classes for in-demand fields, but in the wake of COVID-19, it began to affect everyone: How do you build a classroom experience when you cannot gather all your students together at the same place and time? How do you create meaningful interactions—both direct and peripheral—between students and faculty and among students themselves without synchronous co-location? Why do so many of these remote learning experiments—and distance learning classes before them—lack the feel of a classroom?

This book presents a vision of a "distributed" classroom: a learning experience that retains that classroom environment but distributed across time and space. Rather than defining a classroom as a physical location used by a co-located group of students and teachers at a shared time, a distributed classroom looks at how characteristics of that environment may be shared with remote and asynchronous learners. It describes a view on learning that is not dependent on the typical same-time, same-place assumption of traditional education, but also one that does not swing all the way to the other extreme of full asynchronous remote learning.

It seeks to fill in the entire spectrum of synchronicity and co-location from one extreme to the other, asking students only to make the minimum necessary trade-off needed to achieve a particular level of access to the learning experience. It is not merely a way of teaching remotely, but a way of proactively organizing the classroom experience to exist independent of other constraints. It strives to allow learners to participate regardless of location and time, but without the heavy compromises in interaction and assessment made toward that end by efforts like MOOCs.

More than anything else, the distributed classroom strives to present an optimistic, learner-centric view of remote learning and the future of education, one where every person on earth is turned into a potential learner as barriers of cost, geography, and synchronicity disappear. In the process, it reorients the discussion of online education from a separate mechanism for transmitting content to a new medium for extending an experience.

We developed these ideas in the context of continuity planning for COVID-19, but nothing about this vision is specific to the pandemic; we strongly believe it was coming in the next several decades. This vision provides a plan for designing educational experiences that allow us to survive the present, but also to prepare for the future. In addition, it provides guidelines for how this paradigm can be used to students' benefit rather than the benefit of other competing demands.

Several parallel trends over the past decade have already laid the groundwork for these developments, from the proliferation of learning management systems to the emergence of new course formats like HyFlex and flipped classrooms.[6]

This vision brings them together into a cohesive, prescriptive blueprint for leveraging these trends to solve both old and new problems. For years, there has been a need for lower-cost, more accessible, and more distributed educational options at all levels, from kindergarten through adult learners. The student loan crisis in the United States, the vast discrepancies in learning opportunities based on socioeconomic status, and the concentration of institutions in a small number of countries all need to be addressed. These problems, however, are vague and distant, and there is enormous inertia behind the status quo. The problems presented by the pandemic, however, were clear and immediate, providing the sort of critical mass to realize major change in a short period of time. Just as mRNA-based vaccines like those developed for COVID-19 are now being created to address older viruses like influenza and HIV, so also progress made to make remote learning more widely available during the pandemic can now be pointed at older problems like inequitable access.[7]

The vision of the distributed classroom presents a way to address immediate concerns, but it is not merely a stopgap for the remainder of the pandemic; it is a vision of how education can and should work in the coming decades. COVID-19 has been a challenge, but also an opportunity to address these issues in durable ways that will retain their advantages after the crisis is over. The distributed classroom encourages us to look excitedly to the future rather than longingly at the past—and not to ask ourselves when things will return to normal but rather how we were ever satisfied with "normal" in the first place.

I

WHERE WE ARE NOW

1

THE CLASSIC DICHOTOMY

Students' enrollment in distance-learning classes and programs has been rising significantly over the past several years, bolstered by the growth of online education. According to data from the National Center for Education Statistics, in fall 2018, 34.7 percent of all postsecondary students were enrolled in at least one distance-education class, and 16.3 percent were enrolled exclusively in distance education classes.[1] At the K–12 level, most states now offer public online virtual academies, while there are also significant for-profit players in the space offering fully online class experiences. At the same time, however, many teachers, students, and employers remain skeptical of online education.[2]

We do not bring these studies up to highlight the growth of online education, which you likely already know about; nor do we bring them up to let you know that online education has skeptics, which you likely also already know. We

bring this up to point out that research on online education frequently assumes a clear dichotomy between online
and face-to-face. If your perception is based on the research,
the national conversation, and the legal statutes, then it
appears that face-to-face and online education exist largely
separately. Asking the questions, "How is online education
perceived?" and "How have online programs grown?" places
online education into a separate, largely distinct category.

This distinction has far-ranging implications. For example, the US Department of Education's guidelines contain
dedicated definitions for interaction in online classes, man-
dating that they be "regular and substantive," a term not
applied to in-person classes and poorly defined as it pertains
to new technologies.[3] Financial aid programs often distin-
guish online classes and degrees from face-to-face programs;
for example, the Pennsylvania Higher Education Assistance
Agency State Grant (PHEAASG) is not available to students
taking more than half of their classes online.[4] Students may
not be eligible to apply for visas to enroll in classes proven
to be deliverable online, a point of concern during the rapid
shift to remote education in the wake of COVID-19.[5] Critically, these rules all rely on the existence of a clear distinction between online and face-to-face classes.

That clear distinction exists at different levels. At the
highest level, we can juxtapose entirely online universities
or school systems—like Ashford University and Florida Virtual School—with traditional universities and school systems. We can also segment that down, finding online degree
programs within traditional universities; these may have a
corresponding campus program, like our online MSCS program at Georgia Tech, which grants the same degree as the

face-to-face program, or they may be exclusively online, like the University of Illinois iMBA program, which led to the discontinuation of its residential MBA program.[6] We can often scale down even further, finding specific online classes available to students otherwise enrolled in person, as noted by the PHEAASG regulations; many universities offer online classes to high school dual-enrollment students as well, such as David's own online CS1301 class, Introduction to Computing, at Georgia Tech. But regardless of the level, the distinction exists.

Why the distinction? Implicit in this dichotomy is the need for comparison. How do students' outcomes differ in online and traditional educational environments? How do the costs differ? How does access differ? How can online education be used to reach communities that lack high-quality traditional education? What are the risks of online education to hidden social functions played by traditional education? These questions are asked over and over, reinforcing the either-or dichotomy between the two areas. More problematic, the implication of the different treatment of online classes by the law, financial aid, and public opinion is that online classrooms are in some way inferior. Rarely do we see incentives for more online classes, but we frequently see regulations limiting the number of online classes that students may take. Universities often attach the word *online* to degrees given via online delivery mechanisms, insinuating that the degree itself must be differentiated from in-person alternatives.[7]

These broad comparisons are unfair. Neither online nor traditional education is a monolithic entity consistent across all locales, schools, and subjects. To illustrate the range of possible differences, we take the example of an online undergraduate class we launched in January 2017 at Georgia Tech. In developing this class, we paid close attention to the research showing that learning outcomes often tend to lag in online classes compared to traditional classes. We wanted to ensure that the online class—CS1301: Introduction to Computing—could promise comparable learning gains to the traditional version of the same curriculum before rolling it out to a larger audience. The class we produced ended up turning out students who learned as much as or more than students in a traditional version of the class.[8] Other experiments at MIT and Carnegie Mellon have found similar results.[9] The class has been offered every semester (fifteen terms total) since, totaling over three thousand course completers for credit, and has also been launched as a MOOC; over ten thousand students have completed a MOOC version of the course. This scale was possible only because of the favorable learning gains we observed in our experiments over the first couple of years of delivering the course: without evidence of the learning outcomes, we would have been reluctant to expand the course so heavily.

These results run counter to an influential thread of research about online education, where the finding has been that outcomes suffer in online environments compared to traditional environments. In response to this result, some have argued that students in selective and prestigious research institutions like MIT, Georgia Tech, and Carnegie Mellon are themselves better prepared to succeed in online classes; they possess the discipline and self-regulation skills necessary to monitor their own progress with limited external structures ensuring their continued engagement.[10] Much of the research finding poorer outcomes in online classes comes from community colleges and MOOC providers, and so some argue that the achievement difference is due to differences in the students. Online classes, then, could contribute to a widening of the achievement gap as they allow already well-educated students to move forward even faster based on their ability to succeed in more flexibly-available online courses.

Others—ourselves included—pose a different explanation. These large research institutions have and are devoting significant resources to developing online initiatives. When David developed our online Introduction to Computing class, we spent a full year writing the textbook, filming the lectures, and developing the initial assessments. We had a team of nearly a dozen people supporting David, including video producers, textbook copyeditors, project managers, technologists, and teaching assistants; in many ways, we had far more support than even traditional face-to-face classes have, before we even consider David's own prior experience teaching online. Our online master's-level courses are similarly developed by teams of professors, teaching assistants, instructional technologists, and project managers using world-class facilities. It is perhaps unsurprising that such a large investment of resources creates an educational experience leading to superior learning outcomes.

Although our offerings are all asynchronous, this increased investment can be seen in synchronous environments as well. In 2014, Harvard University launched HBX, a virtual synchronous classroom that had many features—such as virtual hand-raising and a lecture hall–like visualization—that have become major parts of the use of tools like Zoom and Microsoft Teams in the post-COVID-19 shift to remote learning.[11] Minerva Schools at KGI, a joint project between Keck Graduate Institute and the Minerva Project, uses a custom virtual classroom interface called Forum with features for efficient breakout groups, live class polls and discussions, and dynamic collaboration.[12] The same investment we made in high-quality recorded course material and artificially intelligent autograders can instead be made into platforms that support efficient synchronous interactions. Most schools, however, do not typically invest so heavily into individual courses; it is not uncommon for teachers at community colleges to learn only weeks before a semester starts that their class will be online. How can the learning outcomes of these wildly different types of course offerings be lumped together under the catchall category of "online"?

So, comparing online and traditional education is already an erroneous endeavor: there are so many different ways to conduct both experiences. We are not concerned here with which is considered better or worse; our concern is with the extent to which we consider them mutually exclusive opposites in the first place. Our concern is that the question posed to teachers is often first, "Do you want to teach online or in person?" rather than deeper questions about who, what, and how to teach.

THE DISTRIBUTED CLASSROOM

Adopting the dichotomy between online and traditional education introduces numerous problems, but here we are most interested in the extent to which adopting that paradigm limits the design decisions that we make. In electing to teach in person, we take for granted several of the constraints that the decision carries: our class size will be limited, our presentations will be live, and the physical classroom serves as the "home" of all classroom instruction and administration. In deciding to teach online, we may instead assume compromises that need not necessarily be made, such as that instruction will be more one-directional and asynchronous, that interaction among students will be more limited, and that assessments must be more summative and rote. Most important, in teaching online, we risk losing many of the functional and pedagogical roles played by the physical classroom, such as fostering peripheral community, supporting interaction among peers, and facilitating rapid feedback between students and teachers. In effect, we risk teaching without a classroom.

We propose in this book that instead we ought to dispense with the dichotomy between online and traditional instruction. Universities, programs, and classes need not be labeled as specifically "online" or "traditional." The alternative is that we no longer need to view classes as located in specific times and locations at all.

This is the notion of the distributed classroom, the premise of this book. In this context, *distributed* means that the class is not restricted in time or space, but rather can be distributed across multiple locations and multiple times. It breaks the assumption that a traditional class must meet together in a room—as well as the assumption that an online class should exist entirely without a classroom.

By that definition of *distributed* alone, distributed education options are already abundant: MOOCs, HyFlex courses, asynchronous online degree programs, informal learning communities, and more already represent distributed learning. However, the second part of the term—distributed *classroom*—is not merely a throwaway noun to give the adjective something to modify. In the distributed classroom, "classroom" is as important as "distributed." *Classroom* is not merely a stand-in term for any learning environment; rather, it refers to the specific roles that a classroom plays in traditional education, especially those that rely on live, and ideally in-person, communication, potentially making use of affordances of the shared physical classroom. While some underlying functions of the physical classroom may be offloaded to other interfaces—a course forum for questions and discussion, tools like Peer Feedback[13] and Peerceptiv[14] for peer review—there remain others that do not translate evenly into an asynchronous remote environment, like group work on a shared physical artifact, creation of a three-dimensional space conducive to learning that course's content, or the sense of connectedness that comes from simple peripheral awareness of classmates' presence and participation in the course material.[15] Even among those functions that may be offloaded onto interfaces to facilitate remote asynchronous interaction (such as course discussion forums), a degree of connectedness and empathy may be lost when communication is anchored to static two-dimensional images rather than a live video display; Albert Mehrabian famously claimed that 93 percent of all communication is nonverbal, which may be lost in text-only asynchronous online media.[16]

Taken this way, we hope it begins to become apparent how a distributed classroom expands on other innovative learning experiences. A distributed classroom is a class designed such that students can participate in as much of the full learning experience as possible within their individual constraints, especially constraints based on place and time. If they can attend in-person in the live classroom, they may do so; if they can commit to live attendance with a cohort of classmates in another location, they may do that instead; and if they can commit only to remote, asynchronous learning, they may participate that way. No matter their individual constraints, they give up only those parts of the learning experience that are fundamentally tied to that constraint: inability to attend in-person on-campus need not force students into the same remote asynchronous experience as students with additional constraints. Where other initiatives, such as MOOCs, focus on expanding access to a particular core component of the learning experience (typically the content and some assessments), the distributed classroom instead preserves as much of the classroom experience as possible within a given student's or audience's requirements. The important point is that the distributed classroom is interested in the *full* range of interactions and experiences that the physical classroom serves, not merely the ones that draw our deliberate focus, like delivering one-to-many lectures or the mechanics of exchanging reviews in a peer assessment exercise. How do we distribute this full range of interactions? That is the topic of part II of this book; part I describes how other recent trends and developments have set the perfect stage for implementing a distributed classroom, and part III explores the potential this paradigm has for radically changing education for the better.

The goal of the distributed classroom paradigm is thus to move us beyond the constraints of traditional teaching and the compromises of online teaching and instead usher in a view where the classroom is not confined to one mechanism or the other. By adopting a paradigm that diminishes the sanctity of the in-person experience without sacrificing what made it so hallowed in the first place, we can bring to bear the long-promised benefits of online education. Along the way, we also safeguard ourselves from the chaos of the outside world, preparing ourselves for rapid transitions among delivery mechanisms not by developing contingency plans but rather by designing an experience that was durable against outside changes in the first place.

AREN'T THESE JUST HYBRID CLASSROOMS?

We may be preaching to the choir a bit with our readers of this book. That perceived dichotomy between face-to-face and online education has been under attack in various places, from the use of MOOCs to support more traditional classes to the post-COVID-19 shift to more hybrid classes, combining online and face-to-face elements into new hybrid experience. Our critique is not new.

On the surface, hybrid classes themselves tend to be a shift away from this dichotomy. The hybrid model was already emerging before COVID-19, but the pandemic's role in shrinking in-person class sizes has driven a more rapid shift toward hybrid models. Hybrid models proliferated as the answer to many of the challenges presented by the pandemic, allowing schools and universities to implement social distancing while keeping class sizes at their typical levels.[17]

Hybrid classes come in many forms. Prior to COVID-19, flipped classrooms, a type of hybrid classroom, were growing in popularity. Under a flipped classroom model, students might watch lectures in advance, then use synchronous class time for more high-value discussion. Adjustments made for COVID-19 saw a different sort of hybrid classroom emerge: forced to treat classrooms as one-third as capacious, a hybrid model might see students attend a live lecture once a week and a remote lecture twice a week, cycling which students are allowed to attend the lecture in-person. This model closely follows the HyFlex model pioneered by Brian Beatty at San Francisco State University, which calls for students to be able to individually select whether to participate in person, synchronously online, or asynchronously online.[18] In our mental categorization, hybrid models subsume the increasingly popular blended style of instruction, which places greater emphasis on leveraging online materials to improve in-person classes and using synchronous co-located class time for purposes besides lecture, but it offers other instructional models as well.

To be clear, we are big supporters of hybrid and blended classrooms; our colleagues at Georgia Tech even produced a book detailing several successful experiments in blended learning on campus over the past several years, including the aforementioned CS1301: Introduction to Computing class, as well as the use of one of our online MSCS classes to improve the residential experience.[19] These classrooms are an excellent example of investigating our assumptions about how instruction works. Exploring a hybrid model forces deep questions about why we teach certain topics the way that we do and whether better options are available. A hybrid classroom asks questions like: Is listening to the teacher lecture for thirty minutes really a good use of students' time in a shared classroom when it is also the only time they can easily interact with one another? Should all students be forced to answer a practice question within the same general frame of time regardless of their ability, or can instruction wait until they finish to continue? Do I really need to be the thirty-thousandth teacher to teach integration by parts from scratch, or can I provide my students high-quality preexisting resources to learn from and shift my role to more of an individual supporting one?

We are not alone in this optimism: the blended learning incarnation of hybrid classrooms was on the rise for years prior to the COVID-19 era, but accommodations made for the pandemic have accelerated this shift. Anant Agarwal of edX sees COVID-19 as a catalyst in this shift toward blended learning, which he argues will be an improvement on how education has been delivered in the past.[20] Advocates see HyFlex as a perfect mechanism for addressing capacity and attendance issues in the age of social distancing and hybrid modes of delivery.[21] David authored a piece for the *Atlanta Journal-Constitution* that advocated treating COVID-19 as an opportunity to improve remote learning options, which ended up being the first step toward the creation of this book.[22]

So, hybrid classrooms bring many benefits. However, in terms of the dichotomy between online and traditional classrooms, we argue that they merely shift the level of distinction down one more step. Instead of distinguishing between online and traditional education at the school, program, or class level, it exists at the component level: the hybrid classroom has online components and traditional components. However, the dichotomy between them remains, such as in deliberately shifting components between online and face-to-face in a flipped model or in distinctly categorizing students as in-person, synchronous online, or asynchronous online in a HyFlex model.

Perhaps at that level, the dichotomy is no longer meaningful; if it exists between components within a classroom or if students can regularly shift between different categories, then the dangers of the dichotomy we outlined above are largely resolved anyway. It is difficult to regulate how individual components of an individual class ought to be taught the way that entire degrees and universities can be monitored; moreover, a teacher who is already thinking in terms of using both online and traditional components is likely already weighing the benefits of each individually rather than adopting the constraints of one model entirely.

But the greater difference we observe between the hybrid and the distributed classroom is one of scope and impact. The various incarnations of hybrid classrooms emphasize taking the general framework of a traditional class—the number of students, the associated schedule, the strategies for assessment—and augmenting and improving them through online components. This is undoubtedly a worthwhile endeavor. The distributed classroom, in turn, emphasizes how many of those same decisions can be leveraged to achieve large-scale reach and long-range impact. The hybrid classroom asks: How can we use both traditional and online components to improve the classroom experience? The distributed classroom asks: How can we use that design to tear down barriers to access and dramatically expand the number of potential learners in the world?

AREN'T THESE JUST MOOCS?

When we begin talking about access, scale, impact, and cost, a different natural comparison emerges: MOOCs. These are the large-scale initiatives that burst onto the scene in the early 2010s. Their growth and impact is well documented in Rich DeMillo's *A Revolution in Higher Education*, which traces the story of MOOCs through to the launch of the program we now run, Georgia Tech's online Master of Science in Computer Science (OMSCS) program.

In the decade since MOOCs began to emerge, they have followed the typical hype cycle: initially trumpeted as the solution to all of higher education's ills, then maligned for their failure to deliver on that promise, they have settled into a role as a tool for access and outreach. They became popular but did not pose the existential threat to typical higher education that was prophesied at the start of the decade. COVID-19 led to a resurgence in popularity, though; economic hardship and social distancing spell a perfect set of incentives to engage in low-cost, at-home, online education.[23] It is too soon to know if this development will spark a second life for MOOCs or if they will settle back into their previous roles. They have taken on an additional role in the process, however, as many MOOC providers have created programs to let universities borrow high-quality existing content to support courses rapidly shifting to remote instruction.

From the perspective of the distributed classroom, MOOCs represent an extreme end of the spectrum: they are beautifully distributed in time and space, but they lack many of the elements of a traditional classroom. Indeed, for all their successes, many critics note that MOOCs fail to capture critical portions of the learning experience.[24] These criticisms manifest in the student experience as well. MOOCs represent a great compromise: we willingly give up components that are difficult to scale like live interaction with teachers, rigorous open-ended assessment, and personalized feedback for the sake of expanded access, automated evaluation, and reduced cost. For most MOOC learners, the choice is likely not between a MOOC and a traditional class, but rather between a MOOC and nothing at all; there is little evidence that their growth is cutting into traditional offerings, but they are growing nonetheless, suggesting they are tapping into an otherwise unreached audience.[25]

The distributed classroom represents an examination of that compromise but not a referendum. MOOCs absolutely have a significant role to play, and we would argue that a MOOC can and should be part of a distributed classroom—but only *part* of it. The distributed classroom is about filling in that spectrum from a traditional classroom to a MOOC, making only the compromises necessary at each level to introduce incrementally improved scale and access.

TOWARD A SPECTRUM

To illustrate this shift from a dichotomy (traditional versus online in general, traditional versus MOOCs specifically), let us look at the example of the program that commands much of our time: Georgia Tech's OMSCS program. Much has been written about the program in general; we have provided several resources if you would like to read more about the program itself.[26] For the purposes of understanding its place on a spectrum between traditional classes and MOOCs, however, there are a few pertinent details to describe here. Launched in 2014, the program was developed according to a MOOC-like model: all course content is prerecorded, and there are no mandatory synchronous sessions. Beyond replacing live classes with prerecorded content, though, the online program is mostly the same as the on-campus program: assignments and projects are largely open-ended and graded by human teaching assistants at the direction of university professors; questions and discussions take place on a course discussion forum; and standard mechanisms for ensuring academic integrity, such as proctoring tools and plagiarism checkers, are in use. Courses follow the university semester schedule, with term start and end dates, instantiating the cohort model seen in some MOOCs (rather than purely self-paced). As a result, the program holds the same accreditation as the on-campus program: the word *online* does not appear on the degree granted by the online program; rather, it grants the same Master of Science in Computer Science one might earn in Atlanta or at one of Georgia Tech's other campuses around the world. Students can enroll from anywhere and are not required to attend class during working hours. The program has been a runaway success, growing to over 11,000 active students as of spring 2021 (along with over 3,500 alumni). With that enrollment and the reduced demands for in-person infrastructure, tuition is low: the total degree cost is between $6,900 and $8,400 depending on how many classes the student takes at a time, a small fraction of the cost of our and other universities' comparable residential programs. Since launch, the program has inspired two other partner degrees at Georgia Tech, an online MS in analytics and an online MS in cybersecurity; together, the three programs comprised 16,594 students in spring 2021, making up

42 percent of Georgia Tech's total enrollment for the term. Georgia Tech has nearly doubled in total enrollment since 2013 (from 21,472 students to 39,712 students), with 91 percent of that growth coming from these three online programs. Other universities have followed suit, with nearly fifty similar programs now offered, mostly in partnership with MOOC providers like edX, Coursera, and FutureLearn.

Our OMSCS program is billed as the first "MOOC-based" master's degree, but it includes many features that are absent in most MOOCs, such as human evaluation, open-ended assignments, and assertions of academic integrity. The features we borrow from MOOCs include our reliance on high-quality prerecorded course content, our asynchronous but cohort-based (not self-paced) delivery model, our commitment to free public access to content for nonstudents, our dedication to affordability, and our emphasis on scalability. In fact, since fall 2020, we have run the OMSCS program without a formal MOOC partner (such as edX, Coursera, or Udacity), but the hallmarks of MOOCs are still present.

Thus, our OMSCS program adds another gradation to the spectrum from traditional classes to MOOCs: it preserves those components necessary to award a degree—such as human evaluation and integrity verification—and compromises on those features necessary to achieve scale, like synchronous co-located attendance. Through this model, it demonstrates the interplay of scale, access, and cost: increased access yields increased enrollment, leading to economies of scale and reduced costs, leading to further increased enrollment. But critically, the credit-bearing program abandons some of the tenets of MOOCs: it is neither massive (as more teaching assistants must be hired to support more enrollment) nor open (students must be admitted to the program, although the program does subsidize free open access to the course content itself). This is true of the emerging landscape of affordable degrees at scale (or as we call them, Limeades: large internet-mediated asynchronous degrees): MOOC-based master's degrees typically exist by sacrificing some features of MOOCs.

What is critical here is that the sacrifice is contained to that portion of the program that requires that sacrifice; many of those components we must reintroduce to attach degree credit to a course are not necessary for open access to the content alone. Courses in the program exist in both forms: a for-credit variant with human evaluation, integrity verification, and interaction with instructors and open-access variants with public content, automated evaluations, and no enrollment cost. Some programs separate out this gradation further: edX's MicroMasters programs, for instance, introduce a variant between MOOCs and our for-credit classes, where most elements of the course experience—human-graded assignments, proctored exams, and a cohort-based delivery schedule—are preserved but students are not required to apply and be accepted to the program; anyone can enroll. In exchange, students in the MicroMaster's program do not earn full course credit: they earn a credential, and that credential can be applied for advanced standing toward a degree if they choose to move on to the full program. Here, the compromise is trading automatic course credit for expanded and more accommodating enrollment.

The distributed classroom is the culmination of these efforts, an elucidation of a fully developed spectrum from a traditional classroom to an open MOOC with numerous possible combinations of trade-offs in between. This effort is not about identifying the perfect level of compromise, but rather about distributing offerings across the entire spectrum of possible compromises. For those students and classes able to operate in a traditional model, that model ought to remain; for those who can attend with only small compromises, such as needing a different time slot or needing to attend at a distance, only those compromises ought to be necessary; and for those who need the drastic compromises like free access or open admissions, MOOC-like variants ought to remain. A distributed classroom takes the classroom experience and distributes it across these various different delivery modes, allowing each student to obtain as much of the original (or improved, based on new technology and new incentives) course experience as possible.

While theoretically that may seem feasible, is it practical? Who is going to do the work of designing each of these offerings and subofferings? When this challenge is framed as designing multiple distinct offerings, the work it poses is daunting. We argue that this can be resolved by adopting the mindset of a distributed classroom from the outset. By thinking outside the restrictions of a physical classroom or a particular MOOC platform in the first place, it is possible to create educational experiences that can be distributed among these different variants quickly. This is going to require rediscovering many of the components we sacrificed in the shift to online learning in the first place, but that also means this approach is as accessible to novices in online learning as it is to seasoned experts. That is one of the aspirations for a distributed classroom in practice: it ought not require significant additional dedicated staff or complex additional training; rather, it should be accessible to instructors largely within their existing skill sets or with minimal added instruction.

Most important, this vision will provide an antidote to the dystopian future feared by many watching with trepidation as online education expands. This vision does not foretell a future where only a few universities remain as some have predicted,[27] even as individual universities dramatically expand their footprint; instead, it foretells a future where expanded access turns everyone into a potential learner. The distributed classroom does not just break down barriers to academic content as the "democratize education" movement has emphasized; it breaks down barriers to the entire classroom learning experience, including live interactions with classmates and trustworthy assessments of ability. Every school can triple in size without shutting any doors if we triple the number of learners in the world at the same time.

STRUCTURE OF THIS BOOK

This book presents a vision for the distributed classroom, including the what, the how, and the why. Part I lays the foundation for these developments. Here, in chapter 1, we have described the current state of the relationship between online and residential education, and we have explored where we want to go: a classroom distributed in time and space. Chapter 2 defines the two spectra, place and time, and how we break them down into different gradations, emphasizing where and when students sit relative to both the original instruction and to a cohort of classmates. Chapter 3 looks at how existing efforts have already moved the needle toward a distributed classroom, from trends like distance learning and affordable degrees at scale to technologies like learning management systems and classroom discussion forums. Chapter 3 shows that even what we consider to be traditional education is already relatively distributed.

Part II then provides a blueprint for what a distributed classroom looks like in practice. Chapter 4 articulates *what* a distributed classroom is, examining all combinations of place and time from the spectra in chapter 2. To do so, it creates the distributed classroom matrix. Chapter 5 defines the ultimate form of a distributed classroom setting: symmetry. The greatest outcome (in terms of instruction) that the distributed classroom can achieve is a symmetry of experiences such that both students and teachers can move around the matrix at will, delivering or joining from different locations and at different times, without dictating a dramatic change to any particular class or cohort. Chapter 6 delves deeper into the implementation details of making the distributed classroom happen. It unpacks the roles that teaching assistants, technology, and teachers must play to make the experience a reality.

Part III then looks at the broader impacts that a widespread push towards a distributed classroom may have, both positive and negative. Chapter 7 explores the effects of this vision and its impact on different audiences of learners, how it intersects with finances and economies of scale, and how it preserves academic freedom and diversity. Chapter 8 connects this effort to moves to unbundle higher education, looking more deeply into the differential needs of different learners and how a distributed classroom can provide greater access by separating itself from other elements of the educational enterprise. Chapter 9 examines the fears and risks of this approach and how the distributed classroom can be a force for good and positive change rather than a force for further centralization. Chapter 10 provides the long-term dream of the distributed classroom: a world where lifelong learning is the norm rather than the goal, and where it fits into students' lives rather than demanding tremendous sacrifices.

WHO THIS BOOK IS FOR

This book is written for teachers, administrators, instructional designers, and learners. Not surprisingly, these are four roles we have held over the course of our careers. David has taught over fifty online classes and twenty thousand online students; Charles has taught twenty-nine online classes and over twelve thousand students, as well as dozens of in-person classes over the preceding two decades. We both currently hold roles as administrators in the college, Charles as dean of the College of Computing and David as the executive director of online education. Prior to this role, David worked as an instructional designer and course developer, helping other faculty members bring their courses to life in an online environment. And of course, we are both lifelong learners.

If you are a teacher, this book provides a vision for how you can function and educate in an increasingly complex world, burdened by an ever-changing landscape of requirements and constraints. This vision tries to liberate you at least from some of these, allowing you to face conversations about class size, teaching modalities, and individual accommodations with excitement—or, perhaps better yet, ambivalence—rather than fear. Most important, this vision strives to provide a way that you can continue to use all the skills and best practices you have developed over your career rather than having to relearn how to teach online. For a book about education, we actually talk relatively little about pedagogy because this model is designed to let your existing pedagogical knowledge continue to shine in this new medium; our goal is to allow whatever works in the physical classroom to continue to work in a distributed classroom and to open up new environments and opportunities for exploring new pedagogical approaches, whatever they may be.

If you are an administrator, the book pushes for viewing the increase in digital options as a trend to leverage for students' gain in addition to existing goals around reducing costs and raising enrollment. Moreover, it encourages you to adopt an optimistic rather than a survivalist view of the need to more heavily leverage digital options. The distributed classroom holds as one of its tenets the need to increase the number of learners in the world, meaning that scale does not necessitate drawing students away from other schools. Instead, it encourages us all to think first of how we can expand educational opportunities to those who currently have none, or at least none that are compatible with other constraints in their lives.

If you are an instructional designer, this book gives you a new, yet likely familiar, way to look at the design process of new courses. Many of the practical ideas in this book are related to designs you may have already used, like HyFlex and flipped classrooms, but with a new emphasis on the broader impact that these designs can have. Specifically, this book encourages you to consider small, early, low-stakes decisions that can have enormous implications later in allowing your class's content to be shared, reused, improved, and updated without reteaching or redeveloping the content from scratch. Small decisions in these areas can have a massive impact. This book also recommends clearly delineating the functional roles of different elements of course design and their potential to be distributed across time and space; for example, understanding that exams must be accessible to asynchronous and remote audiences in addition to synchronous and co-located cohorts dictates elements of assessment design that can be simple when addressed early but difficult to redesign for distributed audiences later.

If you are a learner (which we hope you are, even if you are also a teacher, administrator, or instructional designer), you have likely been inundated with the growing need to make learning a lifelong endeavor. The world is changing so fast that a four-year degree can no longer supply you with the skills for a forty-year career. The question has never been the need but rather the feasibility: in a world where tuition can cost tens of thousands of dollars and most quality higher education options require attending during working hours and living near the institution, how do you balance being a lifelong learner with having a job, raising a family, and still getting some sleep? Do you compromise on the quality by selecting only what is convenient, or do you make sacrifices in other areas of life? For you, this book is a road map to the minimum amount of compromise necessary, a blueprint for the kinds of educational opportunities to seek to become a lifelong learner without devoting your life to learning.

WHAT THIS BOOK IS NOT

As we were brainstorming and writing this book, a number of topics came to mind for inclusion. Ultimately we observed that to include them all, we would be writing a thousand-page tome of which the distributed classroom would be a small part; we decided instead to focus more narrowly on this core idea. As a result, there are a number of topics you might expect to see in this book that are not here.

First, for a book about education, we discuss actual pedagogy relatively infrequently. The reason is simple: one of the goals of the distributed classroom is to create an infrastructure for distributing the class experience across time and space without requiring that teachers dramatically change what they do in the classroom. Many well-intentioned initiatives in teaching have struggled because they required millions of teachers to completely reinvent their teaching practice in order to be successful. Our goal is to create mechanisms that leverage and channel what teachers are already doing. That means that whatever pedagogical approaches teachers are already employing in their classrooms, we want to make sure to preserve them online. Rather than painstakingly detailing numerous specific approaches, we instead focus on building an experience that preserves as many of the fundamental features of the classroom as possible, ensuring that those specific approaches can remain in use. Within that framework, there are countless excellent resources on teaching in general and teaching online specifically that remain relevant to complement this book's goals.[28]

This should not be taken to suggest that the traditional in-person classroom experience is the perfect, unimpeachable gold standard. While we argue that there are functions—both obvious and hidden—that a live, face-to-face classroom plays that are difficult to transition online, many have noted fundamental strengths that more asynchronous models provide as well. Competency-based education, for instance, is a movement in learning that advocates for allowing students to move forward once they have demonstrated competency in an area, regardless of how much time that takes. The movement is theoretically richly compatible with the self-paced nature of MOOCs, but it can be leveraged in more traditional environments as well; critically, it thrives when delivered via asynchronous online mechanisms because it removes synchronous co-located class time as a constraint on the amount of instructional time a student receives. It is perfectly compatible with a distributed classroom as well, and in fact the distributed classroom provides a framework to design what portions of a learning experience should be synchronous and asynchronous. Our goal with the distributed classroom is to set up a framework that allows whatever happens in person to be distributed across space and time, and for new initiatives to be incorporated into the distributed experience; teachers may decide separately what they actually want to include in that experience. Our goal is to accommodate as much of what they select as possible.

Finally, this book is not a history and overview of our online MSCS program at Georgia Tech. We draw many lessons from it, and we advocate emulating many of the mechanisms that we have put into play in scaling our program. However, this book is about far more than just what we have done within our program: it is about all the other things we know we can do because we have seen the end points of the spectrum. We have seen the value of synchronous, face-to-face classes throughout the history of education, and we have seen the success of asynchronous, remote classes in the much briefer history of our OMSCS program. This book is about putting those two experiences down as extreme end points of a spectrum and exploring all we can do in the middle.

2

PLACE AND TIME

The vision of the distributed classroom calls for distributing the classroom experience across space and time. In order to get started with this vision, we need to have a clear understanding of what we actually mean by "space" and "time." Confusion about these definitions can sow miscommunications at critical junctures. For example, in discussing MOOCs, we often describe courses as either synchronous and cohorted, or asynchronous and self-paced. A "synchronous" MOOC has a cohort of students moving through the program with shared deadlines, aiming to create more of a community feel deriving from going through the same experience at the same time as others. However, in almost every "synchronous" MOOC, there is no true synchronicity: students still complete work on their own time, interacting with one another via asynchronous forums rather than synchronous classrooms. Even those that offer some sort of more synchronous mechanism leave it optional; many MOOCs use Slack or Discord for real-time chat, for example, but typically as an optional additional communication channel. So while these courses are not truly self-paced due to the shared, cohort-based deadlines, they nonetheless are primarily asynchronous, at least as compared to true live synchronicity. This differentiation is just one of the places where descriptions of synchronicity and remoteness may take on different definitions.

THE TIME/SPACE MATRIX

One of the theoretical tools employed by the field of computer-supported collaborative work (CSCW) is the time/space matrix, which looks at interactions among individuals from the perspectives of the two dimensions of time and space (figure 2.1).[1] Each dimension is made of two relatively

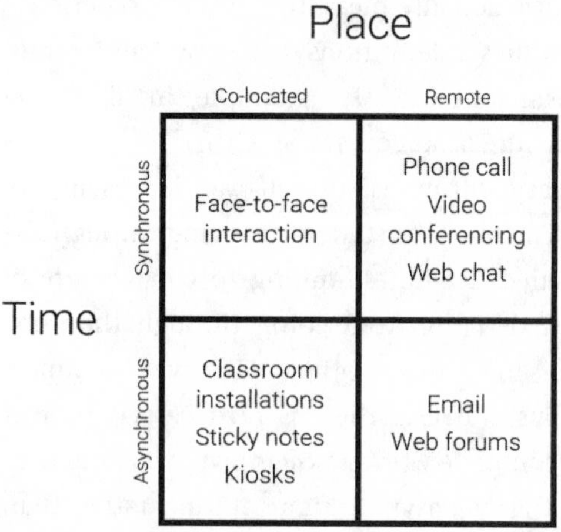

	Place	
	Co-located	Remote
Synchronous	Face-to-face interaction	Phone call Video conferencing Web chat
Asynchronous	Classroom installations Sticky notes Kiosks	Email Web forums

Time

Figure 2.1 The Time/Space Matrix

discrete categories: time is divided into synchronous and asynchronous, and space is divided into co-located and remote. This leads to four quadrants.

We can apply this framework to many existing educational environments. A typical classroom, for instance, belongs in the synchronous co-located quadrant, where students interact with one another and with their teacher live in a shared location. That synchronous co-located time can be used for a variety of purposes, including lectures, class discussion, group work, and testing; the important element here is that synchronous co-location is available to be used.

Remote and distance-learning classes very often implement the synchronous remote quadrant, a synchronous experience where people are not physically in the same place. Often—especially in the wake of COVID-19—this is an instructor teaching via a teleconference, where rather than coming to a physical classroom, everyone signs onto the same link at the same time. This might be performed using existing teleconferencing tools like Zoom or Microsoft Teams, or it might use dedicated synchronous remote classroom tools like Harvard's HBX classroom or the Minerva Project. Sometimes this synchronous remote distance-learning experience is added on to a synchronous co-located experience, where a remote audience can watch a live class. This is our first glimpse at a distributed classroom: a single class is distributed across a synchronous co-located and synchronous remote experience. Viewed this way, all of televised sports and live entertainment can be seen as a distribution across synchronous co-located (for in-person attendees) and synchronous remote (for those watching on TV); shows recorded in front of a live audience are distributed to the asynchronous remote quadrant as well. In the wake of COVID-19, some schools experimented with other variations on the synchronous remote quadrant; one model that emerged was a sort of "study hall" approach where remote students were assigned work to complete during a specific class time but their efforts were largely individual. A teacher would be available to answer questions live via a chat tool or teleconference, but the teleconference was not the main driver of the experience; instead, students worked more independently, albeit at an assigned time.

The obvious candidate for the asynchronous remote (AR) quadrant, then, is the typical MOOC model. Whether students are cohorted with shared deadlines or allowed to pursue the course in a purely self-paced model, these sorts of courses build heavily on material that is persistently available via the internet, breaking the necessity for synchronous or co-located interactions. The AR quadrant is not absent from traditional education, however; the very notion of homework can be viewed as leveraging asynchronous remote environments: the teacher asynchronously provides directions to the student to complete later in their own space. As technology has taken on a greater and greater role in traditional education, asynchronous remote interactions have become more significant: even in classes that meet in person, teachers may use learning management systems to post announcements, collect homework, and return grades, shifting more of the classroom administration into the asynchronous and remote sphere.

The final quadrant, the asynchronous co-located quadrant, is a bit of an anomaly: How can you be co-located without being together at the same time? But it nonetheless plays a significant role in the design of traditional class-rooms. Lower school classrooms may tape students' work up on the wall, thus providing a passive mechanism for communication among different classes. Schools may employ idea walls to gather input or give students room to express themselves. Museum kiosks may let users see the creations of earlier informal learners. From the perspective of the distributed classroom, though, asynchronous co-location will take on new importance as we reinterpret "co-located" to instead carry implications about the features of the space: it may not be important for asynchronous learners to be in the same *actual* space, but rather to individually be in spaces that support the same activities and behaviors.

The time/space matrix has already been a useful tool in rethinking how we use different constructs in designing the student experience. Blended learning, for instance, looks at the fact that the scarcest resource in designing a course is synchronous co-located time; a class may meet for only three hours a week. Those three hours, thus, should be spent on whatever can be accomplished *only* within the synchronous co-located quadrant, as one would find in a flipped class-room model. We may then look at what typically happens during that time—such as a lecture—and determine that it can be shifted to the asynchronous remote quadrant to better use the scarce synchronous co-located time.

The matrix on its own is a valuable way of thinking about interactions, although many of its implications for the design of learning experiences are rather straightforward: often the quadrant within which we may design is given *to* teachers rather than selected *by* teachers. We know at the start, for example, that we are teaching in-person or remotely, and

whether we can expect students to sign in at a particular
time; then we move on from there with our own designs.
The goal of the distributed classroom is to design across,
rather than within, these quadrants—not to design a separate class experience for each quadrant, but rather to design
an overall class structure that covers multiple quadrants.

EXPANDING THE MATRIX

In the pursuit of the distributed classroom, we make two
additions to this general structure: one structural, one
semantic. These changes are made to reflect the reality of
what we are designing for in an educational experience, as
well as to shift focus on what we hope to realize with the
distributed classroom.

First, under the standard interpretation, synchronicity and
co-location are relative to the original delivery of the course,
which is typically framed from the student-instructor point
of view, especially whether students are with the teacher
live in the same room. However, what we often want to preserve are interactions among classmates; or, we may want to
preserve interactions not necessarily with the teacher, but
with what we would commonly call a teaching assistant.
Teaching assistants, under this model, are individuals with
less content knowledge and experience than the teacher but
more than the students in the class, acting under the designs
and direction of the original instructor. They may facilitate group interactions, give individual feedback on work,
answer questions that do not require the expertise of the
instructor, and curate questions to deliver to the instructor

that *do* rely on that expertise. Teaching assistants are common in large programs—our OMSCS program employs over four hundred of them each semester, and our on-campus program employs dozens as well. Analogous roles are common in smaller programs and K–12 classes as well, usually in the form of paraprofessionals with more specific roles like supporting students with Individual Educational Plans (IEPs) or other accommodations. We come back to the relevance and role of teaching assistants throughout this book.

The important point of this observation is that there ought to exist a middle layer of the classic time/space matrix. Both synchronicity and co-location can be thought of not only in terms of the student's positioning relative to the original delivery of the content, but also relative to a cohort of classmates and teaching assistants. This relationship is automatic if one happens to be a student in a traditional model, but attendance in a traditional model need not be a requirement for a student to have some synchronous, co-located classroom with classmates and instructional staff.

Thus, our structural modification of the time/space matrix in support of the distributed classroom is to insert an additional level along each dimension. In terms of synchronicity, we have three levels:

- Synchronous with the original class: Students participate with the original delivery of the class, whether in person or remote.
- Synchronous with a cohort, asynchronous with the original class: Students participate with a synchronous cohort of classmates and teaching assistants, watching or following along with the material as it was originally presented,

pausing to engage with their own cohort at moments when classroom interactions happened in person.

- Individually asynchronous: Students consume the class material entirely on their own time, without a synchronous cohort of students to interact with in a live, designed way.

Then, in terms of co-locatedness, we have three levels as well:

- Co-located with the original class: Students are in the same place as the teacher for the initial delivery of the material.
- Co-located with a cohort, remote from the original class: Students gather in a room together to participate in the learning experience, but that place need not be the location of the original delivery of the material.
- Individually remote: Students may attend from wherever they are, so long as the technology is available to support their attendance.

With these additional layers, we establish the distributed classroom matrix. Chapter 4 expands on how each element of this matrix may function in the real world. However, even before examining the individual elements, it is possible to see the potential power of this approach. In high-demand fields, a key limiting factor in delivering cutting-edge content is the availability of instructors to teach that content. Even in more well-trodden fields with established training regimens for bringing new teachers into the fold (such as K–12 education), individual variation is strong, and teachers are asked to serve far too many functional roles at the same time. Part of the power of this approach is that it may separate out elements of the experience—such as the initial classroom delivery—into reusable commodities. Rather than limiting the number of students an excellent teacher or a subject matter expert can instruct, their delivery of the content becomes something that can be leveraged toward the education of an unlimited number of students without increasing the workload on that teacher individually. For example, each semester, we together teach over three thousand students in classes we originally filmed; delivering live lectures to that number of students would be two full-time jobs on their own, but instead we teach the classes in addition to our roles as executive director of the program and dean of the college because we are able to leverage this commodity. Perhaps more interesting, professors who have moved on from Georgia Tech continue to have an impact—in some cases, continuing to teach their Georgia Tech classes from new positions at other universities, and in others allowing a new instructor to continue to leverage their content. These approaches allow classes to be taught that might otherwise be retired when the professor with the necessary knowledge moves on.

This on its own, of course, is nothing new: it can be traced back to the broadcast of lectures via radio and television through initiatives like the United Kingdom's Open University (which has been ahead of its time in a multitude of ways). Those efforts, however, fall squarely in the asynchronous remote quadrant (or the synchronous remote quadrant before the advent of convenient individual remote communication) where classroom interactions are difficult. The distinguishing factor brought by this new dimension is the potential preservation of classroom dynamics and interactions coupled with the distribution and reuse of the initial classroom presentation. It may no longer be necessary to sacrifice the authentic classroom experience for the convenience of mass distribution; a compromise between the two, preserving their benefits, may remain possible.

That shift on its own, however, would be somewhat limited in its impact. If we merely viewed the distributed classroom as a way for a teacher to teach a cohort of students that is separated in space and time, then it might seem to be of narrow usefulness: How often is it really the case that a cohort of students can gather together at a time and place an instructor cannot reach? There might be use cases for training workers in remote areas, but that does not intersect with the larger majority of education.

This leads into the second modification of the time/space matrix, one that is more semantic than structural. While it is not deliberate, the majority of applications of the time/space matrix we have seen situate initiatives squarely within a particular quadrant: an interaction is synchronous co-located, synchronous remote, or asynchronous remote. The goal of the distributed classroom is different: rather than positioning teaching in a particular cell of this matrix, its goal is to design learning initiatives that span many cells with as little additional labor as possible.

Every cell of this matrix represents a compromise. Given the choice, we have no doubt that most students would choose to participate in the original room with the teacher instead of with teaching assistants if both options were equally accessible. However, in many subject areas, synchronous co-located participation is impossible for the vast majority of students who would benefit from the experience. For many of these students, the existing alternatives—asynchronous MOOCs or playlists of prerecorded lectures—sacrifice far more of the experience than those students need to give up. The focus of the matrix is on offering a suite of potential compromises from which to select, such that students may maximize their benefit and minimize their sacrifice, without adding tremendous extra work on teachers to accommodate each set of constraints.

3

PROGRESS SO FAR

The distributed classroom is more feasible now than in the past due to the significant progress that has been made in distributing elements of the learning experience across space and time. This feasibility is partially due to technological innovations like video streaming services and learning management systems and partially due to the emergence of more asynchronous and remote options in general. However, the progress we have made has not been deliberately in service of a distributed classroom; instead, it has been toward expanding access, improving existing systems, and addressing emergency situations. The result of these developments, however, is a landscape ripe for a more cohesive vision. To understand how well suited we are for a shift to a distributed classroom, it is useful to interpret some elements of the current state of affairs through the lens of this approach.

To unpack this idea, we look at five current trends in education through the lens of the distributed classroom: the growth of traditional distance learning; the increasing importance of learning management systems; the rise of open educational resources and shareable content; the emergence of local cohorts to complement online programs; and the development of new models to allow in-person teachers to rapidly shift online in the wake of the COVID-19 pandemic. All of them seek to take something that previously has been located within a particular place and time and distribute it across one or both dimensions. What we will find is that even our traditional classrooms are already becoming distributed, while more traditionally remote or asynchronous options are becoming more and more part of the mainstream as well. Taken together, the observation here may be that distributing the classroom experience itself is actually the *last* step we need to take, not the first. We will see that there already exist classrooms in various cells of the distributed classroom matrix with potential to be easily extended to other cells as well.

A word of caution: because we are deeply involved in Georgia Tech's online education efforts, we approach many of these ideas from the perspective first of what we have done in our programs. Some of these ideas are novel, pioneered by us and picked up by others, but many more are common across other schools and universities. It is not our intent to suggest that these sorts of initiatives are unique to Georgia Tech, but rather that we have the familiarity to talk about our own progress in greater depth. Many other schools have taken similar steps in these directions, which should reaffirm the progress of the education enterprise as a whole toward a distributed classroom.

TRADITIONAL DISTANCE LEARNING

The idea of distributing learning across space and time is certainly not new: distance learning has pushed for breaking these barriers for almost two hundred years. Sir Isaac Pitman first taught a correspondence course on the Pitman shorthand writing system in 1840. The University of London began offering distance-learning degrees in 1858; the University of Chicago began offering correspondence courses in 1892. These programs were conducted by mail between students and instructors. As technology advanced, so too did distance-learning offerings. The University of Wisconsin began recording lectures via phonograph shortly after the turn of the century, mailing these recordings to students to use for their studies.[1] John Wilkinson Taylor pushed the idea of college classes by radio in 1948.[2] The United Kingdom's Open University began transmitting course content via television in the 1970s. Vocational programs targeted at flexible job training thrived in the 1980s and 1990s, mailing students videotaped classes to watch on their home VCRs.

From the perspective of the distributed classroom and the time/space matrix, it is easy to see where these different initiatives sit. They are largely positioned in the asynchronous remote quadrant; students are separated in both place and time from the original teaching materials and receive them via some asynchronous means, then return their work later for grading. Some, like the radio and TV broadcasts of college classes, sit in the synchronous remote quadrant, requiring live remote attendance, but in these cases, there is little evidence that the synchronicity was used to improve the learning experience by allowing remote students to interact with one another live; instead, synchronicity was a technological constraint. At the time, at-scale distribution of content could be achieved only live over the airwaves; asynchronous content distribution required still slower mechanisms like the postal service.

The experience of distance learning during these times would not be argued to be comparable in any way to a traditional experience. Instead, distance learning presented opportunities for students who would not typically be able to participate at all due to cost or location. The function would differ based on the individual program, of course, but they would most reasonably be interpreted as outreach or expanding access.

DISTANCE LEARNING AND THE INTERNET

Modern technology has changed this experience. The internet allows for more symmetrical participation by remote audiences. We can see this in one modern incarnation of online schools and classes, where a teacher teaches live via teleconference exactly as in a classroom; rather than sitting in desks, students sit at home on their computers. This situates distance learning more deliberately in the synchronous remote quadrant, where synchronous interaction facilitates learning experiences that are difficult in the absence of live back-and-forth communication.

The mesh of classical distance learning ideas with modern technology has given rise to a form of distributed classroom. Many distance-learning programs operate in a sort of two-function model, using existing face-to-face classes as the foundation for creating distance options. Some students attend class in person, and equipment present in the room lowers the overhead of capturing and disseminating that in-person experience. A virtual audience of remote learners then registers for the same class and attends virtually at the same time, using the equipment in the room as a stand-in for in-person attendance. Out-of-class portions of the experience are then handled the same way for both groups of students by way of a learning management system, which we describe in the next section.

These more synchronous remote models are where we see the clearest modern example of a partially distributed classroom in action. This model distributes the classroom across two quadrants, the synchronous co-located quadrant and the synchronous remote quadrant. The in-person cohort of students is synchronous and co-located together, while the remote cohort is synchronous with the in-person cohort (as well as with each other) but individually remote. Most critical, the course exists in both quadrants at the same time: it is *distributed* across the matrix. It is also easy to see how this could be extended to a third quadrant, the asynchronous remote quadrant, where those lectures are recorded and made available afterward as well. If a class offered in this model does not require synchronous attendance, then it essentially already exists in all three of those quadrants at once.

Online programs leveraging this model (as well as pure asynchronous remote models, like our OMSCS program) have grown in popularity over the past several years; however, they have not threatened traditional programs. Instead, the growth of these programs comes largely from people who would not have otherwise been students at all: they require the compromises that come with distance learning. This is true in our OMSCS program: the enormous majority of our students would not have enrolled in a traditional program if they had not been accepted to our asynchronous remote program.[3] Thus, there are two frontiers for potential growth in distance-learning models: they can continue to grow to open access to more learners who could not otherwise participate, and they can increase in sophistication to the point where they pose a viable alternative to traditional models.

WORK STILL TO BE DONE

While this model—using a synchronous co-located classroom to build synchronous and asynchronous remote offerings—is promising, it does not guarantee equitable treatment of students in the remote cohorts. Interactions between a group of co-located students and a group of remote students are still technologically difficult; the slight lag in online communications or a lack of familiarity with the room's audio volume can leave remote students uncomfortable with interrupting or participating. This also often restricts the face-to-face interactions only to students able to attend in person rather than deliberately facilitating interactions among remote students. It also leaves students unable to attend synchronously on their own in a MOOC-like paradigm, bringing up the issues of isolation and social presence common among purely asynchronous experiences.

Most problematic, though, students often pay a *premium* for this subpar experience: while the landscape is too varied for general claims, it is not uncommon for online degrees to actually cost more than their on-campus counterparts.[4] There is a logic here, of course: online students are paying more money for more convenience, able to complete their education from the comfort of their couch rather than trekking to school several times a week (to say nothing of the need to live near the school in the first place). But by that same logic, Netflix (or other movie-streaming services) should cost ten times more than a movie ticket because it is also much more convenient. Of course, a month of Netflix actually costs roughly the price of a single movie ticket: the at-home viewing experience is considered inferior to the movie theater experience, and economies of scale drive down the cost to individuals. Both of these dynamics may apply to these remote learning experiences as well. Distance learning can accomplish scale beyond what is possible in a fixed-size, in-person classroom, but the experience—at least so far—leaves out features of the in-person classroom that students may find desirable. There may not be observable differences in learning outcomes between well-designed in-person and online classes, but other factors, like the ease of forming social and professional connections or the access to other in-person artifacts or resources, may nonetheless offer a superior experience to traditional students, justifying a premium on in-person tuition.

To be clear, we believe that online learning experiences can be as good as in-person experiences. We actually believe they can be *better* than in-person experiences, for a wide variety of reasons that are largely out of the scope of this book. But we do not believe that distance-learning experiences built solely from sticking a camera in the back of a room fulfill that potential. That potential can be realized only by building in far more deliberate opportunities for interaction between students and teachers, as well as among students themselves. The experience must be designed *for* remote audiences rather than just made available *to* these audiences. That has not been common so far (although individual initiatives have made significant progress), and when coupled with the scale they enable, we should thus not be seeing distance education costing more than in-person education, despite the rational argument about paying more money for greater convenience.

Nevertheless, we clearly have a promising start. The progress made in distance learning over the past ten years has demonstrated in various ways the feasibility of all the components of the distributed classroom. This new effort is toward unifying these types of offerings into a cohesive vision, one where students can receive as much access to authentic experiences and recognized credentials as possible given their individual constraints. The distributed classroom is about treating these remote experiences as fundamental parts of the classroom design rather than afterthoughts, incorporating them more universally into more classes, and making remote learning more comparable to a face-to-face experience.

LEARNING MANAGEMENT SYSTEMS

Under the narrative of distance learning, we see the efforts starting with the core assumption—distance—and working backward, adding elements of the in-person experience while preserving the fundamental assumption that students are remote. The narrative of learning management systems can be told from the opposite angle: we start with a traditional classroom and look at what components can be digitized.

Online learning management systems have emerged alongside the internet over the past thirty years, dating back to tools like FirstClass in the early 1990s. As the internet has become more and more ubiquitous, they have taken on an expanding role. It was largely the existing reliance on learning management systems that allowed schools and universities to continue remotely in the wake of COVID-19 in the first place; an infrastructure was already in place for distributing portions of the learning experience over the internet, and so the transition could focus on moving the remaining face-to-face components into that infrastructure as well. The four largest players in this area are Canvas, Blackboard, Brightspace, and Moodle, and their market share has been growing over the past decade; at the time of writing, they together command over 90 percent of the market, led by Canvas with 35 percent.[5] Other options abound as well, with some schools using proprietary solutions while others leverage open-source or open-access tools like Sakai and Google Classroom. Among these options, nearly every school in the United States at every level from kindergarten through postsecondary now uses some form of learning management system depending on the needs of their level.

The relationship between learning management systems and the classroom can be thought of in many ways. From the perspective of the distributed classroom, though, we are most interested in how learning management systems shift interactions among quadrants in the time/space matrix and how those shifts pave the way for more distributed efforts going forward. This section follows that structure: it examines components of common learning management systems to see how they shifted interactions and then how those already-shifted interactions make a distributed classroom more feasible.

ASSIGNMENTS AND FEEDBACK

Before learning management systems, students would generally bring their work to class and hand it in directly; teachers might come around and collect work or have students leave it in a box at the front of the classroom. Once graded, it would then generally be handed out in class, taking a significant amount of time to find each submission's recipient. The interactions largely took place during synchronous co-located class time, using that valuable and scarce resource on a highly mechanical process.

Learning management systems digitize that process, allowing assignment submission and grade return to occur asynchronously and remotely. The system gives directions (although they may be reiterated in class or in the syllabus), accepts submissions, and delivers submissions to instructors for grading. Once graded, the system delivers grades and feedback to students, as either plaintext comments or annotations to the documents themselves. Assignments still have deadlines, but students may submit any time before the deadline to the virtual system, and grades may be posted as soon as they are ready rather than waiting for the next class session. Many learning management systems now have mobile apps, sending push notifications to students as soon as new grades are available.

We could discuss at length the surprisingly far-reaching effects of this development—but we personally think that it may have a negative impact, making it more difficult for students to compartmentalize. Notifications of bad grades can come at any time, interrupting a night out or peaceful slumber. We encourage students to disable these notifications. Remote submission also removes an implicit mechanism for requiring class attendance; in the past, classes might not require attendance on days when an assignment was due because attendance was required to turn in that assignment. Now, class attendance and assignment completion have been decoupled, forcing us to think of either more creative or more deliberate ways to ensure attendance—or whether to ensure attendance at all, if we view required attendance as merely a subpar proxy for assessing whether the student achieved the learning goals of the day. But we digress.

From the distributed classroom perspective, this shift paves the way for remote and asynchronous audiences to participate more fully. The system that even on-campus students use for assignment submission is not in any way affected by a student's inability to be on campus. As teachers, we have already seen, "I have to miss class. Can I turn in the assignment late?" disappear as a common excuse. Again, there are downsides to this, such as forcing ill students to decouple, "Am I too sick to attend class?" from, "Am I too sick to do this homework?" but the mechanism paves the way for equitable participation from remote, asynchronous students.

GRADING AND TEACHING ASSISTANTS

Implicit in the previous section is grading: between assignment submission and grade return is a phase of grading where the teacher looks at each assignment, assigns it a grade, and provides feedback on the student's successes and failures on the assessment. In small classes, this may be accomplished entirely by the teacher, limiting the need for a fancy system to help. At larger scales, though, teachers often employ teams of teaching assistants (TAs) to grade assignments.

Before learning management systems, teaching assistants might be handed a pile of papers to take home and grade, bringing them back when done. Working on a teaching team might mean attending several synchronous "grading parties," where we would order pizza, lock the door, and refuse to let anyone go home until all the assignments were graded. There are significant benefits to this: working in the same room together meant having conversations about common trends, deductions to assign, and potential biases, much the same way that live conversations enhance the classroom experience. There are drawbacks as well: writing grades directly on student papers makes it harder to analyze for trends at a high level and even harder to adjust if discrepancies are observed. For example, if one TA assigned a ten-point deduction for an error for which another assigned a five-point deduction, correcting that by hand would be time-consuming; if the gradebook is instead digitized, correcting it may be trivial. Modern tools such as Gradescope attempt to bring the benefits of live collaboration into this digital arena, allowing rubric categories to be created and adjusted dynamically.

But there is a greater drawback: this sort of scheme mandates that only people who could participate in those sorts of grading workflows could work as teaching assistants. TAs are typically students who performed well in the course the previous term because those are the people present on campus to participate in grading. Digitizing the submission and grading process brings to teaching assistants the same benefits it brings to students: they can be anywhere, working at any time. Efforts must be made to ensure consistency when TAs are not gathered in a room together, but this mechanism opens up a large new world of potential TA candidates.

One of David's roles as the executive director of our online MSCS program is overseeing the process of hiring TAs. When we launched the program, we operated under the assumption that online students would be uninterested in working as TAs: with full-time jobs and families, they are far busier than on-campus students, and the amount we pay pales in comparison to what they are likely earning in their existing careers. So for the first several semesters, we hired students from the on-campus student body to work as TAs for the online audience. On-campus students receive lucrative tuition waivers in exchange for helping in this way, and so the pool was adequately large to scale to the first few thousand students.

One drawback of that approach, however, was that most on-campus students leave for the summer for internships or vacations, while online students would generally rather use summer to continue progressing—on-campus enrollment in graduate computer science classes during summer semesters at Georgia Tech is 9 percent as high as enrollment during spring and fall semesters, but online enrollment is 74 percent as high in summer as in spring and fall. If the program is to rely on on-campus TAs to support online enrollment, summer semesters become infeasible.

So in summer 2015, David tried something new: he emailed the 463 online students who had taken CS7637: Knowledge-Based AI the previous two semesters. He told them that we were interested in offering the class in summer, but our original teaching assistants were unavailable; if he could find two or three good candidates, we could offer a section to a hundred or so students in summer. We opened up the applications, and of the 463 students who had enrolled in the class the previous two terms, more than 70 applied to help out as teaching assistants. He selected 10, allowing 370 students to enroll, and taught the course with fantastic results. Not only were there sufficient TAs to offer the course based on numbers alone, but their performance as teaching assistants outperformed that of our previous staff. One imperfect but objective and easily calculable metric was length of assignment feedback: these teaching assistants wrote on average twice as much feedback per assignment than the previous team did. The new team was also far more responsive on the course forum and more interactive during meetings of the instructional team. They also participated in research while working as teaching assistants, and their work was published the following year at ACM's Learning @ Scale conference.[6] Most stayed around as teaching assistants for several more semesters, and two of that original team of ten are back helping five years later as part-time instructional associates.

We feared this might just be an early-adopter effect, but six years later, the trends have held strong. Today, the program must employ over four hundred teaching assistants every semester; one-third of them are current online students and one-third are program alumni. We regularly have hundreds more applications than positions; during the most recent hiring season, David received 276 applications for his four classes but needed to hire only 7 new TAs, due in part to very low turnover from his previous term's teaching teams. Other trends have persevered as well; while on-campus TAs are excellent, the online students have a unique perspective due to their experience in industry and as online students themselves. They have a better understanding of what other online students need. They are also motivated differently: nearly all are motivated either by nonmonetary benefits of the role (networking with professors, improving their résumés, reinforcing their understanding of the material) or by altruistic desires (the desire to support the program or to help their classmates).[7]

These trends all connect back to that initial distribution of TA responsibilities in time and space. By removing the constraint that these students had to be present on campus to help as teaching assistants, we drew a much larger audience with varying motivations—and, critically, much more professional experience in the field. On top of that, they stay far longer, bringing valuable stability and experience to the role. David's longest-tenured teaching assistant, Ken Brooks, has been working on the program for eighteen semesters over six years. Professionally, he is a former executive with several major textbook publishers in New York City; he could never help out as a teaching assistant if it required him to attend physical grading meetings regularly in Atlanta. What he brings to the role, however, goes far beyond what one might see from a typical teaching assistant, and it is possible only because of the distributed grading process.

Going forward into the distributed classroom era, this is a key component of the ability to scale. Scale in the distributed classroom is linear and uncapped, but not infinite: we require extra human assistance to support a greater number of students, unlike infinitely scalable MOOCs. Learning management systems allow these individuals to support the class asynchronously from a distance, but only if the individuals are actually available; if they are not, the model would not work. Our experience has shown that when you break some of the requirements to help out in the role, the number of interested parties rises considerably. Even today, we barely hire a fourth of the applicants we receive because there are so many interested individuals.

Q&A

Another classroom interaction that happens in face-to-face classes is the opportunity students have to ask questions of the teacher and the teacher to ask questions of the students. This interaction exists along a wide spectrum, from simple clarification questions to the sorts of inquiries that can spawn broader, more back-and-forth collective class discussions.

The ability for students to ask teachers and professors open-ended questions is one of the critical parts of the class-room experience. One common critique of MOOCs is the inability to scale this interaction: MOOCs are often unmoni-tored, with students left to support one another or monitored only by volunteers. At the same time, it presents a challenge to synchronous courses: questions are plentiful and often relevant only to the individual (such as grade inquiries or something of interest to only a small subset of the class), but class time is limited. Stereotypes abound about students who ask advanced questions that derail the overall lesson or stu-dents who ask a great number of basic questions, holding the rest of the class back. Classmates often blame the students themselves for these patterns, but the fault ultimately lies with a system that so highly values synchronous co-located time that student questions can seem to be a waste if they are not relevant to all in attendance.

Office hours are often the mechanism employed to push these questions to an "overflow" space, but these similarly face a challenge of scale: a single student may need a full hour of one-on-one support through office hours, which may be all that is available for the entire class. Teams of teaching assistants may pool together to offer help desks, which are more frequently available; these can offer students the support they need, but at a cost. By shifting this question-and-answer to individual office hours, the rest of the class is no longer able to benefit from discussions that *were* relevant to them.

Taken together, this is one of the challenges presented by the limited amount of synchronous co-located time available to a traditional class: the time is scarce and must be used for everyone's collective maximum benefit. A class discussion relevant to only 10 percent of the class's students— whether they are the 10 percent high achievers interested in advanced topics, the 10 percent low achievers needing extra assistance, or the 10 percent with some special interest like chemical engineers in a computer science class—is not a good use of the entire class's shared time. Yet 10 percent can be a large number of students, and those discussions can be some of the most valuable learning opportunities for *those* students. The scarcity of shared time encourages a one-size-fits-all approach to designing class agendas, and yet one-size-fits-all quickly becomes one-size-fits-none because no one gets the best experience possible for them.

All of those issues arise even before getting into prominent issues regarding gender, race, ethnicity, and equity in the classroom. For example, research has shown that women are less likely to ask questions in seminars[8] and Black

students are encouraged to ask fewer questions by teachers.[9] These issues were on Pooja Sankar's mind when she
started Piazza, a tool that has become one of the most widely
used tools in higher education. Piazza is a forum tool but
designed with certain goals in mind. Sankar writes, "I started
Piazza so every student can have that opportunity to learn
from her classmates. Whether she's too shy to ask, whether
she's working alone in her dorm room, or whether her few
friends in her class don't know the answer either."[10] One of
the defining features of Piazza is that teachers cannot prevent students from posting anonymously, at least from their
classmates' perspectives. The goal is to allow students to post
freely without the fear of being judged for their gender or
ethnicity: a woman in a computer science class, for instance,
can post a question without fearing, "As soon as they see
this post comes from someone named Rebecca, they'll just
assume I don't belong here."

Our own research confirms this use case is still alive today:
while women in our online undergraduate CS1 class post
approximately as often as men in the class, they are almost
twice as likely to post anonymously. This trend applies to
posting both questions and answers; women are more likely
to post questions anonymously and more likely to post
answers anonymously. Interestingly, this may actually represent a place where anonymous posting is working against
us: each woman posting anonymously may feel more alone
due to not knowing how many of those other anonymous
posts—both questions and answers—are from other women
in the class.

But embedded in Sankar's description of her creation
of Piazza is a reference to what we are defining here as the

distributed classroom: that the student can be working alone in her dorm room. This small observation shatters the grip on class Q&A previously held by synchronous meeting times or live office hours. With tools like Piazza, Q&A is distributed in time and space; students can ask questions later from anywhere rather than having to ensure they are answered during lectures. Because they are asked in a public forum, the questions and answers remain available for everyone, so as with in-class discussions, others can still benefit. Because they are asked asynchronously, they do not demand that the student be comfortable asking in front of a live captive audience. And because they exist separate from synchronous class time, no student is required to wait for a discussion that does not interest them to end before class can continue; they may instead divert their attention to a discussion that does interest them.

The benefits of this development are more far-reaching than just supporting more questions and discussions. In 2016, based on our first year of experiences teaching in the online MSCS program, we (with Ashok Goel) wrote a short paper titled, "The Unexpected Pedagogical Benefits of Making Higher Education Accessible."[11] The paper outlines eight ways we observed that the online experience is arguably better than the in-person experience; seven of these are derived from forum interactions. While Piazza was developed to complement in-person classes, we observe that it takes on a new relevance when it is the *sole* place where student-teacher and student-student interaction can officially take place; then, based on this new relevance, new advantages emerge. An asynchronous forum does not demand any synchronous time, meaning that students do not have to consume every discussion as they must while attending in person; thus, those three different hypothetical 10 percent groups described above can initiate discussions on their own interests rather than rely on the class as a whole to align with their priorities. The forum gives students the ability to propose class discussions in a way that would be awkward in person; it is hard to imagine a student raising their hand and saying, "I know there's a lesson plan for today, but I came across a really great article I think we should discuss instead!" But that exact behavior can be accomplished online because their article discussion need not compete for a scarce time resource. All of these discussions can then proceed for days on end rather than having to be curtailed at the end of the scheduled class time, allowing them to develop more deeply while remaining accessible to a larger audience.

The success of forum tools like Piazza in complementing an existing in-person classroom experience shows that distributing components of the experience beyond just lectures is possible; even more important, though, it shows that it can bring benefits to the student experience itself. These tools are not merely about being "good enough" to expand the classroom; they are about fundamentally improving the experience itself, even for those who are otherwise participating in person. Piazza was started as an initiative to—in our vocabulary—distribute the classroom, and it shows how distributing the classroom improves the existing class as well.

TESTING

Among the topics discussed so far, testing is likely the least inspiring. Testing can be a valuable learning and teaching tool—research shows frequent testing leads to better learning outcomes[12]—but it is not one that many people get excited about, like giving interesting projects or conducting deep class discussions. Yet it is also a task that has typically commanded that scarce synchronous class time as well: in order to ensure integrity, students take their tests together in one room. The only time when students gather together in one place is spent forcing them to sit independently and silently.

The drawbacks of this structure are immense. It wastes that scarce synchronous class time on a task that, aside from integrity validation, is largely agnostic to time and place. That wasted synchronous class time usually forces teachers to give a small number of high-stakes assessments rather than give up more class time for more frequent testing, losing the main benefit that testing has been shown to provide. Moreover, it forces students into high-stakes assessments on someone else's schedule rather than the one best for them. All students can likely recall a time when they performed poorly on a test for a reason unrelated to their understanding of the content—for David, it was having to take a final in cognitive psychology an hour after discovering his car had been broken into overnight.

Testing is one of the features now supplied by learning management systems. In our experience, this feature is primarily used by online programs; until COVID-19 drove all classes into some online modality, most in-person classes we observed still did testing in person. And yet this feature provides a way of distributing one of the biggest wastes of synchronous class time. By letting students take tests outside class, instructors can recover hours of instructional time per semester.

The limiting factor here is obvious: integrity. Take-home exams are not a new idea, but many fields need stronger assurance that students did not collaborate. How do you handle that? Now there are digital proctoring services. This was a niche area as recently as 2012, but it has grown tremendously in popularity over the past decade before exploding in the wake of COVID-19 as instructors have frantically tried to find ways to guarantee test integrity when there is no physical classroom. Over a dozen vendors operate in the space offering features like AI-based proctoring, human review of exam sessions, Web traffic monitoring, browser lockdown, and more.

We are both avid users and critics of these services. We believe they have a critical role to play in programs that lack other structural obstacles to widespread misconduct. In an online program, for example, trying to find someone to take a test for you means trying to find someone to log into your account or jump on a screen-sharing session with you, which is far easier than trying to find someone to enter a physical classroom to take an exam for you in person. At the same time, they are inherently invasive, they introduce additional stress on test takers already going through an anxiety-inducing experience, they add a nontrivial additional workload on teachers and teaching assistants to review flagged behaviors asynchronously, they still demand some rethinking of test design to account for behaviors that are hard to detect, and they are expensive. But from the perspective of the distributed classroom, they provide the minimum necessary functionality: they allow another activity typically performed in the classroom to be distributed in time and space.

Even if a teacher's discomfort with digital proctoring services is great enough to deter them from using one altogether, many learning management systems provide other options for ensuring integrity in a distributed classroom. These include simpler lockdown browsers to prevent easy sharing of exam content to classmates taking tests at other times; question banks to ensure that a student does not receive the same exact assessment as a classmate that may have shared test content with them in advance; and parameterizable questions to generate effectively infinite variations on the same problem. These may be coupled with other design decisions—such as opting for many small quizzes rather than a few high-stakes tests—to offer more guarantees of integrity while improving learning at the same time. For the many faculty uncomfortable with springing digital proctoring on students who signed up for an in-person experience, David has authored a guide to designing trustworthy unproctored assessments that is available through Georgia Tech's Center for Teaching & Learning.[13] The chief takeaway here is that there now exist options, whether through proctoring services or other features of a learning management system, to shift assessment from the synchronous co-located quadrant into the asynchronous remote or synchronous remote quadrants.

THE OMSCS CONNECTION

As we have noted, this book is not about our online MSCS program, which lies near one extreme of the distributed classroom spectrum, short of true MOOCs. Nevertheless, it is worth discussing it a bit more because it provides an excellent example of how the work done with learning management systems so far has set us up for success in pursuing a distributed classroom.

When asked about how we run the OMSCS program, the questions we receive often reflect a deep misunderstanding of what the program is. We have been asked, "Do you really think it's possible to give a master's degree just on the basis of passing a bunch of multiple-choice tests?" The answer: absolutely not, and almost every class in the OMSCS program is project based.[14] We have been asked, "I watched ten courses on Udacity.com. When do I get my diploma?" The answer: you don't; earning course credit requires far more than simply watching the class videos. We estimate that engaging with videos is only 5 to 10 percent of the time students spend on our courses; student reviews regularly report that the total time required for a course is ten times more than the raw length of the course video content. We have been asked, "Do you really trust peer grading enough to give graduate degrees on the basis of peer-assigned grades?" The answer: we use peer review a lot, but for pedagogical purposes, not for assigning grades. Research has found that peer-to-peer feedback is highly valuable as a pedagogical exercise: putting students in a position to critique work rather than generate it forces them to view content from a different perspective, and receiving feedback from a wider variety of reviewers raises the likelihood that the recipient will understand and internalize the feedback.[15] Other research has found that peer grading can even be reliable compared to expert grading in very specific circumstances;[16] however, our primary concern is with the reliability of the feedback, and so our grades and feedback are still given by trained human TAs.

The truth is that despite lying on the far other end of the distributed classroom spectrum, classes in the OMSCS program run remarkably similar to their on-campus analogues. Semesters start and end on the same dates. Students submit assignments to and receive grades and feedback from the same learning management system as on-campus students. Students in both campuses use class forum tools like Piazza, Campuswire, or EdStem (albeit more heavily in the online program). The difference is that while on-campus classes meet together in a classroom at a shared time, online students have custom-filmed asynchronous instructional content. Most other administrative and structural details remain the same.

Many classes go even further than that: many are offered online and on-campus by the same instructor in the same semester. In some of these cases, the instructor may merge the online and on-campus classes in the learning management system and course forum, and the same team of teaching assistants may grade students in both sections. This structure is part of why we have been so confident in asserting that the online program is equivalent to the on-campus program: many times, they are not even delivered as if they are different programs. One of our first experiments with this came in fall 2015, when Ashok Goel taught CS7637: Knowledge-Based AI simultaneously online and on-campus; David was a teaching assistant for the class at the time. While we did not merge the classes in the forum, we did use the same assignments, exams, and projects in both sections, along with the same course schedule, and students in both versions were graded by the same team of teaching assistants; when grading, those TAs did not even know if an assignment came from an on-campus or online student. We found that on every assignment, online students either met or exceeded the performance of on-campus students.[17]

Our most ambitious experiment with this arrangement came in fall 2019. During this term, David co-taught CS7646: Machine Learning for Trading with Dave Byrd, a research scientist at Georgia Tech's Institute for People and Technology. This online section was also offered to students in our online master of science in analytics program. Meanwhile, Dave was teaching an on-campus section of CS7646, which itself was cross-listed with CS4646, the Machine Learning for Trading class for undergraduate students. So we put all the students together into one large section in the learning management system, led by a team of 26 teaching assistants. More than one thousand students (785 online, 292 in person) began the class, and 929 (649 online, 280 in person) completed it. Online students watched custom-filmed class videos from the course's original creator, Tucker Balch, while on-campus students attended Dave Byrd's lectures in person (but could watch the online lectures if they wanted to as well). The two sections completed the same projects, which were graded by the same teaching assistants. The different sections were given different exams, with the on-campus students' exams reflecting content Dave taught that was not in the online lectures, while online students' exams featured questions on content in the online lectures Dave did not cover in person. The course went by largely without a hitch— primarily, we would argue, due to the incredible job done by Josh Fox, the head TA for the class that term (for which he quite deservedly won the college's Outstanding Graduate TA award).

The details for designing for that scale, including negotiating the different constraints and demands of those different sections and audiences, could probably fill an entire book on its own, but that is not exactly what we are interested in here. What is important is that our on-campus teaching is already so distributed that when we went to launch the OMSCS program, we were able to leverage a massive amount of the face-to-face program's structure. We did not have to figure out how to have students submit assignments from all over the world, ask questions regardless of their time zone, or get individual feedback even in a class of three hundred. Those needs were already taken care of by technological developments over the past decade. All we had to do was take the small number of remaining things that still were reliant on a physical classroom and nudge them over to the asynchronous, remote side. The reason we are confident that the online MSCS program is equivalent in rigor and prestige to the on-campus program is that it shares such a large amount of the same content, designs, and infrastructure: the same professors teach the classes, the same teaching assistants grade the work, and the projects and assignments are the same for the online student body. That is because the traditional program was already so distributed that the online program could be designed on its foundation rather than built up from scratch.

The same foundation may apply to other schools, other programs, other subjects, and other levels. Classrooms are already distributed in many ways. Making them fully distributed is the last step, not the first.

SHAREABLE CLASSES

Distance learning and learning management systems can be seen in many ways as two trends converging on something resembling a distributed classroom. Distance learning starts with the premise that learning must be at a distance and then preserves whatever it can from the in-person experience. Learning management systems start with in-person learning, then look piece-by-piece at what can be distributed across place and time to expand what the course can offer, improve the course experience, and maximize the usefulness of live shared class time. Bolstered by modern technology, these efforts have begun to converge; distance learning can be remarkably similar to on-campus classes because both are now so reliant on the same shared technologies.

These next three examples—shareable classes, distributed co-location, and emergency remote classrooms—are less foundational to future initiatives; rather, they are examples of how elements of the distributed classroom have already been realized.

EXPANDING REACH THROUGH SHARED CLASSES

The first of these notions is that of a shareable classroom. Under a traditional model, an individual teacher's reach is usually linearly related to the effort involved. Teaching twice as many students means teaching twice as many sections of the class, delivering twice as many lectures, grading twice as many assignments, and so on. Some of these things may be shifted to more flat costs; developing good assignments and rubrics takes the same amount of effort regardless of whether they will be completed by fifty students or five hundred. Other components may scale with support staff; if a TA is hired for every fifty students, the teacher's reach can grow without necessarily increasing their commitment by the same rate.

Nonetheless, teaching more students almost always incurs more demand on the teacher ultimately in charge of the class: even if it is not delivering more lectures or grading more students, it is managing more teaching assistants or handling more edge cases, such as grade complaints and individual accommodations. Some of these responsibilities have little to do with knowledge of the subject matter, however. The idea of making a class "shareable" would be to ask at what level a class—including its instructional content, assignments, rubrics, and so on—can be shared from one teacher to another, especially with regard to what level of content knowledge is necessary for a new teacher to deliver a class designed by someone else. The more a class is shareable without requiring the knowledge necessary to design the class in the first place, the greater reach it can attain without increasing the workload on the original teacher.

This is not a particularly new idea: viewed in a particular light, numerous existing initiatives mirror this desire. MOOCs are an obvious example, but textbooks themselves are in many ways an effort toward making a class more shareable. Authoring a textbook requires a level of knowledge of the material that goes beyond that needed to teach a class on the same content. Teachers using a textbook need not write enormous numbers of practice problems, learn professional-level equation editors, or consider all the content dependencies for a particular lesson. These are provided by the structure of a well-written textbook. A teacher equipped with a strong textbook may be able to deliver a class that they would struggle to teach by their own efforts alone.

Still, these obviously carry large compromises. Using a textbook in a class still requires the teacher to have significant content knowledge, just not the sort of expert-level knowledge necessary to prescribe how the class ought to be taught in the first place. MOOCs are similar: rather than finding a way to distribute the content-agnostic responsibilities of teaching a class in person, MOOCs largely avoid those responsibilities in the first place. What level of compromise between these extremes is possible?

SHARING CLASSES IN OMSCS

In the previous section, we briefly referenced teaching CS7646: Machine Learning for Trading. David began teaching this class in the OMSCS program in spring 2019 and as of the time of writing this book has taught it for eight semesters; three of these he co-taught with Dave Byrd and five by himself. David is not an expert in machine learning for trading or computational finance. His knowledge of the field extends beyond what is taught by the class, but not far enough to have developed the class by himself. In terms of a matrix related to the types of knowledge necessary for teaching, he is high on pedagogical knowledge, but more average on pedagogical content knowledge and content knowledge. He is not teaching the class from scratch, though; instead, he is executing a class designed by someone, Tucker Balch, with all three types of knowledge. David is able to use the original lecture videos, the original assignment descriptions, the original rubrics, and the original structure. He is also supported by a team of incredible teaching assistants who evaluate assignments and patrol the course forum for questions. Tucker remains involved at the level of being able to discuss ideas and being available to answer questions that no one else can answer, but the time commitment represented by those two tasks is relatively minimal.

This is not the only class to undergo such a transfer; of the forty classes available in the program at time of writing, five other classes have undergone a similar handoff. Three have undergone a partial handoff, where the original professor has remained involved but more administrative responsibilities have been handed off to a co-instructor; this allows the professor to focus on those content questions that are truly their area of expertise. Another class has been traded back and forth between two professors for multiple semesters. On the surface, this is not unusual: many college classes are taught by one of multiple professors depending on the term, or multiple instructors during a single class term. What is remarkable here is the extent to which the class content and structure remain consistent across these handoffs.

Similar ideas exist at other universities as well. Professors at Stanford University have developed CS Bridge, a program that describes itself as "a model for cross-border co-teaching of CS1."[18] Part of the development of this program is the CS Bridge Course-in-a-Box, an "open-source and free to use CS1 curriculum-in-a-box: assignments, a clonable website, slides, lesson plans, and more." The goal here is similarly to create a fully developed course that is easily shareable with new instructors, significantly lowering the amount of expertise and effort needed for a particular individual to offer an additional section of a class. Stanford's CS Bridge program has been offered in countries around the world; in some places, a local section is managed by and includes direct interaction with the original authors, while in others, individual instructors pick up the kit on their own and offer their own section with little to no direct input from the original authors.

There are drawbacks, of course. This focus on shareable and reusable content also may allow content to become outdated, especially in rapidly developing fields. This is a natural consequence of models that encourage a significant amount of upfront development to create content to be reused over time. The distributed classroom model attempts to address this issue: rather than one-time upfront development, it encourages low-overhead mechanisms for making existing in-person experiences—which themselves are somewhat naturally updated as the content is redelivered each semester—more distributable. We discuss this more in chapter 4.

But the important point here is the way in which a shareable class may be used to expand a teacher's reach. While our sharing has happened within our program, there is little technologically or pedagogically to prevent a class from OMSCS being taught at another university in another program. Another university could create a class built from our lecture material, our assignments, and our rubrics, administered by their own teacher and teaching assistants for the purposes of assessment and discussion. Like the promise of MOOCs, a single professor may be able to reach thousands of students, but unlike MOOCs, this reach may retain much more of the original experience and rigor through these more deliberately distributed models.

SHARING CLASSES IN K–12

Our bias in this section shows that we work in graduate-level computer science, an upper-level field whose biggest difficulty is often hiring professors and instructors when industry can offer much greater incentives. What about in a field where teachers are more plentiful?

We revisit this question in chapter 9, but this connects to the long-held fear that these sorts of initiatives will be used to replace teachers. In a field like quantum computing, where the number of people qualified to and interested in teaching the content is highly limited, a distributed classroom holds obvious appeal to expand the reach of that small number of individuals. But what about in fields like calculus or history, where teachers are generally more plentiful?

In these cases, rather than expanding reach, the goal of the distributed classroom becomes to improve outcomes. Teachers already teach with textbooks and leverage assessments provided by publishers; "distributing the classroom" means making more such resources available to them. For example, rather than having to individually grade every student's work, grading responsibilities can be distributed to a wide audience of evaluators; research has already found some success in creating this sort of crowd-sourced assistance.[19] Or, rather than having to be one of thousands of teachers delivering generally the same lecture on integration by parts (a topic in calculus) on a given day, teachers may leverage distributed resources to flip their classroom and focus on individual practice and support.

Teachers are already asked to play far too many functional roles in the classroom. It is, in our opinion, unreasonable to ask any single individual to deliver an engaging live class experience, write excellent individual feedback on essays or homework problems, handle tough disciplinary issues, support at-risk and disadvantaged students, engage and challenge high-performing students, monitor external standards for adherence and compliance, and all the other responsibilities teachers are asked to fulfill. Beyond asking individuals to excel at too many vastly different responsibilities, the quantity of work that results is too high as well. A 2012 report by the Bill & Melinda Gates Foundation found that teachers work on average ten hours, forty minutes per day,[20] and bring work home 30 percent of the time.[21] Distributing the classroom opens the opportunity for distributing these responsibilities as well. Imagine, for instance, a school system with ten individual high schools, each with its own calculus teacher; under a traditional model, each of these teachers fulfills all of the above roles. What if instead a single teacher, the most gifted presenter, was tasked with presenting the core class content to all ten schools, freeing up the remaining teachers to focus on answering individual questions and giving high-quality feedback? What if a particular teacher specialized in cases where students struggled most mightily, allowing them to devote more individual attention because they are not forced to also be the sole source of instruction and grading for an entire additional class? Of course, feedback cycles are necessary: the person delivering the class content benefits from seeing the errors students are making, but these can be built in without also requiring the instructor to be the grader for a large cohort of students on their own.

This is not a new idea, of course: it's similar to the vision of open educational resources, standardized class designs, and more. Teachers ought to be able to select from precreated, high-quality, thoroughly vetted materials rather than recreate everything from scratch. There are also fears about these approaches, and they are not unfounded: these ideas can be used to students' detriment as much as to their benefit. A teacher can thoughtlessly turn on a video and hand out a worksheet without deeply attending to the students' current progress or alignment between such resources. There *are* cost-cutting opportunities here in an industry already far too underfunded in many areas. Like any other tool, the outcome of distributing functional roles across teachers and creating more reusable content is based on how these initiatives are used.

DISTRIBUTED CO-LOCATION

In discussions of distance learning, hybrid classrooms, HyFlex models, and other models related to the distributed classroom, we find that one characteristic is often taken for granted: the idea that the students themselves are likely to be individually isolated. The common framework for distance learning is that students are attending from their own homes or offices. In the distributed classroom matrix we described in chapter 2 and further detail in chapter 4, this design paradigm jumps straight to designing for purely and individually remote audiences.

Despite this, there are several signs that this may step too far toward pure distance learning. Students may not be willing or able to travel to a campus thousands of miles away to attend classes, but they may nonetheless be willing and able to travel to meet with other students in their area. This presents the opportunity to preserve co-located interactions even among students who are remote relative to the home campus. We have seen two such examples of this phenomenon, and we have begun making plans for a third.

LOCAL MEET-UPS

Taking the OMSCS program as an example first, we enroll at the time of this writing over eleven thousand students from all over the world. Accordingly, in several major cities and tech hubs, we have numerous students. One study found that "as many as 80 percent of OMSCS students in the United States live within two hours of one of ten major population centers."[22]

Those shared locations have given rise to an abundance of local meet-up groups. Clear data on these local meet-ups is hard to come by as they are organized in large part by students in unofficial channels rather than by the program or institute. That is not to say that they should not be officially organized, but rather that students have consistently moved more quickly than we possibly can to create the things they want to see. We know, though, that meet-ups have occurred in cities around the world. In the student-run OMSCS Slack organization, numerous channels are dedicated to finding connections to local classmates. During the first weeks of a semester, course forums are often filled with threads seeking nearby classmates for study groups.

To date, most such meet-ups have either been purely social among local students in the program regardless of their current class enrollments (including alumni in many instances) or smaller, more dedicated study groups for a particular course. This is in large part due to the asynchronous nature of the program: the material itself is built assuming a remote asynchronous audience, and so when students gather together, the structure of the course is not inherently conducive to shared participation in a more live learning experience. It is not a far stretch, however, to imagine an arrangement where rather than merely watching an asynchronous lecture, a remote cohort of students instead participates in real time with the lecture taking place elsewhere or with a recording of the lecture built with dedicated pauses for practice problems or discussions to replicate a more typical in-person experience.[23] The existence of local meet-ups, even in the absence of any formal incentive to participate in them or structure to facilitate them, suggests that the spectrum between co-located and remote has more gradations than previously leveraged.

This phenomenon is not unique to OMSCS, of course; many of the most popular MOOCs have a culture of local meet-ups as well. Harvard's popular MOOC CS50, for instance, has spawned numerous local meet-ups. Early in its history, MOOC provider Coursera experimented with Learning Hubs, a sort of combination of local meet-up space and internet café targeted at areas of the world where high-speed internet access is less ubiquitous.[24] MOOC provider Udacity similarly experimented with in-person offerings through Udacity Connect in 2017.[25] Other student-led initiatives to create local meet-up opportunities are well documented.[26] In some instances, universities have been more proactive in managing local cohorts: Harvard's CopyrightX program, for instance, has had affiliate courses at dozens of universities around the world, which are effectively local cohorts for a distributed course.[27]

We might wonder, though: If there truly is sufficient demand for creating co-located experiences from otherwise-remote classes, why were MOOC-based initiatives like Coursera Learning Hubs and Udacity Connect ultimately discontinued? Why do in-person boot camps and similar programs still dominate the in-person, not-for-credit space rather than these sorts of distributed experiences? We can speculate many reasons why, but we would argue it largely comes down to the same issues that lead to MOOCs' low engagement and completion rates. MOOC credentials are wildly varied in their rigor, scope, and trustworthiness, which means that it is unclear why a person should dedicate the time and energy to attending an in-person gathering.[28] To explore the potential for such remote meet-ups, they need to be attached to the types of incentives that are more likely to coax a student into such high-effort engagement. Unofficial local meet-ups associated with OMSCS classes are one such promising area, but what if such groups were more official?

DISTRIBUTED CAMPUSES

Many universities have multiple campuses. Some, like the State University of New York (SUNY) with its sixty-four campuses, are defined by that variety of locations. Others, like Georgia Tech, are more clearly structured as a core campus and multiple satellite campuses. We, for instance, have a campus in Lorraine, France, as well as our newest campus in Shenzhen, China. The typical model would be that classes taken at any campus are usable at any other campus, and that different campuses would offer all classes necessary to complete some subset of the total number of programs. For example, SUNY has a bachelor's in applied computing program specifically available at its SUNY Polytechnic Institute campus. Campuses would have their own faculty, or sometimes faculty would travel among campuses; Georgia Tech faculty regularly spend a semester teaching at Georgia Tech-Lorraine, for instance. On the whole, the model is built more on the idea of exchange (whether of credits, students, or faculty members). The university's influence is increased, but with an additional expenditure of resources.

When our OMSCS program launched in 2014, one early question was whether the model could be used to expand some of our course offerings at other campuses. Students in France apply to and enroll in the OMSCS program; it would seem silly if students at Georgia Tech's campus in Lorraine could not also enroll in the program's classes. For years, a small number of students at Georgia Tech-Lorraine each semester have joined up with the OMSCS program's much larger student body. For instructors teaching some of these classes, the process is administratively trivial, requiring only a few minutes at the start and end of the semester to merge classes or export separate final gradebooks. The students in Lorraine, however, have a built-in local cohort of classmates to interact with as they move through the course.

The numbers in that case are small (often only two or three students at the Lorraine campus in a class), and so there are limited options to leverage that local cohort to improve the student experience. In fall 2020, though, we began a greater experiment: a dozen students at the Georgia Tech-Shenzhen campus enrolled in David's CS6750: Human-Computer Interaction class. Like the Lorraine students, they were merged into the same section in our learning management system and shared the same course forum, but they also had an in-person component to complement their participation online. With a dedicated local co-instructor (program alumnus and one of Forbes' China 30 Under 30, Fandi Peng), they had their own in-person recitations to discuss the course material, work together on team projects, and participate in their own peer review cycles. They even planned their own field trips, such as a visit to Huaqiangbei, the largest electronics market in China, to investigate the design principles they learned in the course. They were graded by the same teaching assistants as the rest of the class, ensuring the same rigor and expectations are applied, but they had opportunities to take advantage of having a local cohort of classmates with whom to interact.

While on the surface this is similar to initiatives like Udacity Connect, the participation is tied to a heavyweight credential, a graduate degree in computer science, with all the trappings that go with the program, including human grading, formal transcripts, and a recognized diploma. Through these incentives, we see greater engagement than in MOOC-based programs and a preview of the model of the distributed classroom.

GEORGIA TECH ATRIUM

The programs in France and China are already underway; students at Georgia Tech-Lorraine have enrolled in OMSCS classes for several years, and students at Georgia Tech-Shenzhen started in fall 2020. There is a third idea within this general category of leveraging a heavily distributed student body to reintroduce synchronous co-located interactions, one that we expect to ramp up in the coming few months.

Georgia Tech's 2015 Commission on Creating the Next in Education report described five initiatives for the future of education. The fifth of these initiatives, A Distributed Worldwide Presence, follows the same principles as this argument for an overall distributed classroom. The focus of this initiative is on the notion of the Georgia Tech atrium, "an open space that can be programmed to suit the needs of learners, a venue for performances and events, and a way to provide social glue for learners, professors, and others who want to be associated with Georgia Tech."[29]

This design breaks the common assumption that a remote, online degree program means that students will work on material from their own homes. Rather, it may provide the sort of common area students find in university libraries and student centers, where they may go to interact with classmates and access services like high-speed internet. One can imagine that these spaces may be used to extend access to certain facilities common on campus that cannot be easily distributed all the way to students' homes, like spaces for chemistry labs or three-dimensional printing.

Viewed through this lens, the Georgia Tech atrium becomes another instance of modifying the compromise between traditional and distance only as much as necessary. Historically, opting for distance learning has meant giving up such synchronous meeting spaces and high-cost facilities for the sake of the flexibility to attend from a distance, but models like this show that compromise need not go quite that far. We will revisit the relevance of these ideas in chapter 8, "The Distributed Campus."

EMERGENCY REMOTE CLASSROOMS

The rapid shift to remote learning sparked by the COVID-19 pandemic had both positive and negative effects on efforts toward distributed learning. The crisis forced widespread experimentation with online technologies, leading thousands of faculty members to start looking almost overnight at what can and cannot work in remote teaching. This sudden enormous investment of attention into remote learning has led to some novel insights into the ways in which it can be done well, as well as a growing understanding of what does not work. The results of that exploration appear to be positive: a survey by Tyton Partners in August 2020 found 49 percent of faculty members view online learning as an effective method of teaching, up from 39 percent only three months earlier.[30]

At the same time, the rapid shift to remote learning obviously did not occur under the best circumstances. Teachers and students were not trained for remote learning, did not self-select into remote learning, and made the shift while dealing with likely the most uncertain time in their life spans. It would not be fair to judge the potential of online education based on the reality of this rapid shift. We noted in chapter 1 that when we developed our online undergraduate CS1 course, we worked for a year with a team of almost a dozen well-qualified people. Even setting aside our prior years of online teaching experience, how can the results of that investment of expertise and resources compare to individuals forced to make the transition largely on their own in a two-week time period? And yet a pushback against remote learning is underway using negative results from this rapid shift as evidence of a hypothesized fundamental weakness in remote learning. We do not doubt for a moment that teaching remote or hybrid classes during the pandemic has been an enormous challenge for many teachers; but we also argue that the potential of these initiatives cannot be fairly assessed based on their performance under the worst of conditions.

During this rapid shift to online learning, several of us who work on the OMSCS program quickly pivoted to a support role helping our on-campus faculty with their transition. We participated in the emergent national dialogue on this shift and supplied our own guidance and suggestions. Throughout these experiences, we gained a sort of informal catalog of the different approaches that faculty members are using. These approaches are by no means exhaustive, and there may certainly be many other models used in other places, but the models here cover those that we witnessed most often in our work during the crisis. The relevance of these models here is that they provide mechanisms that may be further developed and used to support a distributed classroom under favorable circumstances in the future, so it is worthwhile to explore teachers' experiences with these mechanisms under these unfavorable circumstances.

THE SYNCHRONOUS MODEL

As described earlier in this chapter, most classes already had many of their structures available in a distributed manner. Many were already using a learning management system to receive assignment submissions and return grades and feedback. Some were already using a forum for asynchronous Q&A, although the degree to which teachers were involved prior to the crisis varied. The major question that emerged was the actual classroom experience.

The default approach we observed during the early part of the pandemic was a one-to-one substitution of the in-person classroom with a teleconference. Rather than coming to a particular room at class time, students would sign on to the class's videoconferencing system. From there, the teacher conducted class live. Lecture material was delivered just as if the teacher was standing in front of the classroom. Some teachers used slides, while others experimented with virtual whiteboards on writable tablet computers or screencasting live interaction with some software. Questions were often asked via the chat function or built-in "raise hand" features in the videoconferencing platform. One common observation from teachers was that social norms were not well established in these classrooms; unless students were informed to do so, they often held back from interacting in the chat or using such features of the system. This led to our guideline to future instructors to include specific instructions for how they want students to interact with them so that students may know what behaviors are expected.

A large number of classes function according to this model: these are either large lecture classes with limited opportunities for back-and-forth interaction in the first place or small classes with significant back-and-forth interaction feasible even within the videoconference. For classes that use their synchronous class time for more interaction, however, teachers often experimented with tools like breakout rooms to give students the opportunity to interact in smaller groups. Teachers could then move between the breakout rooms to participate in the conversation, similar to how a teacher might go around a room while students engage in group work. We observed that there were often nontrivial technical hurdles to this experience—directing students to breakout rooms and bringing them back together was far less trivial than in person (although other interfaces, like the Minerva Project, may make this much simpler). We also observed that as with the other interactions, students needed detailed guidance on how to participate because the social norms of classroom participation were not readily transferable. We observed, for example, an odd asymmetry when it came to students in such breakout rooms who did not turn on their cameras, and yet we also understand that students may be uncomfortable appearing visually from an area of their home they had not intended to share with their classmates.

As more schools pursued reopening in fall 2020 and spring 2021, this synchronous model gave way to a more typical distance learning model where some students attended in-person while others joined remotely. This allowed social distancing to be maintained in the classroom without cutting class enrollments. On reflection, however, many teachers we spoke to noted that this could be even more difficult; some felt as if this model required them to effectively teach two classes at once. Remote students reported sensing more inequity as well; questions raised by remote audiences could be overlooked by the instructor for extended periods of time as they catered to the visible in-person audience.

THE ASYNCHRONOUS MODEL

While these synchronous models are common, they create a nontrivial additional burden on teachers, especially those lacking a general comfort with technology. Teachers are forced to juggle both technical administration with content delivery and classroom organization, dramatically increasing the complexity of teaching live. Social media in the wake of the shift was full of humorous and embarrassing stories from students about faculty members forgetting to turn on their camera or microphone, forgetting about what was visible in other tabs on their computers, or forgetting what could be seen in the background of their webcam feed. In response to this, we advocated for faculty members to instead deliver content asynchronously, filming the presentation of their core material on their own rather than attempting to present it live. This would allow them time to learn the technology without the pressure of a live audience, and it would ensure that faculty were comfortable with the results *before* they were visible to students. The model had other benefits as well: teachers can match the length of a presentation to the content rather than external constraints such as scheduled class time, and students can interact on their own schedule, which is more compatible with their new normal.

Of course, a synchronous remote class can be recorded as well, and most such classes we observed or assisted with did in fact capture of the remote class experience. This too gives students a persistent resource they can refer back to on their own time and helps students more disproportionately affected by the crisis to engage as they are able. A student who was forced to return home overseas, for example, might be asked to attend class at 3:00 a.m. local time, but recorded material allows them to stay up-to-date within their local time zone. Recording live remote lectures introduced other issues, however, most notably that it created more pressure

on students who otherwise wanted to ask questions or interact live: they had to do so with the pressure of knowing
that their questions or interactions would be recorded and
published to the rest of the class. An embarrassing question
would be recorded and reshared—potentially even outside
the class—rather than forgotten five minutes after class
ended.

The asynchronous delivery model posed other issues as
well: it meant a lack of live interaction between teachers and
students. Students' questions were no longer anchored to
particular places in the content as they are when asked during a synchronous class (either out loud or via a chat tool),
but rather were somewhat disembodied as a separate forum
post. Courses that involved synchronous class discussions
or group work suffered as well, although we saw some success with requiring students to record such group interactions and submit them as a sort of assignment. As schools
shifted to partial reopenings, some teachers continued to
favor asynchronous options for content delivery and opted
to effectively flip their classrooms. In-person class meetings
became supplementary touchpoints that relied on students'
prior interaction with the asynchronous course content.
Anecdotally, of the models we saw develop during this time
of reduced in-person attendance, this one received the most
favorable reviews from both teachers and students, but relatively few attempted it.

THE HOSTED MODEL

It was from these different sets of pros and cons that a sort of
hybrid compromise between synchronous and asynchronous

emerged, especially during the early part of the pandemic when classes were entirely remote. The term *hybrid* is so overloaded in this domain, however, that we tend to use a different term: we call this the "hosted" model. Under this model, teachers adopted an approach where they record the core material in advance, but then host (like a television host or master of ceremonies) that material during a live interaction. For example, if a class meets Tuesday and Thursday at 9:30 a.m. eastern standard time (EST), the teacher films their material on the previous Sunday. On Tuesday at 9:30 a.m. EST, the students sign onto the videoconferencing system. The teacher briefly appears on screen to welcome everyone and then plays the video. Students ask questions in the chat box while the video plays, and the teacher answers them live without interrupting the video; thus, students do not feel their questions must be worth pausing all their classmates' experiences. If the teacher receives a question that they think is worth presenting to everyone, however, they do: they pause the video, appear on screen again, address the question, and then continue with the prepared content. The teacher may also build into the video dedicated breakpoints where students are expected to work problems on their own, engage in group discussions, or move to breakout rooms for small group interaction.

On the surface, this model may feel silly. If the video is prepared in advance, why bother requiring students to attend live? Why play it for them instead of just requiring them to view it on their own time? In practice, though, the model preserves the opportunities for live interaction anchored to the course content while also preserving the polish and comfort possible with prepared material. As with other ideas mentioned throughout this book, it presents a compromise only at the necessary level: synchronous interaction need not be sacrificed for the sake of the benefits of asynchronous production. But as with any other model, there are drawbacks: live feedback from students can no longer alter the way the teacher presents the content. Many teachers we worked with, however, felt that their presentation was so much better with the benefit of asynchronous production that it made up for whatever on-the-fly changes they might make based on live interaction.

Once developed, the model also presented other advantages. Students in time zones far removed from the school may still receive a recorded presentation, just as they could if a live class was captured; however, capturing a live class forces other live attendees to be comfortable having their questions and discussions recorded. Under this hosted model, live questions and discussions take place separate from the recording that is shared for later viewing. Teachers who simultaneously teach multiple sections of the same class could focus on teaching a particular lesson well once, then reuse it across all their sections rather than redelivering the same content two or more times. As universities moved to partial reopenings, this benefit emerged for faculty members teaching the same class to both in-person and remote students: prerecorded content either made it easier to cater to both audiences at once or allowed teachers to add a second class meeting time dedicated to remote students without dramatically increasing their teaching workload. But these benefits only begin to scratch the surface of what advantages we believe are possible by pursuing these ideas to their full potential.

THE DISTRIBUTED MODEL

All of these models demonstrate some of the hallmarks of the distributed classroom. All allow students to be geographically remote. Some allow students to participate on their own time. The hosted model captures the notion of offering different sets of compromises to meet different student needs: students who can attend live may do so (without consenting to themselves being recorded), and students who cannot are not locked out of the content altogether.

Going back to the time/space matrix, the synchronous model generally exists in the synchronous remote quadrant, although it may offer resources for limited asynchronous engagement or may be built from a synchronous in-person experience. The asynchronous model exists in the asynchronous remote quadrant, allowing only asynchronous remote interaction, while losing the advantages of synchronous interaction. The hosted model is remote but distributed between the synchronous and asynchronous quadrants: there exists a synchronous mode, including the advantages of synchronous interaction, but there also exist asynchronous remote options for those unable to participate with the synchronous model. As in a HyFlex design, the compromise is made at the student level: inability to participate synchronously does not prevent students from engaging altogether, but rather alters the components of the course with which they can engage. Only components that require synchronous interaction are inaccessible to asynchronous students.

Here, these compromises are relatively straightforward. It is seemingly natural that when a class session is already being delivered via videoconferencing that it be recorded. Even if a school is not affected by students being sent home to different time zones (such as more local K–12 schools), recording the session creates a resource students can use to study after the class is over; these recordings also make it simpler to support students with accommodations or disabilities that hinder synchronous attendance. Allowing ill students to stay up-to-date with the content requires little additional work from the teacher when such recordings are already captured and disseminated. These are some of the benefits we have witnessed firsthand in our OMSCS classes; problems that previously vexed us, such as ensuring students with excused absences could catch up on course content and accommodating class sizes that exceed a typical lecture hall, are addressed almost passively by these models.

These advantages are tremendous, and yet they are easily accessible only because the classroom experience has already been digitized. Going back to the time/space matrix, technology is already required to create a remote classroom experience, and that technology is what supports distributing it across time as well. That suggests that these advantages are preservable only if we stay in the remote half of the time/space matrix.

Are these advantages worth sticking to a remote classroom even when there is not a global pandemic forcing students to stay at home? It appears not. Despite the health risks, universities and schools experienced enormous pressure to reopen in-person experiences as quickly as possible. It is evident that significant parts of the co-located, synchronous experience are highly valued. They are not all pedagogical; many may coincide with the social role of formal education, providing the shared venue in which friendships can form. Others may align with the structural role that education plays, giving students a place to go so parents may return to work. Nonetheless, students and teachers alike express a fondness for the in-person classroom itself as well. This may be due to some fundamental superiority, or it may merely be due to familiarity, but in any case, there is significant pressure to bring back components of the in-person experience that have been lost in this transition. But does returning to an in-person experience mean losing the benefits of these alternate models?

The answer from the perspective of the distributed classroom is emphatically no. In-person interactions have a place in a distributed classroom as well. Just as the hosted model distributed the remote classroom experience between the synchronous and asynchronous quadrants, the distributed classroom seeks to distribute it even further, including synchronous co-located classes, as well as the middle tier of synchronicity and co-location introduced in chapter 2, where students may have their own synchronous or co-located cohort separate from the original class. We may bring back the synchronous in-person experience for students who can commit to participating within its requirements, allowing them to retain whatever benefits come with it, but we may also use what we have learned over the past several months to extend a classroom-like experience to remote and asynchronous students and cohorts of students as well.

In the process we may reap significant benefits. We may increase our ability to equitably accommodate audiences that struggle with the requirements of synchronous co-location, whether due to disabilities that make navigating a physical campus challenging or family obligations that preclude committing to full-time education. We may expand the diversity of our programs, catering to students who bring rich personal and professional backgrounds to class discussions and groupwork that enhance the experience for their classmates. We may improve the education experience itself by creating more opportunities for self-paced learning, embedded practice, and formative feedback through asynchronous options without sacrificing the benefits of live interaction. And we may accomplish all of this without dramatically changing our expectations of teachers, requiring neither dramatically different skillsets nor significant extra time; in fact, we may even allow teachers to further specialize and focus on their strengths.

II

WHAT WE DO NEXT

4

THE DISTRIBUTED
CLASSROOM MATRIX

Part I set the foundation for the distributed classroom matrix. Chapter 1 notes that the dichotomy between online and traditional education is already breaking and that it should continue to break to maximize and combine the benefits of each modality. Chapter 2 then set a framework for interpreting educational initiatives in terms of time and space, borrowed from work performed in the computer-supported collaborative work community. Chapter 3 interpreted existing trends in education through the lens of this framework, specifically to emphasize how close we already are to a more distributed experience.

In part II, we delve deeply into how to create a distributed classroom. We start in this chapter by more clearly defining the distributed classroom matrix with its extra dimension along both axes. We then provide a series of vignettes or scenarios describing a classroom in each cell, including how it is distributed across other cells as well. We close this chapter by speculating a bit about the cells that are less intuitive but nonetheless may carry valuable lessons.

In chapter 5, we tie these various cells together into one larger scenario, showing distribution across many dimensions, and pose the notion of symmetry as the ultimate form of the distributed classroom: symmetry would be attained through the design of a classroom where it does not even matter where the teacher is in the broader distributed ecosystem. While this is an ambitious idea, chapter 5 closes with an extended illustration of where a distributed "classroom" has already occurred and, we would argue, achieved symmetry, albeit in a very different domain.

THE EXPANDED TIME/SPACE MATRIX

In chapter 2, we proposed an additional level in each axis of the time/space matrix, one that differentiates synchronicity and co-locatedness with the original class delivery from synchronicity and co-locatedness with a cohort of classmates and dedicated instructional support. This augmented time/space matrix is shown in figure 4.1.

This matrix provides nine different classroom types based on their relationship to synchronicity and co-locatedness. The six lighter squares represent classes that have relatively intuitive implementations. The three darker squares are a bit more speculative; these cells ask whether it is possible and meaningful to preserve more co-locatedness than synchronicity. In a classroom context, is it meaningful to have students meet in the same place but not at the same time? This chapter focuses on the six lighter squares, but it closes by

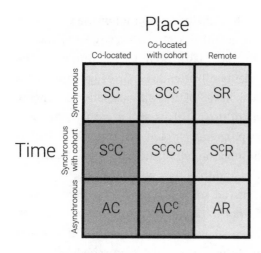

Figure 4.1   The Distributed Classroom Matrix

briefly speculating about how implementations within the darker squares might be meaningful.

The focus of the distributed classroom is not on selecting which one of the cells in the distributed classroom matrix a classroom fits within; rather, it is about trying to distribute the classroom across as many cells in the matrix as possible, giving many more students the chance to participate in the content while making only the trade-offs necessary for their individual participation. However, in order to understand the different cells, it is perhaps useful to consider what it would mean to design a classroom that sits specifically in a particular cell.

We'll start with the most familiar classroom design and work toward the less familiar cells. The SC classroom is straightforward: it is any class where students are together in the same room at the same time. This is the standard model for education. Much of the disruption following COVID-19 was because the standard model was exactly what was no longer feasible. Instead, classes were largely thrown to the SR classroom: students still attended courses synchronously, signing on to whichever of the various teleconferencing systems their school used. This is also a model that some distance-learning programs employ. Importantly, the class remained within only one cell of the matrix: students were initially co-located, and then they were remote.

Some classes instead shifted to an AR classroom (asynchronous remote, not to be confused with augmented reality), recording material rather than presenting it live and allowing students to watch on their own schedule. This is the model we use in our online MSCS program, as well as the model MOOCs use. This model was also common even before COVID-19 in many dedicated virtual K–12 programs. Importantly, the model itself does not imply anything about the rigor of the assessment, the quality of the feedback, or the amount of support. These may all remain the same as in a traditional environment. The AR model is solely a way in which students and teachers interact with one another and with the material itself.

That leaves three intermediate cells of the distributed classroom matrix. An SC^C class—synchronous and co-located with a cohort of classmates—that was not derived from any other cell in the matrix would entail a classroom of students being taught by a remote teacher. Remote guest lectures in an in-person class take on this model, with a guest speaker teleconferenced in to speak to the class live.

An S^CC^C class—synchronous and co-located with a cohort of classmates but asynchronous and remote relative to the original class experience—keeps a group of students that is separated from the original presenter but adds asynchronicity as well. For example, a guest lecturer might instead film a lecture to be shown to the cohort later and then answer questions asynchronously via a course forum. Importantly, the students themselves are still gathering together in the same place at the same time to watch the presentation together, potentially with the support of a teaching assistant. A model like this could be used, for example, by a teacher living in Vancouver to remotely teach a class in Cairo, despite the two locations having no overlapping working hours.

Finally, an S^CR class—synchronous with a cohort but individually remote rather than in a room together—retains the notion that the cohort of students will meet synchronously with one another but removes the requirement that they be in the same place. For example, imagine that a teacher had been remotely teaching an S^CC^C class in Cairo from their home in Vancouver when COVID-19 occurred. The Cairo students would no longer be able to meet together to attend class but could still participate synchronously by signing on to watch the prepared material at the same time. Such a model could also be used to teach a class to a local cohort with specific needs but who themselves were too dispersed to attend physically together. For example, one organization we have spoken to has described teaching students in Vietnam how to set up wireless data systems; the students participate from all over the country and thus cannot gather physically, but they share a common language, cultural context, and time zone, and thus they benefit from meeting and interacting synchronously.

These examples are not hypothetical. In the vast array of educational opportunities in the world, every one of these models has already been realized. Some universities offer overload rooms for large lectures, where students watch a video feed of the live class; even if the real class is taking place one room away, this represents some level of distributedness into the SC^C area, breaking the sanctity of the original classroom's walls while connecting these distributed students with their own cohort. Models like SC^C and S^CC^C have played a significant role in expanding educational opportunities to underprivileged areas without requiring teachers to spend semesters abroad, as with Stanford's CS Bridge program. Harvard's CopyrightX uses an S^CR model to support twenty-five-person remote cohorts of its course that participate in weekly synchronous seminars with a dedicated Harvard teaching fellow, facilitating their participation with otherwise asynchronous course content.

These examples largely (though not exclusively) design a class from the outset to function in one of the cells of the matrix. The distributed classroom proposes designing classes that instead can exist across the matrix, leveraging work that is already being done for greater reach and allowing students to sacrifice only as much as necessary to attain the knowledge, experience, and credential that they want to achieve. There will still be compromises, of course—a student wishing to earn a degree will need to participate in more assessments, which may require live presentations, proctored exams, or greater tuition costs than students who merely want access to the material—but the menu of compromises will be more flexible.

DISTRIBUTED CLASSROOM SCENARIOS

With that in mind, let us explore how a class might be distributed across different cells in the matrix through a series of scenarios focused on how an SC classroom in particular can be leveraged to support classes in other cells. A distributed classroom does not have to start from the SC classroom, of course; we explored previously the idea of recording a remote synchronous class for later consumption by students unable to attend live, thus distributing the classroom across the SR and AR cells. However, the SC classroom demands the most from students—move close to campus, pay lots in tuition, attend typically during working hours—and so it often makes sense to start with this classroom and move across the axes from there.

We will begin with the more familiar models and work toward the more novel ones. Even for the familiar models, however, we emphasize the ways in which the experience may be cultivated to preserve more of the in-person classroom dynamics. It is worth noting that these models assume some minimum classroom capture functionalities. To use in-person material for a distributed classroom, it must be recorded, including speaker audio, video of the teacher and in-class visual aids like whiteboards, and screen capture of whatever happens on a projector. This is typically referred to as "lecture capture," but we call it "classroom capture" because other class structures, especially those that involve more active learning, can similarly be captured and distributed. We revisit these practical considerations in chapter 6, but for this chapter, it is worth noting that the requirements will not be daunting. Although nicer equipment and infrastructure will lead to a better product, the tools used to present in the classroom in the first place will generally be sufficient to record a class for distributed use.

THE AR CLASSROOM

To understand how an SC class may be distributed to the AR quadrant, it is useful to first consider the strengths and weaknesses of existing AR classrooms. Between MOOCs and MOOC-based master's degrees, AR classrooms are often deliberately designed with custom-created material. Classroom capture (that is, filming an in-person class session) is in some ways frowned upon as overly opportunistic and a waste of certain affordances of the online medium. When producing media designed from the outset to be consumed by an AR audience, designers can take greater advantage of the medium: lessons can be designed based on their natural scope rather than scheduled class times, opportunities for active work can be integrated without regard for the individual time required to complete that work, and teachers may have far more opportunity for reshoots and revisions even within the original recording session. David, somewhat infamously, recorded a course where he spoke nearly every sentence three or four times until he was comfortable with it; the product after editing was excellent, but we doubt the video producer tasked with editing out all those retakes will ever forgive him. Hidden in this anecdote as well is the observation that most schools do not have the luxury of dedicated video editors to do this work; that luxury is not a necessity to pursuing this model, however.

We love the custom production model for online courses. It makes the process of creating a new class much more deliberate and forces the instructor to rethink the structure and organization of the course. It also gives lots of opportunity for cross-referencing content. During the design, the teacher knows that at any point students can jump to another lesson or video if they need a reminder of some concept. The resource investment that goes with this custom production model means there are also other possible features we can use that are too demanding for a traditional class structure. For example, a class can devote significant time to having an animator create a rich demonstration of a complex concept. For another, multiple faculty members can co-present material. Michael Littman, a professor at Brown University, co-created our CS7641: Machine Learning with Charles. It would be infeasible to have them co-teach the class in-person every semester, but because they only had to film it once, the course could draw from both of them.

However, the AR classroom does have significant weaknesses. For one, it requires far more resources to bring a new course to life. Our online courses typically require six to nine months of production time, during which we tell professors to expect about ten hours per week of additional work, even if they were already teaching the course in person. Second, that resource investment creates a strong need to create material that will be durable; courses in fields that are undergoing frequent change risk becoming outdated. When teaching in-person and re-presenting the same material every semester, this latter issue is handled somewhat naturally and iteratively; with prefilmed content, it is easier to become complacent with outdated material. This model of filming material deliberately to be used in an AR classroom is thus well suited to highly requested classes in well-established fields; these two criteria justify that upfront cost because the content will be durable and enrollment will be consistent.

Highly requested classes in well-established fields, however, have a relatively small area for potential impact, especially given the prior observation that in-demand fields are often the ones that struggle to find instructors because the careers are so lucrative. For other classes, how can these problems be mitigated? We would argue through a distributed model, designing a class to function in both the SC and AR cells. Let us say that Ana Rodriguez teaches CS3750, a class on human-computer interaction, Mondays and Wednesdays at 9:30 a.m., to an in-person class of twenty-five students. Her presentation style features slides, as well as some live demonstrations of different interfaces on the screen. The class session is recorded, including a live video feed of Ana presenting, an audio feed of her speech, and a screen recording of the live demonstrations and presentations. These are synchronized by the recording interface, which itself can run on the computer from which she is presenting. Thus, at the end of class, Ana has a recording of the entire session.

This recording is then edited. *Edited* can be an intimidating word. For some people, it calls to mind fancy software for graphical overlays, intro and outro music, storyboarding, and more. Research has generally found that these steps toward higher production values may not have much meaning for engagement and learning outcomes, however.[1] Instead, we use *editing* here to refer more to the minimum work necessary to make the video portable to a distributed audience: removing dead space or technical issues, editing out student questions if students did not have the opportunity to consent to be included in the recording, or breaking it into smaller, more easily navigable chunks. Little in the way of technical expertise or powerful software is required; Ana herself could handle this minimum editing, or a teaching assistant or dedicated audiovisual specialist could take care of this step relatively quickly using only freely available software. This content can then be shared using the class's learning management system. Those twenty-five original students can use it as a learning resource, or students who missed that day of class can use it to catch up on what they missed.

Nothing we have actually described so far is revolutionary. At Georgia Tech in the mid-2000s, one of the calculus teachers famously taught his class Mondays, Wednesdays, and Fridays at 8:00 a.m. but recorded and shared every session; attendance was not mandatory, and students could keep up based on the recordings. The class was still structured as if it was an SC class: only students who were on campus, who had that spot in their schedule open, and so on were able to enroll. The AR features were a bonus.

Distributing the class across the SC and AR cells would mean treating the asynchronous remote students as asynchronous and remote from the outset. Systems would need to be added to allow them to complete the course without coming to campus, such as remote submission of course assignments and asynchronous mechanisms for asking questions—the same features we documented previously as introduced by modern learning management systems. It is thus already feasible to distribute a class across the SC and AR cells, letting asynchronous remote students participate in the class fully, submitting the same assignments, receiving grades and feedback, and earning credit. In fact, in fall 2020, Georgia Tech's Office of International Education issued the guidance that all classes offered in a hybrid format (the majority of classes for that semester due to COVID-19) should also be accommodating of purely remote students to cover those unable to return to campus due to visa issues.

Of course, there remain drawbacks: these students lack the ability to participate in live class discussions, conveniently participate in group work, or synchronously present their own work to classmates. There are mechanisms to recreate some of these things, but our own work has found paradoxically that even in a program where everything is supported asynchronously, students still value synchronicity. This is what we call the synchronicity paradox—the phenomenon where students require a program to be asynchronous in order to fit in with their work or family constraints, but within that program still crave synchronous interactions as long as they do not present an obstacle to participation altogether.[2] In this scenario, does synchronicity really have to be sacrificed, or can it be preserved without putting up additional obstacles to enrollment? We explore this in the other classroom structures moving forward.

This structure of using an SC class as the foundation for an AR offering has been used for MOOCs as well. One of our favorite MOOC series, Columbia University's Civil War and Reconstruction XSeries on edX,[3] was built from live lectures captured in a for-credit class. This is another instance of distributing the class across the SC and AR cells, but it comes with a large compromise: AR students do not receive course credit, human feedback on their work, or notable access to experts in the field, although students in the SC section do. MOOCs still play a role, but it is important to note that distributing to the AR cell does not necessitate throwing out the high-value assessments or credit-worthy credentials. Hybrid classes in the wake of COVID-19, for instance, distributed the experience across the SC and AR cells but preserved the same assessments, rigor, and feedback for AR students as for those in the SC section.

In some ways, we have used this model in our online MSCS program as well, albeit with caveats. A professor who delivers a course online and in-person at the same time often will give the in-person students access to the videos filmed for the online class. These then become part of a flipped classroom, letting the in-person students use scheduled class time for more active learning activities. In fact, this has proven to be one of our professors' favorite parts of teaching in our online MSCS program.[4] Under this model, teaching assistants, course calendars, grading rubrics, assignment directions, and so on are still shared among the SC and AR audiences. This represents a move toward a distributed classroom, albeit one that uses the AR class to enhance the experience of the SC class rather than vice versa. Plans are underway now to experiment with teaching more online MSCS classes on the foundation of an SC class to see how the model may be used to create more course opportunities and keep content more up-to-date.

THE SR CLASSROOM
Distributing across the SC and SR cells is similarly relatively well established; this is the distance-learning model that many universities already use. Under this model, there is a class meeting in person in a distance-learning classroom, which supports remote learners watching the class live. Just

as with the AR classroom, this means that these distance students can participate as full members of the class with respect to submitting assignments, taking tests, and so on. Unlike the AR classroom, it does require students to be available at a particular time, but in exchange for that added requirement, it offers SR students the chance for live engagement. Notably, these are not mutually exclusive: there is no reason that the SC class, already set up for classroom capture, could not be live-streamed to SR students and then shared to AR students. We revisit this idea in chapter 5.

The existing popularity for distributing a classroom across the SC and SR cells means that we probably do not need to belabor the point about its possibility very much, especially after establishing it as an instance of the distributed classroom in action. However, we do think it is worth reflecting on a common issue we have witnessed and on how the classroom can be more distributed across the two cells—that is, how the SC experience can be more adequately persisted in the SR experience.

From our observations of this sort of synchronous distance learning built from a co-located class, the emphasis is largely on access. Remote students are *able* to access the material. However, distributing the classroom is about distributing the full experience, not merely distributing access to the material. In many places, the remote audience risks becoming a second tier of students: they are given the ability to watch the "real" class through a camera in the back of the room, but they are not themselves students in that "real" class. Interactions between co-located and remote students are difficult due to internet lag and an uncertainty among remote audiences in how they are appearing and sounding to the in-person students. If the class uses small group discussions or group work, these may not be meaningfully extended to the remote audience; the most we usually see is a token, "Remote students work with each other," which ignores some of the realities of that experience. We have no doubt that some teachers, classes, and schools have found ways to excel in this area, but our observations suggest that is a relative minority.

We see two ways to address this asymmetry, which we illustrate with an example. Let us say that Sergei Rabinoff teaches INTA6002, a strategic decision-making course in the university's graduate-level international affairs program. The program is extended to a distance-learning audience; Sergei presents to the in-person students in a distance-learning classroom equipped with cameras and sound capture equipment, and his presentation is live-streamed to the remote audience as well. One way in which Sergei can more symmetrically distribute the in-person experience to the remote audience is with certain deliberate behaviors and actions to treat those students as first-class members of the class. At the start of the class, Sergei may take a moment to directly address the camera and welcome remote students into the experience. At various points in the class, he may ask for questions; during these times, he may deliberately solicit questions from the remote audience as well, creating a time when they need not worry about interrupting an in-person question due to lag or uneven audio. Or he may use some features of modern teleconferencing software to allow these students to raise their hand virtually. In terms of group work or small group discussions, the remote audience might be preemptively segmented into small groups that will move into breakout rooms to complete their discussions. At the end of class, Sergei might remain on camera as the in-person audience exits for a dedicated Q&A session with the online students. The purpose of these actions is twofold: to share the full range of the in-person experience with these remote audiences and to deliberately communicate to the remote audience that they are valued and equivalent members of the class, entitled to the same level of interactivity and personal attention as the in-person students.

That overall model of making small overtures to the remote audience has significant potential, but only if the remote audience remains at a relatively manageable scale. However, one goal of the distributed classroom is to expand reach. A hallmark of our online MSCS program is that in most classes, enrollment can grow linearly with the availability of teaching assistants with no hard cap. What if there were five hundred students interested in enrolling in Sergei's class but the room could only hold twenty-five? Would the remote section need to be capped as well?

Thus, the second model for distributing across the SC and SR cells is to implement a tiered approach to instructional support. Let us consider first a single remote section of fifty students, too many for Sergei to manage while simultaneously teaching the content of the course live. This large section is assigned a dedicated teaching assistant whose sole role during the live session is to facilitate the experience for the remote audience. She would be able to answer questions through chat facilities during the live lecture, direct students among breakout rooms during small group discussion times, and curate questions that she cannot answer to deliver to the professor. This narrows Sergei's role in accommodating the remote audience from monitoring fifty students to collaborating with a single colleague; it also provides the large remote audience with a dedicated individual whose sole live role is to assist in their experience.

Now, instead of fifty remote students, let us imagine that Sergei's class draws 500 remote students, certainly far more than he can manage live while teaching the content—and more than a single teaching assistant can manage live as well. As before, that audience of 500 can be segmented into separate remote sections, each hosted by a particular teaching assistant who is that section's dedicated point of contact. These teaching assistants can collaborate on their own to curate and prioritize questions from the remote audience to deliver to Sergei to address at the end of the lecture, perhaps managed by a head TA overseeing them all. This provides a live classroom experience to all 525 students, including a dedicated point of contact for all audiences, without tremendously raising the burden on the live instructor. It relies instead on adding teaching staff linearly with enrollment numbers, but critically that added teaching staff need not have the main instructor's level of expertise. Combined with the existing infrastructure for distributing assignment submission, grading, asynchronous Q&A, and so on, these remote students may not only fulfill the requirements for credit but also receive an experience far more analogous to the in-person classroom.

As with many examples in this book, this one is framed largely in terms of higher education, but it has the potential to apply to K–12 education as well. Let us take as an example the state of Georgia in the United States. Georgia's population is concentrated in the Atlanta metropolitan area;

about 60 percent of the state's residents live in metropolitan Atlanta, although it represents only 14 percent of the state's geographic area. The largest high school in the state at the time of writing is Norcross High School with 3,817 students.[5] Among the courses it is able to offer with such a large student body are Jewelry & Metalsmithing, 3D Design, Marketing & Entrepreneurship, and Engineering Applications. The state also has forty counties where the county's only high school has fewer than five hundred students.[6] These counties certainly do not have the number of interested students necessary to hire faculty and offer all the courses that a behemoth like Norcross High can offer. But by distributing the classroom across the SC and SR cells, they may not need to; if each of those forty counties has only a single student interested in taking engineering, then a synchronous remote course supported by a single teaching assistant could be offered to coincide with the live course at Norcross High. Distributing the classroom can thus similarly open up opportunities for students in less populated areas to enroll in niche courses without making all the compromises that come with AR distance learning. Of course, this trivializes real challenges like scheduling such a live meeting across so many different systems and districts, a topic we revisit when we discuss the remaining classroom structures to explore how it can be further resolved.

THE SC^C CLASSROOM

The SC, SR, and AR classroom designs cover what we have seen as the most common approaches to distance-learning design, whether designed specifically to target one of those cells or distributed from one cell to another. The three combined represent a powerful menu of options to offer to students; this power has been seen in the success of HyFlex course designs, which target these three modalities specifically. A program that leverages an SC classroom to offer SR and AR classes can accommodate any student, at least as far as time and space demands are concerned, while also resolving some of the issues regarding high production costs and aging content.

The compromises these students make, however, are nontrivial. There remain many components of the in-person experience that do not transition well to distance learning. One major part is the social component. Our research has found that the absence of synchronous interaction is a major hindrance to forming social relationships in an online program,[7] and other research has found similar negative effects on retention or community formation in distance-learning programs.[8] In many classes, there are significant materials or resources that are similarly feasible to share only when many students are gathered together in one place, such as a shared robot in a robotics class or authentic prototyping materials in an architecture class. Students are forced to compromise a significant part of the student experience when participating in distance learning, and while that compromise may be justifiable, is it necessary?

Let us say that Shuchun Chen teaches AE3333: Advanced Aerospace Vehicle Performance, a hypothetical class in which students construct prototype vehicles using real components. The vehicles are then tested in one of the working wind tunnels Georgia Tech has on campus in order to learn how to perform analyses of drag, as well as to evaluate the prototype itself. These experiences do not easily distribute to remote audiences; components may not be affordable on an individual basis, and access to real wind tunnels for testing requires university infrastructure. How, then, can this class be distributed? Distributed students might instead work on simulated versions of the project if such simulations are available. They could also be partnered with in-person students to perform tasks that can be completed at a distance while participating peripherally in the in-person steps. If the remote students are truly all over the world, this might be the best that can be done—and keeping with the theme of making only the necessary compromises, perhaps that is a fair compromise for a student who has no other way of participating in the class, and perhaps it is still sufficient to award equal credit. Perhaps it is not, though; an instructor might argue that the hands-on experience of working with the prototype in a real wind tunnel is a necessary part of the learning objectives of the class and thus that these remote students are not entitled to equal credit.

However, let us say that AE3333 is taught simultaneously at Georgia Tech in Atlanta and at Georgia Tech's Lorraine campus in France. The class meets at 10:00 a.m. EST, corresponding to 4:00 p.m. at the Lorraine campus. As members of another campus environment, the Lorraine cohort can count on a number of assets: a cohort of multiple students to interact together in person, an investment in local infrastructure to make certain projects feasible, and a location for shared resources such as parts of a vehicle. Students at the Lorraine campus may thus participate in parallel with the class in Atlanta, using their own local infrastructure and materials. Importantly, Shuchun is now able to teach the class in two places at once without an enormous extra expenditure of effort. Offering the class in Lorraine one semester, for instance, does not require skipping a semester of offering it in Atlanta or finding another subject matter expert to teach at the new location. As with the SR and AR models, local instructional support is still necessary, but the expertise for this role is that of a teaching assistant (likely a former student who could act as a TA while taking their own study-abroad semester) rather than a full instructor.

That example may sound niche, but it can be generalized further. As noted previously, we estimate 80 percent of students in our OMSCS program live within two hours of a major urban center. That provides ample opportunity for creating more local groups. Were a class like AE3333 offered in our program, rather than creating a dedicated section at another formal Georgia Tech campus, it may instead be possible to create teams leveraging local maker spaces or entering agreements to share lab space with other universities for the pursuit of these projects. This would formalize the local meet-up design described in chapter 3 into an actual classroom. For classes that do not need significant materials or infrastructure, this mechanism may still be used to introduce greater social interaction and community building into the experience, providing to those students willing to commit to attending at a particular place and time (so long as it remains local) a true co-located cohort.

This returns to the notion of the minimal necessary compromise. Students who are willing to commit to attending a class in person at a particular time in order to have a more traditional classroom experience are able to as long as they live in an area with other students willing to make a similar commitment. Students who do not live in such an area or whose lives are not conducive to such a regular commitment may instead compromise more of the traditional experience for the sake of their access, participating in an SR or AR mechanism that does not require them to travel even a short distance. Part of this compromise may be the inability to participate in certain activities that can be done only in person, such as those in AE3333; that may carry additional compromises regarding the type of credential that can be attached to the course. It may be determined that without that in-person experience, course credit cannot be granted; the number of students who must resort to that level of compromise, however, is far lower than when course credit relied on attending synchronously in Atlanta specifically.

As with the SR classroom, there are possible applications of this to the K–12 space as well. One problem with offering a diverse course catalog in K–12 is the need to have a critical mass of students interested in a particular class; a second problem is the need to find a teacher once that critical mass is established. A major challenge to efforts to encourage greater access to computer science education at the K–12 level is the lack of teachers.[9] Even if a school has enough students to offer a computer science class, a teacher may be unavailable. At a school using an SC^C model, the course could be offered by pairing with an existing course at another school. The class would still require local instructional support, but that support would not need to be a subject matter expert capable of teaching the class themselves. A local teacher may be able to handle classroom administration, while content support could be curated and diverted to the original teacher—or even distributed further with a network of remote teaching assistants.

THE S^{C}C^C CLASSROOM

The picture we have painted of the SC^C classroom is admittedly a bit rosy. Technical issues (which we revisit in chapter 6) take on a greater significance when the risk is wasting synchronous class time. Scheduling constraints typically go together with geographical constraints. An SC^C classroom would be plausible only among multiple locations that share a reasonable working hour; courses distributed within particular countries are feasible, but beyond that, the available time windows become narrow. Even if the effort were to distribute within a time zone (such as offering a college class to cohorts in Atlanta, New York, and Boston) or within a state (such as offering a K–12 class to students at Norcross High School, Jasper County High School, and Emanuel County High School in Georgia), it is unlikely that different schedule constraints would match up to allow synchronous remote class meetings. Returning to the idea of compromise, the mechanism is feasible only to a relatively small and more deliberately designed set of classrooms. Are the others forced into the AR compromise if they cannot attend synchronously, even if remotely?

The middle cell of the matrix, S^{C}C^C, offers a better compromise. An S^{C}C^C classroom builds on three of the constructs already introduced as part of the other classroom structures: the initial recording of the classroom experience, the presence of dedicated instructional support for distributed audiences, and the existing distribution of other classroom activities in time and space.

Let us return to the AE3333 example. Instead of offering a section at Georgia Tech-Lorraine, imagine instead we are offering a section at Georgia Tech-Shenzhen. Shenzhen is eleven or twelve hours removed from Atlanta depending on the month; there is no time of day when a class can meet in Atlanta where it is reasonable for a simultaneous class to meet in China. So instead of attending synchronously, students in a section at the Shenzhen campus instead gather together to participate with the lecture that occurred twelve hours earlier. They are synchronous and co-located with their cohort and may have access to the types of infrastructure that can only be offered to a critical mass of in-person students. Alongside that, they submit their work to the same learning management system, ask questions with their classmates in Atlanta using the class forum, and receive grades and feedback from the same graders.

What is crucial to keep in mind with this model is the structure of the classroom experience. If the class in Atlanta is merely a lecture where students sit and listen for forty-five minutes asking the occasional question, this mechanism for distribution is somewhat silly; instead, the Shenzhen section could be flipped, with students watching the recorded material prior to the class meeting time and then using the scheduled time for group work, activities, and discussion. But distributing a class lecture experience is not a major challenge in the first place; MOOCs have shown the relative ease of that model. The S^CC^C classroom is more geared toward distributing classroom experiences that have been resistant to scale—those involving more interaction and more active work, which are also those considered more pedagogically sound.

Thus, under this model, the original classroom experience would involve points where students are directed to participate in discussions, work on active projects, engage in peer review, and perform other activities that are more easily administered in a synchronous co-located environment. The S^CC^C class would complete these as well and at the same points as in the original presentation under the direction of their dedicated teaching assistant.

Sitting at the center of the distributed classroom matrix, this holds the greatest promise for expanding reach and access while preserving most of the classroom experience. Under a model closely connected to the original class, a single course could be distributed to sections around the world without heavy regard for time zone alignment or local scheduling constraints; local sections would have flexibility within fairly broad time scales to decide the optimal meeting place and time. To participate with the original live course (for example, including a shared forum, shared instructional team, shared assignments), a class would just need to follow the same semester-level schedule as the original class. Within that, the only compromise these cohorts make is regarding the synchronous interaction with the original teacher and class. They still follow the same class schedule, complete the same work, receive feedback from the same shared team of graders, and are able to ask questions of the original instructor through an asynchronous mechanism.

Within the same cell, another layer of compromise is also plausible. It often may not be feasible for a particular cohort to adhere to the same semester schedule as everyone else. There may also be several other reasons a cohort should not be grouped in with the original class; for example, a cohort of high school students may be able to go through a college class but need to spread it out over a year instead of a semester. But the nature of the recording and distribution process means that there exists a sort of enhanced "textbook" for the course, consisting of its classroom sessions, assignment descriptions, rubrics, and more. A school may be able to pick up these materials, just as any other class could pick up a textbook, and implement its own delivery of the course. This was the case of Stanford University's CS Bridge program, which allowed local cohorts to pick up and deliver synchronous classroom experiences based on prepared materials. Here, the schools would need to supply their own credit options and bring in their own instructional support; the demands of this instructional support are lower, though. They need not be able to deliver the course from scratch; they need only to grade work in the class, give feedback, and answer questions. This, of course, is no small order; significant domain knowledge is necessary to fulfill these responsibilities, but not as significant as that required to teach the course without such materials.

This model, in fact, is one we have begun to pursue with the Georgia Tech Constellations Center for Equity in Computing, but originating from a different cell in the matrix. As we mentioned before, we developed an online CS1 class that was designed from the outset to be an AR class; no synchronous or co-located activity is required even though the class is primarily (in its original form) offered to on-campus students. Built into the material are all instructional videos and hundreds of assignments. The course is complete enough that students can move through the material with no instructional support; the MOOC version has drawn thousands of course completers who required no additional human effort. Now, the course is being used as a foundation to develop CS classes to deliver to schools in the Atlanta Public Schools system where computing classes are typically unavailable. Students will meet together in a classroom at the same time and work on course content together, and they will be aided by teaching fellows who can answer questions on the content; the instruction and grading, however, may be taken care of by the prepared CS1301 material.

This usage of CS1301 is interesting in part because rather than recording a traditional class (SC) and distributing it to the S^CC^C cell, it instead develops a new S^CC^C class from AR material. The S^CC^C class benefits from custom-prepared video content, which is in many ways superior to classroom capture. We noted previously the benefits of classroom capture as well, but these benefits can then be reintroduced in the S^CC^C class, such as more recent or local applications of the content. But more important, the greatest benefit to the S^CC^C class is that it can exist where it may not have been able to otherwise; without its own dedicated teacher, there would be no foundational content on which to build the S^CC^C experience.

This is not the only place we are using this model. As we mentioned in chapter 3, in fall 2020, we experimented with offering a section of our online CS6750 class at the Georgia Tech-Shenzhen campus. This class is offered as an AR class in our OMSCS program, and students attend from all over the world; there are no required synchronous class components. As part of this experiment, a cohort of a dozen students at Georgia Tech-Shenzhen joined the class. They themselves had a co-located recitation supporting their enrollment, with their own local co-instructor. During this shared time, they watched lectures, participated in peer review activities, and held their own discussions. The persistent presence of the AR class material is thus used as the foundation of an $S^C C^C$ class. Beginning in fall 2021, this model will be the foundation of an entire in-person MSCS program at Georgia Tech-Shenzhen.

Nonetheless, these AR-turned-$S^C C^C$ classes carry some of the weaknesses of the AR model documented previously: the classes are relatively static due to the difficulties in updating prepared video material, and they require significant investment to develop. They are used in these contexts in large part opportunistically because that investment has already been made. The model of recording SC classes to use as the foundation for $S^C C^C$ classes offers a leaner path to creating and maintaining content (as it is being redelivered each term anyway). Importantly, this cell also offers the smallest compromise: learners may still retain the majority of the student experience, including the course content, the classroom structure, and the presence of dedicated instructional support, as well as potentially even the same assignments, grading procedures, and course credit. In exchange, they must commit to synchronous co-located participation with a local cohort, but those cohorts may be constructed all over the world instead of being tied to a particular city or time slot. In large metropolitan areas, it may be feasible to have multiple cohorts meeting at different times in the same city; in smaller areas, it may be feasible to find enough students to offer at least one local section. Dedicated instructional support may even be offered online if no local support is possible; an in-room teaching assistant is preferable, but even if this assistant must be remote from the $S^C C^C$ class itself, a large portion of the experience may persist, depending on the specific demands on that class.

THE S^{C}R CLASSROOM

With the foundation laid by the SR, SC^C, and S^{C}C^C classrooms, the S^{C}R classroom comes out relatively intuitively. Imagine, for instance, that Sachin Reddy teaches MGT6165, a course on venture opportunities targeted at those wishing to develop their own start-up. The nature of computer science now is that many students are interested in learning CS in order to start their own telecommerce businesses, and so such a class would be of significant interest to students in an online MSCS program. However, the nature of the content is that the class must be highly discussion driven, and these discussions must be fast paced and interactive; although it may be an interesting exercise to experiment with teaching such a class using asynchronous forums, in its existing form it necessitates live interaction.

Can such a course be offered in this predominantly AR program? Some compromise is necessary, but what form must that compromise take? While it is true that the majority of students live near a small set of major metropolitan areas, there remain many who are outside those areas; still others, despite living in such an area, may lack the flexibility to leave the house in the evenings to attend S^{C}C^C classrooms. Our own research has noted that synchronicity is more important for community building than co-location.[10] Is a compromise among these competing needs possible?

An S^{C}R classroom designed around MGT6165 might see small sections—perhaps 15 people each—scheduled multiple times during the week. A large class (our average class size in the OMSCS program is 350) may then be divided into 25 smaller sections, based entirely on when individuals are able to commit to attendance. This preserves a significant amount of the flexibility associated with the program while also preserving the synchronous communication necessary for the course. Each such section would follow the pattern of the in-person version of the course (in our case, two ninety-minute meetings per week), meeting twice a week to follow the original classroom structure, supported by a recording of its original delivery (if necessary; some classes may be entirely discussion-driven) and a dedicated teaching assistant. Notably, the synchronous demands for teaching assistants would be moderate: a new section would require three extra synchronous TA hours per week. If this is their only responsibility, then a single TA can cover the sections for 75 students. Importantly, this section can still participate in broader asynchronous activities with the rest of the class, such as forum discussions and asynchronous peer review. In spring 2021, in fact, we launched our first class following this model, CS8803: Systems Issues in Cloud Computing. Taught by an experienced OMSCS professor—Kishore Ramachandran, who has taught CS6210: Advanced Operating Systems since the inception of the program—the class offers students asynchronous core content like other classes, but further requires them to attend a synchronous 90-minute session once per week to work through more hands-on activities at the live direction of a teaching assistant.

These designs cover only the minimum necessary structure to largely recreate the classroom experience; once created, additional benefits begin to emerge. The structure expands access to student bodies that previously could not have participated in such a course; no longer is it available only to those who are able to take time off work and away from family and who live in the right place. In a discussion-oriented class, that pays ongoing dividends: not only are more students able to access the class, but their presence and the greater diversity it brings improve the course experience for the rest of the students. Flexible structures might further bring them into collaboration with a greater number of classmates. Students could, for instance, have different classmates in the two sessions they attend each week, expanding the number of viewpoints to which they are exposed. This builds on the existing greater interactivity and ownership present in an online classroom.[11] Those benefits are all present even if we remain within the framework of students in a single online master's program; if we start to expand it to students from other programs and at different levels, the benefits may become even greater.

Other applications of this structure flow relatively naturally from some of the prior examples. In a K–12 setting, for instance, it is entirely likely that students scattered across smaller schools around the state are interested in taking a particular class, but there are not enough students in any one of those places to hire a teacher and offer the course. Synchronous co-attendance with the class as it is offered at a larger school in the state (the SC^C model) may be infeasible for practical scheduling reasons. Larger schools unable to hire their own teacher may offer the course in an S^CC^C model, but this still excludes students who attend schools too small to offer a section at all. Still, through an S^CR model, these students may be aggregated into one online section that meets synchronously (likely after school, with a dedicated study hall during the day to attend to the class's work and avoid increasing each student's overall course load), thus opening up access to the course to a greater audience.

With the S^CR model completing the picture, it becomes clear how a single teacher teaching a normal number of class sections in a single place can have their material become available to students around the world—not in a MOOC model where access is defined minimally as the ability to watch the content, but in a more flexible model where each student need sacrifice only the minimum amount of the course experience to attain the access desired. For some who are interested only in personal growth, that may be the MOOC model; for those desiring course credit or other formal recognition of their achievement, that is likely some sort of more similar and rigorously assessed course experience.

Somewhat surprisingly, our hope at this point is that you are underwhelmed. We hope the ideas we have presented so far seem straightforward and that you are aware of places they are already occurring. As we mentioned in the first chapter, one of the goals of this book is to communicate how close we already are to realizing this potential; all that is needed is a little more push to embrace these designs more fundamentally and systematically rather than opportunistically.

In the next chapter, we trace through one class as it might be taught across numerous different cells in the distributed classroom matrix. The goal there will be to show the enormous potential that develops from systematically embracing these relatively simple ideas. Before we get there, though, we pause and speculate a bit about the less intuitive half of the distributed classroom matrix and what it might mean for us as we design these classroom experiences.

ASYNCHRONOUS CO-LOCATEDNESS?

The previous section focuses on the top-right side of the distributed classroom matrix. The implicit idea is that we must drift toward more remote options before we drift toward asynchronous options because breaking synchronicity before breaking co-locatedness does not seem to make logical sense. What does it mean pedagogically to be in the same place at different times?

There are examples of this in the real world. For example, a classroom (likely in the K–12 space) that is used by multiple sections of the same course each day may see earlier sections leave artifacts for later sections. There might be a whiteboard exercise that students add to as the day continues, building on the work of previous sections, or there may be displays around the classroom where each section's work is shown for other students to see at different times of day. These would exist in the S^CC space: a synchronous cohort is co-located, but asynchronous with the original section that generated these artifacts or future sections that may add to them.

Ideas like these, however, are not approaches to designing overall classroom experiences; they may lead to some novel activities but creating such an activity does not distribute the classroom experience itself across the matrix so much as it distributes a particular set of artifacts the students are creating. If we were to consider distributing the entire classroom experience into the S^CC space, we would likely be discussing the same sort of design as the S^CC^C space, but with the asynchronous cohorts coincidentally in the same classroom where the material was originally recorded. But the classroom itself, from a physical point of view, does not appear to be particularly special if the synchronous class is not occurring there at the same time, so what benefit would the S^CC approach bring that goes beyond an S^CC^C approach?

There are two ways we might think about this question, and each brings some additional features for us to select as we design our classrooms. The first is to think of co-locatedness as more of a spectrum than a binary property. The second is to think of co-locatedness not in terms of an *actual* physical location, but rather the properties of the location.

A SPECTRUM OF CO-LOCATEDNESS

One of the online classes that David teaches is CS1301: Introduction to Computing. Unlike his other classes, this one is for undergraduate students. Unlike in the OMSCS program, these students for the most part are physically on campus: they live in dorms or in near-campus apartments, they are enrolled in other classes on campus, and they have direct access to campus resources.

We have described CS1301 as an AR class because from the classroom perspective, that is what it is: the course content is prerecorded and students never have to come to any physical location to complete the course. In fact, while we generally assume students are on campus, we know that there are many who were not even before COVID-19: students sometimes take the course while completing internships, while home for summer vacation, while participating in study-abroad programs, and so on. It has also been popular among older students working full-time jobs as well as students battling chronic health problems, both situations that make in-person attendance difficult. But it remains that most students are contained within a relatively small geographical area during the term. They are remote in the sense that they do not have to come to a very specific location, but the variation in that remoteness is more limited.

This goes against how we have discussed co-locatedness so far. In the distributed classroom matrix, co-locatedness can be expressed in terms of two binary values: whether you are co-located with the teacher and original presentation of the class content, and whether you are co-located with a cohort of people. We take it as a given that if you are co-located with the teacher, you are also co-located with a cohort. But if we rethink co-locatedness as more of a spectrum, we may start to see how an AC classroom functions. In CS1301, we take advantage of students' general nearness in multiple ways. There is a room in the College of Computing building we call the CS1301 help desk; all TAs hold their office hours in this room, and so students need only to come to this room to get live help. We also offer a recitation, an optional, synchronous, co-located class that meets once a week for seventy-five minutes; here, students receive supplementary instruction, work problems together, and get feedback from the TAs. Finally, each week David holds about three hours of office hours where students can come and ask questions live. The fact that these individual environments all support live interaction leaves it a bit nonintuitive that this is an "asynchronous" design, but the key point is that there is not one shared synchronous time for all students. These synchronous interactions are optional, supplementary, and far more flexibly scheduled.

We might ask, though, if the students are on campus anyway, why are they choosing to take an online class? Our early studies found students who selected the online section valued the flexibility to work on the class anytime, anywhere; a significant number also reported preferring to be able to go at their own pace. The in-person section's students, by comparison, reported valuing the live lectures and the structure of a traditional class.[12] The distributed classroom paradigm suggests the design of a single course that can meet these different students' needs along with other permutations (such as students desiring live meetings but needing flexibility with regard to proximity), rather than two distinctly different versions of the course altogether.

The recitations, help desk, and office hours all build on the fact that we are located in the same physical proximity, even if we are not meeting in a truly co-located classroom. It would be senseless to offer these environments to our OMSCS students given the far greater variation in their distance from campus. By thinking of co-locatedness in terms of degrees rather than binary values, we may find additional environments we can design and offer. We can then extend this further to an AC^C classroom: if a cohort of students has enrolled in a class together from the same geographic location, we might offer them on-site support resources. Under the $S^C C^C$ section, we noted how students at the Shenzhen campus have their own dedicated recitations, supplying the S^C component. But even in the absence of those recitations, those students would still be in a relatively small geographic area, and it would make sense to offer them the same sort of on-site support we offer to our local CS1301 students. They would thus be in an AC^C classroom: there would be no mandatory synchronous component as recitation remains optional, but they are still sufficiently co-located with a cohort to justify some on-site resources.

In some ways, this is similar to what we discussed when considering SC^C and S^CC^C classes: we considered whether students were already in relatively close proximity to one another, and then we built truly co-located environments out of that geographic proximity. Here, we take that a step further, and note that there may be environments we can design based on that close proximity that do not require the cohort to gather all together at the same time and place. We might do that to offer extra levels of support to students, or we might do that because a physical place might have relevance: there might be infrastructure or equipment that can only be accessed in a particular place. This is more similar to the next idea, to consider co-locatedness in terms of the characteristics of the space rather than the space itself.

CHARACTERISTIC CO-LOCATEDNESS

Under its original interpretation, co-locatedness refers to multiple people being in the same place, albeit potentially at separate times. This is why asynchronous co-locatedness, on its surface, does not appear to be a useful idea. Why does it matter if people are in the same place but at different times if our focus is on the interaction among them?

Another interpretation that may help this make sense, however, is if we do not think of co-locatedness as referring to the same *literal* location but to a location that supports the same behaviors and activities. Here, "being in the same place" does not mean a geographically identical place, but instead a functionally identical place. Under this interpretation, we can introduce topics like lab classes and studios into the distributed classroom framework.

We already described the idea that a place may have some important characteristics to it using the example of a hypothetical course, AE3333: Advanced Aerospace Vehicle Performance. In some ways, the idea of tying infrastructure to a place is orthogonal to the idea of co-locatedness with a cohort. An individual student with access to that infrastructure could still participate in some of the work involved in the class even in the absence of a co-located cohort; the cohort just justifies the expense of securing the infrastructure. This could provide us with an interpretation of what it would mean to offer an S^CC and AC classroom structure. AE3333 itself could be thought of as S^CC rather than S^CC^C due to its reliance on specific features of the classroom environment: it is not co-located in the same place as the original class, but it must be located in a place that supports the same activities. An S^CC^C class, by contrast, would occur anywhere the cohort can gather to achieve co-locatedness, regardless of the details of the environment in which they are gathering.

While this distinction might seem pedantic, it may have powerful implications for the design of particular distributed classrooms. For a class that typically requires some in-person materials or infrastructure, could we design it so that it may be completed by both a cohort with access to the necessary infrastructure and by one without such access? At Georgia Tech, Michael Schatz has developed an introductory physics

MOOC that follows this idea: rather than removing the lab component from physics in order to meet the demands of MOOC scale, he instead redesigned the lab experiments such that they may be completed by anyone with a smartphone. Rather than manipulating materials in a lab, the course sends students out to film sequences in everyday life, like a car traveling at constant speed or a ball following a parabolic trajectory. These videos are then analyzed by software to allow students to perform the same analyses that they would in a more controlled lab. In this way, students with access to the laboratory can complete the course with one set of assessments, and students without such access can complete a reasonable approximation worthy of credit nonetheless.[13]

This, then, gives us a starting point to consider what an AC classroom would be: asynchronous and co-located need not mean that the students are coming to the same place at different times, but rather that despite the asynchronicity, their physical location supports the same activities. This could mean, for instance, that the class activities are built from resources that are commonly available wherever they are, or that the resources necessary to succeed in the class can be sent to the students directly with relative ease. Under this interpretation, co-locatedness becomes more generally about what can be accomplished at the student's location. When considering the minimum compromise, the activities supported by the student's location can be considered: students who can complete the full activities associated with the original class should be able to, and students who cannot should be offered alternatives. These alternatives, however, may have an impact on criteria like whether the class is considered equivalently credit-worthy.

PLACE BEFORE TIME

We believe this exploration of the possible meaning of asynchronous co-locatedness poses some valuable ideas to the design of distributed classrooms. It encourages us to think outside of the typical prescheduled class times and instead consider the structures that support the course, like meetings with instructors at office hours, dedicated study areas, or TA-led review sessions.

However, as we move forward, we continue to favor the side above the diagonal of the distributed classroom matrix—those boxes where co-locatedness is lost before synchronicity. First, although the idea of considering co-locatedness more functionally than literally provides valuable insights for distributing classes that heavily rely on classroom infrastructure or physical artifacts, the majority of classes we have observed can be distributed with relatively little attention paid to the physical space in which the class meets. So long as students have the ability to watch a video (whether streamed or downloaded in advance), interact with one another, use domain-specific software, work problems, and take notes (whether on paper or on their own devices), most classes are distributable. Lab classes, studio classes, and other classes that require more interaction with an in-person artifact will need to consider the ideas in this section more deliberately, but many classes will not need to. For many classes, the question of whether the course is distributed to the S^CC cell will be pedantic because there is no notable way in which S^CC is distinguished from S^CC^C.

Second, our research has found that time is more important than place in supporting student interactions and community building.[14] Students have reflected that they do not have much difficulty forming relationships with people who are a long distance away, but they do have difficulty if they are not able to interact with those people synchronously. So, while asynchronous co-locatedness may have particular relevance in certain content areas, it will not be one of our focuses going forward. We will look primarily at the area of the distributed classroom matrix where classes are always distributed across space first and time second.

5

SYMMETRY

As we mentioned toward the middle of the previous chapter, our perhaps unintuitive hope is that the ideas we have proposed so far are underwhelming. As you have read through these ideas, we hope you have come up with examples of where you have seen classrooms already built and deployed that implement some of these proposals. We hope you know of high school classes that are using materials like MIT OpenCourseWare, of study-abroad programs that have students tele-attend lectures with students back home, or of school districts that offer online classes to students whose local school has more limited offerings.

The fact that these ideas have already been used in so many places is exactly what makes this direction so promising. We have already seen dozens of individual use cases. That is what makes us confident that this is the direction in which education is moving anyway, but rather than let it happen slowly and inadvertently over time, we have the opportunity to push it forward in a deliberate, organized fashion.

In this chapter, we show how the familiar, established building blocks we discussed in the previous chapter can be combined into something revolutionary by touching all of the various cells of the distributed classroom matrix (those above the diagonal anyway). Then we discuss what we will argue is the ultimate form of this sort of design: symmetry. *Symmetry* in this context will mean that classes can shift among cells in the matrix with relatively little impact. When symmetry is achieved, the distributed experience is very close to the core, original experience that we are seeking to scale. This chapter closes by looking at a very different enterprise through the lens of the distributed classroom matrix to demonstrate the feasibility of this overall vision. It has already happened in other contexts, so why not now in education?

A FULLY DISTRIBUTED CLASSROOM

To illustrate a fully distributed classroom, we use as our example CS4643: Deep Learning. CS4643 is an undergraduate class, but it is cross-listed as CS7643, a graduate-level class, so undergraduate and graduate students already take the class together, complete similar assessments, and so on. We are choosing CS4643 for three reasons:

- Deep learning—a subset of machine learning—is one of the hottest fields in the world at time of writing, so the class is always in high demand. It regularly fills up and could easily support additional sections if other instructors were available.

- The skill set necessary to teach deep learning is highly prized, meaning that anyone qualified to teach the course would likely need to willingly forgo the larger income they would make in industry.
- The materials needed to do deep learning can be entirely digital. Students do not need any special equipment beyond that needed to watch videos and access cloud resources.

CS4643 therefore presents an ideal candidate for this sort of distributed classroom. It is a course that many schools struggle to offer due to the difficulty of finding teachers to teach it, and yet it is a class that many students want. A mechanism that can expand access to this content could have enormous impact in numerous ways.

Of course, as a result, there are already many alternate solutions: MOOCs, vocational programs, boot camps, informal learning communities, industry programs, and more. Each alternative has significant drawbacks, though, from high cost to questionable quality to weak credentialing. The drawbacks of our existing course are the various barriers to entering college in the first place (tuition cost, time demands, geographic requirements, competitive admissions driven by limited space), which are the exact barriers the distributed classroom aims to circumvent. In fact, an online version of CS7643 delivered in our OMSCS program has already resolved those issues for this exact content: tuition is relatively low ($540 for the class) compared to other tuition costs or those associated with boot camps and vocational programs, the course is remote and asynchronous built with working professionals in mind, and anyone who meets the program's minimum standards is granted admission. But with those solutions come new drawbacks, especially the loss of synchronous interaction with classmates and instructors. The goal here is to distribute the experience across the matrix rather than offering only two versions located at the extremes.

GETTING STARTED: CAPTURING THE SC CLASSROOM

We start with a traditional offering of the course. In this particular semester, let us say that Dhruv Batra, the course's creator many years ago, is teaching the course on campus in a traditional environment, Tuesdays and Thursdays at 9:30 a.m. During the semester, Dhruv's classes are captured by cameras in the room, as well as screen capture on the device he is using to present. He presents with a microphone each time, with students' questions captured by the room's distributed microphones. Software is used to automatically pair the multiple audio recordings with the two (or more) video feeds, captured and available for live streaming. After the class, some lightweight editing removes dead space in the recording (such as when students are working independently or in groups), removes questions from students who did not opt into being recorded, and potentially switches between camera feeds as focus transitions between Dhruv himself and the screen contents. The conclusion is a quality capture of the live class.

Based on this description alone, a variety of advantages and criticisms already start to emerge. One advantage is obvious: Dhruv has time to teach the course only once per year, and presumably he may no longer have time to teach it at all at some point. He is also the original architect of the course, as well as one of the world's foremost experts in the field; by capturing it, it may be reused in semesters when he is not teaching, exposing hundreds more students to the course.

The more general advantage, however, is that the approach we are discussing expands the reach and impact of a single delivery of a class. That might mean simply expanding the reach of an existing class, but it may also mean that individuals who otherwise do not have time to teach could be encouraged to do so by radically increasing the impact associated with relatively the same amount of work. This is not a hypothetical situation. A class in a similar circumstance is CS7641: Machine Learning, which Charles still teaches online (despite having moved on to become Dean of the College of Computing) because the preparation of the course content dramatically lowers how much time he needs to devote while teaching the course; this reduced commitment is the only reason he is able to remain involved. The course was co-developed with Michael Littman, another of the world's leaders in the field; it would similarly be impossible to have them both co-instruct a single section of an in-person class, not least of which because they live a thousand miles apart; however, the promised impact of years of reusability provides sufficient reason to do so. This is especially pertinent in in-demand fields like machine learning, although it has relevance in more universal subjects as well, as we will see.

That advantage aside, we can think of at least two criticisms of this approach based only on what we have described here. The first would be a critique of our rosy view of technology: we make it sound like creating such a recording is trivial, but in reality it requires a significant investment in in-room infrastructure and a notable amount of work to convert in-person recordings into a watchable video experience. But while these resources are great if available, they are not actually necessary to accomplish the goal; they are an incremental improvement but not a fundamental requirement. We discuss this more in chapter 6, which looks at the practical details of making this sort of distributed classroom happen.

The second criticism is regarding the mechanism we have described. In online education, this recording mechanism is typically called "lecture capture": there is a live lecture, and we are merely capturing it. We instead refer to it as "classroom capture" because the classroom experience need not be a lecture in order to be captured. In Harvard University's Poetry in America MOOC series (sadly no longer available), classroom capture is used to record class discussions among students. A similar mechanism could be used to capture the instructional portions of a classroom experience, rapidly intercut with time for students to work on their own, work in teams on shared problems, or participate in group discussions. Once the experience is distributed, a dedicated facilitator would ensure these portions of the in-class experience are redelivered as well.

Overall, the mechanism is to capture some class session that is already happening, regardless of what is happening within that session; however, this view is generally considered inferior to custom-producing new content to be used online. Classroom capture is not what we do in our OMSCS program; we specifically boast about the quality of our custom-produced content in creating a superior online experience. (You can view any of our course videos at our program website; they are available free to the public.[1]) Most MOOCs similarly do not use classroom capture, although there are exceptions.

The truth is, though, we believe that we in the online education community may underestimate the value of classroom capture. Classroom capture has been executed poorly in many different places—for example, with tinny, indecipherable audio, grainy video, and long spaces of dead silence—and that has given it a bad reputation, but we do not generalize prior poor execution to mean it lacks potential altogether. We have seen classroom capture done well. We mentioned in chapter 4 the Civil War and Reconstruction XSeries from Columbia University. That course is filmed in classroom capture, but the quality of its presentation surpasses nearly any other MOOC we have completed.

This idea is not in conflict with the literature; although research found that "high quality prerecorded classroom lectures are not as engaging when chopped up for a MOOC," researchers use that to give the guideline, "If instructors insist on recording classroom lectures, they should still plan with the MOOC format in mind,"[2] an indicator that the mechanism has potential but must be proactively and carefully designed. In the Civil War and Reconstruction XSeries, classroom recordings are well filmed, intuitively divided, and bookended by short custom videos filmed for the online audience.

Our argument is that classroom capture has significant potential as a medium for creating distributable materials and that the steps necessary to realize that potential are not overly burdensome. We revisit this second portion of the argument in chapter 6. Even if classroom capture has fundamental disadvantages, however, those must be weighed against other benefits to the medium. First, a common critique of MOOCs and other prerecorded online courses is that the content risks becoming stale over time, especially in rapidly changing fields. This critique takes on new significance when considered next to the high production costs of custom course material, estimated to run between $29,000 and $325,000 depending on the course and the analysis.[3] These high costs are justifiable only if the content will be durable. Classes presented live, however, have a natural defense against this staleness: someone is actively re-presenting the content each term. When content is asynchronously produced, the teacher must select whether to reuse an old video, for which the work involved is trivial, or to record a new video, for which the work involved is substantial. When teaching live, teachers must select whether to present old content or refresh the content before presenting; in both cases, they will be presenting again, which represents a significant amount of work that must occur either way. There is also more immediate pressure to do so: they will be asked questions about their immediately preceding presentation rather than an older filmed video. If these captured lectures are then used as the foundation for the distributed versions of the class, there is a natural update cycle built in without overwhelming additional work as long as the class continues to be offered live.

Second, the fundamental goal of the distributed classroom as an alternative to MOOCs is to reintroduce elements of the classroom experience to the core material used to support the class. When filming a course deliberately to be delivered asynchronously, we do not often build in time for class discussions or group work; these are trusted to occur in parallel on forums or via other mechanisms. Our goal with capturing the lecture is to capture a version of the class that can be shared with a synchronous group of students at another location or with asynchronous cohorts who will use the presentation to structure their attendance and participation in a classroom-like environment. Classroom capture preserves a structure geared toward that in-class engagement.

Third, as part of the distributed classroom design, we attach a certain value to synchronicity with the original classroom context. Participating truly live gives some level of more direct access to the class, whether it be sending questions to the live instructor (likely curated by an intermediate teaching assistant) or participating in live activities that the instructor observes. This sort of live interaction by definition requires classroom capture—although the "capture" itself is not actually necessary so long as it is streamed. Still, if the class is already being captured digitally for live streaming, then preserving it for future reuse is a small additional step.

Note that we are not saying that classroom capture is better than custom-recorded material. The equation to determine the optimal recording mechanism is complex and has many variables. David, for example, struggles mightily with presenting in person. He thrives with a camera and with the freedom to try a video eight times before he settles on a version that he likes. Charles, in contrast, thrives with a live audience; in his two OMSCS classes, CS7641: Machine Learning and CS7642: Reinforcement Learning, he co-teaches with Michael Littman, which in many ways re-creates a live audience dynamic as the two take turns teaching one another. Many teachers we have found say teaching to a camera is depressing and unfulfilling. Resources also factor into the equation: If resources are not available for an expensive custom production, is classroom capture better than nothing? Our argument is that if the distributed classroom is feasible only with classroom capture because resources are unavailable for a custom production, then the distributed classroom is feasible. Classroom capture is good enough—and in some ways it can be better, especially for this use case.

All that said, you do not have to agree with this portion of the argument to follow the design of the rest of the distributed classroom. If you believe that only custom material with high production values is good enough for this design, so be it. For the SC classroom, that custom material can be used as the foundation for a flipped class, where students in person perform activities based on the knowledge they gleaned from watching videos before class. Distributed cohorts may then participate in those same activities, supported by the same prerecorded videos, facilitated by their own dedicated instructional support. Nothing about the distributed classroom is reliant on classroom capture as a mechanism, but classroom capture provides the most immediately available avenue to start building distributed classrooms. The lectures are already happening, why not capture and leverage them?

So, to continue this exploration, we filmed a session from Dhruv's CS4643: Deep Learning class. Now what?

SYNCHRONOUS WITH THE ORIGINAL CLASS

We start by staying within the synchronous row but supporting students outside the Atlanta area. The natural first jump when thinking about an SC^C classroom is to a separate campus, but before we go there, we may start with something closer to home. We mentioned previously that CS4643 fills up easily. How can we offer it to more students on campus? At present, the only mechanism is to offer two sections, requiring Dhruv to deliver the same class twice a day (or, alternatively, requiring us to find a second teacher for the class). Why two sections? Because lecture halls generally accommodate up to three hundred people. Consider, though, that the course content may be the same, the course assignments may be the same, the students may be graded by the same sets of graders following the same rubrics, and so on. A second section may thus instead be scheduled at the same time but in a different classroom. The second section would have a dedicated teaching assistant to set up the live broadcast of the lecture, to collect and curate questions for delivery to Dhruv, and to facilitate smaller discussions at the appropriate times. These students would retain full access to the breadth of campus resources, such as visiting live office hours. The net effect of this is that at Georgia Tech's Atlanta campus, as many students as want to take CS4643 can do so as long as teaching assistants are available for the tasks that scale linearly (such as assignment grading, answering forum questions, and live office hours). This is an SC^C class: these students are co-located with their cohort and synchronous with the original class.

The same arrangement there extends to another campus with relative ease. As we mentioned at the beginning, deep learning is an in-demand field. For Georgia Tech's campus in Lorraine, France, finding a dedicated instructor to teach CS4643 has been difficult, so while the Atlanta cohort gathers at 9:30 a.m. on Tuesday and Thursday, students in Lorraine gather in a classroom at 3:30 p.m. their local time. With them in the classroom is a teaching assistant for the course, someone with sufficient knowledge of the course content to answer basic questions and intelligently curate advanced questions for delivery to Dhruv. In their classroom, they turn on the live feed of the class occurring in Atlanta. When the class breaks for discussions, they break into their own discussions as well. When students in Atlanta are given problems to work on their own, students at Lorraine work on them independently, too. As the session progresses, students in Lorraine share their questions with their local teaching assistant, who either answers them directly or curates and delivers them to Dhruv to answer when he begins to take questions. This is also an SC^C variant of the class, but with the co-located cohort far more removed from the original class.

The added value to this live participation is that there exist avenues for direct access to Dhruv as he is presenting. Questions are sent along to him to answer on video for both cohorts. If there are in-class activities that ask students to, for example, complete a clicker question where they register a live response to a class poll, this remote student body at Lorraine can participate in these activities as well. Peer instruction techniques can operate even better online by allowing more seamless formation and shuffling of groups.[4] The Minerva Project's interface has dedicated features for quickly creating small student groups for peer instruction, peer review, and group work. This entire approach can be simpler than classroom capture: the lecture itself is live, removing any expectation for editing, albeit in exchange for increasing the pressure on technology to work because synchronous time is being consumed.

This arrangement covers students who are enrolled for credit at Georgia Tech's Atlanta and Lorraine campuses. However, there are certainly many, many students who are interested in the course who do not reside on one of these campuses. This is not speculative. The online section of CS7641 already draws hundreds of students per semester, and CS7643 (the graduate equivalent of CS4643) was the most requested course for years prior to its launch in fall 2020. The technological infrastructure used to broadcast the class in Atlanta to the class in Lorraine may just as easily be used to broadcast the class to individuals located around the world. Rather than going to a physical classroom to attend at the campus in Lorraine, France, a student in South Africa may sign on at the same time and watch from their own home. This remote cohort may then be gathered together into a typical teleconferencing room where they may chat with each other and with a dedicated online teaching assistant (who may be anywhere in the world). Just as with the local teaching assistant at the Lorraine campus, this online teaching assistant may answer some questions and curate other questions for delivery to Dhruv to answer at determined points in the lecture. If, as with our existing section, hundreds of students are interested in this form of attendance, then they may be divided into multiple sections, each with a teaching assistant to support Q&A, facilitate small-group discussions, and perform the other duties associated with running the classroom. This is the SR group: these students attend synchronously but entirely remotely.

Outside of that synchronous class time, however, these students may all be treated as one large cohort. We already do this with our OMSCS classes, where hundreds of students in a section of a class are grouped into a single section in our learning management system, a single course forum, and so on. Adding in a large cohort of students who themselves are in one place does not affect this design because the functions of the learning management system were never place specific. Students never needed to be on a campus to submit work, receive grades and feedback, and ask and answer questions in a forum. One large team of teaching assistants, themselves distributed across the world and working together, can accommodate the entire breadth of this distributed class audience. Even exams may be delivered remotely using the learning management system, potentially augmented with online proctoring solutions. Not only does this extend the full range of the assessment to these remote students, but it frees up synchronous class time to use on more valuable activities.

This is all easy for us to say, of course. As part of our online programs, we already have the infrastructure to accept applications and enroll students from all over the world without expecting them ever to visit campus. For other schools, the idea of enrolling students who are nowhere near any physical campus may be so unfamiliar that it prevents these ideas from taking off. Or the infrastructure may be there but largely segmented off; many schools' distance-learning departments operate relatively independently of their on-campus programs, as more of a university-branded extension school rather than an equivalent part of the campus audience. Part of the core appeal of this distributed classroom view is that what is distributed is the complete product students might otherwise obtain on campus. That means those integrations between distance learning and campus must be built more strongly.

But the benefits of this approach are enormous. Some are obvious: more students are able to complete the class—not just watch from a distance but participate, complete assessments, receive grades, and earn credit. Economies of scale kick in to lower the cost of enrollment, opening up access further. (We discuss these benefits more in chapter 7.) But what should not be underestimated is the benefit of this arrangement to students who were going to enroll in the class *anyway*. Under a normal arrangement, the more than three hundred students attending the class in Atlanta are in a classroom with a relatively homogeneous audience: most of our on-campus master's students are a year or two removed from completing their undergraduate degree and have limited professional experience. Under this distributed arrangement, these students are now grouped into forums and classes with a much more professionally diverse audience: some are working professionals in the field seeking to update their skill set; some are professionals in other domains seeking a career transition or to add some computer science to their repertoire; and some are hobbyists or entrepreneurs seeking knowledge that may help them with their individual endeavors. These individuals are now participating in forum discussions, asking and answering questions and contributing to the class experience for everyone; as we have noted, this online environment gives students much more access to and influence over their classmates.[5]

Again, this is not hypothetical or speculative. This has been one of the major advantages we have observed in our

OMSCS program. Students enroll in classes alongside individuals at very different points in their career trajectories and work together (peripherally or directly) for an extended period of time. One student described this as an inadvertent seventeen-week job interview because he was ultimately offered a job by a classmate's company that had observed his helpfulness over the course of the entire semester. In one class, CS7637: Knowledge-Based AI (developed by Ashok Goel and now taught by David), we frequently discuss IBM's Watson. During our first semester offering the course, we were stunned to find out that a student in the class was part of the Watson research team. He brought that expertise to class discussions throughout the semester, which themselves were made persistently available because they occurred in asynchronous text. These anecdotes only scratch the surface. We have teachers (or spouses of teachers) giving peer feedback in our Educational Technology class; we have employees for social media companies chiming in on our ethics discussions in Human-Computer Interaction; we have financial managers and accountants seeking a career transition to computing answering questions in our Machine Learning for Trading class. These are skill sets and viewpoints we could never incorporate so organically into a traditional course. When we distribute the class, we make access easier, and when access is easier, a more professionally diverse student body joins and improves the experience for everyone.

Returning to the notion of trade-offs, it is important to pause and take stock of what these designs ask students to do and whether other compromises are possible. Under these synchronous designs, students are expected to commit to attending at a prescheduled time; this locks out some working students who cannot take time out of the workday to attend, but we will accommodate them in the S^CC^C, S^CR, and AR variants (and importantly, none of those are in conflict with access to the same shared forums, graders, and so on). We also are expecting students to commit to the remaining structures of for-credit education, such as completing projects, taking tests, and receiving grades. This carries with it an expectation of prior knowledge and time commitment: students must be qualified to take the class and must commit to the class's workload. This is not a trivial commitment; these classes are hard. Students in Charles' CS7641 estimate the course requires twenty-one hours per week.

But must they commit to that? On-campus programs often have the notion of auditing a course, signing up to attend a course's lectures but not complete its course work or receive a grade. In our experience, that is rarely used in person as it still requires a heavy commitment to physically go to class at a particular time. We have most often seen it used by students who are enrolled in other classes on campus; without the promise of course credit, it is not appealing to potential students who are not already physically present. Online, the story is different: the class content is already set up for live broadcast, so it is as if everyone who is on the internet is already "on campus." Is there any reason to restrict it to those enrolled for credit? A more open audience would not need access to the learning management system, would likely not be in the same forum as the for-credit students, and may not have dedicated instructional support because they may not be paying any tuition, but under this design, distributing the content openly to a live SR audience may be trivial. This is very similar to (perhaps even indistinguishable from) MOOCs, but for a fraction of the production costs because most elements necessary to achieve MOOC scale were already in place. This opens up entire new avenues for outreach and access.

So we now have a live lecture in Atlanta being simulcast to a classroom at Georgia Tech-Lorraine (and perhaps other local cohorts), as well as to a distributed audience of more remote but still synchronous students. We have distributed the classroom across the top row of the distributed class-room matrix: location no longer needs to constrain whether a person can complete the course. Now, what about time?

SYNCHRONOUS WITH A COHORT

It is now 11:00 a.m. in Atlanta. CS4643 has just ended for the day. Classroom capture generated a video recording of Dhruv's presentation, a video recording of the screen con-tents during the presentation, the audio of his presentation, and potentially the audio in the room. Depending on the presentation, some editing might be desired. If the recording starts with a few minutes of students entering and settling into their seats, for instance, that may be removed. Small group discussions may be removed with the knowledge that the distributed versions of the course will pause and perform a similar activity at the same time. Students who do not opt into being recorded should similarly have their questions removed from the recording; keeping this option available accommodates privacy-minded students who may not want to be recorded while preserving the potential of distributing the class. What is important here is that the editing involved is not onerous, likely involving no more than cutting out some segments. For some sessions, just the capture itself may be sufficient.

While all that was going on, the students at Georgia Tech-Shenzhen, halfway around the world, local time 9:30 p.m., were likely getting ready for bed (or, more realistically, probably studying for their other Georgia Tech classes). The next morning, they wake up and go to a classroom. Their local teaching assistant cues up the video of the in-person class from Atlanta the day before. When the recorded class pauses for group work or small group discussion, the teaching assistant similarly pauses the video and facilitates the same activity in their classroom. When students have questions, the teaching assistant may pause the video and answer their questions live, file the question to send to Dhruv later if they feel that it warrants a response directly from him, or direct students to share the question on the course forum. This is the $S^C C^C$ class: these students are synchronous with their own cohort and co-located with their own cohort but asynchronous and remote relative to the original class.

At the same time (9:30 p.m. in Atlanta), a group of online MSCS students from around the United States have finished work, put their kids to bed, and so on. These students are unable to attend the synchronous remote sections in the morning due to work or family obligations, so instead they have their own cohort that meets synchronously in the evenings. Together with their own dedicated teaching assistant, they watch the recorded class in a teleconference together. They ask questions in the chat box or pause the class to ask questions live. The teaching assistant answers some and directs others to Dhruv or to the forum. These students similarly participate in their own discussions. This is the $S^C R$

class: these students are synchronous with their cohort but individually remote, attending from their own living rooms or home offices.

Under these conditions, the experience for the students in Shenzhen and the remote students in the United States is very similar to that of the synchronous students. The component that is lost is the ability to have more immediate impact on the content of the lecture: they cannot ask live questions for Dhruv to answer on camera or participate in class polls or other collective class activities with the original cohort, although they do have their own polls and activities with their own group of classmates instead. What is gained is more flexibility and control over their cohort's own watching experience; they can, for instance, pause the recorded class to ask questions out loud or determine for themselves how long group discussions should go. The dedicated TA under these circumstances has more freedom to tailor components of the delivery to the audience; if the cohort is specifically interested in machine learning for health care, for example, the TA may tailor the discussion to those use cases. As always, all of these students retain access to the instructor and the rest of their classmates through asynchronous mechanisms as well.

That seemingly minor use case carries major potential. Traditionally, class cohorts are formed based primarily on shared availability: the people who meet in the classroom in Atlanta at 9:30 a.m. on Tuesday are those who are committed to and enrolled in the in-person program, interested in machine learning, and available to meet at that time and place. Those constraints already segment the audience down to the point where further segmentation based on shared unique interests may be only sparingly possible. By breaking these scheduling constraints, however, much greater tailoring becomes feasible. The online section of CS7641 enrolls a thousand students per semester, and our online section of CS7643 will easily reach those numbers. We might imagine breaking those one thousand students into twenty- to thirty-student sections, each of which meets twice a week for ninety minutes to follow the class in Atlanta. Enrollment in a section would be restricted to students who are available at that time, but students would have more sections to choose from. Many students would likely be available for multiple sections, and intelligent assignment could pair students with deliberately common interests—or deliberately diverse viewpoints. As with the synchronous sections, these asynchronous sections may continue to participate in the same course forum, complete the same assessments, and be graded by the same teaching assistants. Although these sections are asynchronous relative to the original session, they still follow the same semester schedule. This keeps them naturally eligible for the same course credit.

Just as we considered synchronous audit audiences in the previous section, though, we might also consider another compromise here. There are many use cases where people may leverage this recorded material for other purposes. Workplaces might use these to run their own training sessions, where learners instead apply the concepts to their own work projects rather than course assessments. Other universities, unable to hire their own teacher for the subject matter, may use the course content and assessments but offer their own credit; they would need to hire teaching assistants, but these TAs would not be tasked with designing and executing the entire class on their own (we discuss the feasibility of teaching assistants for this task in chapter 6). For course content that might feasibly be used by younger audiences (such as precollege students), high schools might build their own courses with their own assessments on the foundation of the recorded material.

These initiatives are already happening. We regularly receive emails from teachers asking if they can use our free MOOCs as the de facto "textbook" for their classes. They assign students work in the MOOC and use the grades students earn in the MOOC as a component of students' grades in their actual course. More remarkable, this happens invisibly to us: we know that it occurs because some teachers email us to let us know that they are using our material, but there is no requirement that they alert us. We have no doubt that other teachers are also using the material to support their existing class sections, just as Stanford's CS Bridge program was picked up by teachers around the world. Many classes already use repositories like MIT OpenCourseware and Khan Academy not just to supplement their existing material but to provide a foundation for their course design. The open educational resources (OER) movement formed specifically to facilitate these use cases, where materials developed in one place can be reused in similar contexts elsewhere (such as one university using another's content) or even in radically different contexts (such as a summer camp built around the content of a freshman-level course). In the wake of COVID-19, both Coursera and edX formalized programs to make it easier for instructors to use their massive MOOC libraries in this way. Coursera for Campus[6] and edX Online Campus[7] were started for teachers new to online instruction to easily select from existing high-quality online content to use as the foundation for their newly remote class. Coursera even authored CourseMatch, a tool "that ingests a school's on-campus course catalogue and matches each course to the most relevant courses in Coursera's catalogue of 3,800 courses."[8]

The potential of these approaches is evident; next we must design for them more deliberately. That includes accommodating them more in the original course experience—such as enrolling remote students in the first place and facilitating the formation of local cohorts—and packaging content for smoother distribution to other contexts.

VARIOUS FORMS OF ASYNCHRONICITY
Finally, those efforts translate fairly naturally into the remaining cell of the distributed classroom matrix, the AR cell. There are pedagogical and social benefits to interacting with the material with a synchronous cohort, whether that cohort is face-to-face or online, but there will always be individuals who cannot commit to such interaction. Some may have schedules that are too fluid and unpredictable to make a regular commitment. Some may need to move through the material more slowly than a cohort would easily support, such as a student for whom English is not their first language. Some may not be able to locate the kinds of classmates necessary to form a cohort; a high school student interested in machine learning as a hobby may not be able to find other students at a similar level to participate in the class but may still want to learn it for their own curiosity.

All the steps that have preceded this level accommodate these asynchronous remote audiences in one form or another. There is no reason to lock any students out of accessing content that was already produced. This is what we sometimes call the "subsidized" model of online education: students paying tuition to enroll in our OMSCS classes for course credit toward a master's degree pay the bills associated with developing content, but once it is developed, it costs us essentially nothing to make that material available to others. The direct costs are minimal with the internet's existing support for video streaming, and we do not believe there are any opportunity costs. We doubt there are many students who would have paid to enroll in the full program if the video material was not available for free as the video content alone represents such a small fraction of the degree experience.

As with the other sections, the form that the AR class takes can again represent multiple compromises. Our OMSCS courses are already offered in a purely AR format; for students who wish to earn course credit and are able to follow the semester schedule, they can similarly be grouped in with all the other sections in the same learning management system, with the same forum, and under the same instructional team. This material also becomes the foundation for MOOCs; lightweight, automatically graded assessments can allow learners to complete some more formally organized version of the course with a credential (such as a MOOC certificate) that itself is not equal to course credit but is nonetheless shareable and verified in some fashion. The content can also be offered directly for free via dedicated open websites, similar to MIT OpenCourseware. Each of these offerings, all lightweight to construct based on the work already performed, brings yet another audience into the fold.

These efforts help all students in all previous sections. One of the most-praised parts of online learning is the ability for students to go back and rewatch the material; recording removes the scarcity of content. This simple change has widespread ramifications: falling ill no longer dooms a student to frantically trying to catch up by reading a textbook; a family emergency no longer forces a student to try to focus on class content while preoccupied with other issues; and students with extra accessibility needs may have those met in a more consistent and deliberate fashion, in line with the principles advocated by Universal Design for Learning.[9] Persistent access to the material is a boon for all learners in all sections.

SYMMETRY IN THE DISTRIBUTED CLASSROOM MATRIX

Let us briefly summarize the process we have described so far. We start with the normal synchronous, co-located (SC) classroom experience, which is already happening thousands of times a day at schools around the world. Wherever possible, we stay close to what teachers are doing anyway in order to minimize the work necessary to distribute the classroom across time and space.

From there, the content is captured and live-streamed to synchronous classrooms—the SC^C class—around the world, each with its own dedicated teaching assistant to facilitate the interaction for students in that classroom. Students unable to gather in a physical classroom may instead gather in a shared virtual space—the SR class—to interact with peers and teaching assistants. This distributes the class experience across space as it already existed. That is not to say there is no extra work on the part of the original teacher; steps can be taken to make the in-person presentation experience more conducive to this synchronous distribution, and these steps require some additional effort. However, the effort required is far lower than developing custom video for an entire course. For example, a teacher can make a remote audience feel significantly more welcome in the class by briefly welcoming them directly to start the lesson and acknowledging them periodically throughout the class period; this does not add significantly to the work involved but can nonetheless have a big impact. So through these efforts, a teacher may now—technologically and pedagogically at least, leaving issues of recruitment aside—have a worldwide synchronous classroom of students.

Later, cohorts of students around the world may gather in their own classrooms. These may be physical classrooms co-located with one another—an S^cC^c class—or stand-alone teleconference-based classrooms in an S^cR model. Together with their cohort, they replay the class as it was recorded earlier. The recorded lecture provides these cohorts of students the time to pause and engage in their own small group discussions, work problems themselves, or ask questions of their teaching assistant, thus preserving more of the classroom experience. Synchronous communication with other students and teaching assistants is thus part of the fundamental fabric of these distributed classrooms, preserved wherever possible.

Finally, not all students can commit to this level of regularity; their schedules may be unpredictable, or a cohort of students may not be available at their needed time slots. These students may continue to engage asynchronously, watching the course content on their own. They do not receive the benefits of these synchronous interactions, but this does not lock them out of participating altogether.

At the same time, all students across all of these different contexts may be grouped together in a single learning management system, completing the same assignments, asking questions on the same forum, interacting in the same asynchronous venues, receiving grades and feedback from the same teaching assistants, and earning the same course credit toward a degree. Compromises may be made to the nature of the individual student's experience based on that person's synchronicity and co-locatedness with a cohort, but the assessments that generate the grade need not differ. Then, separately, further efforts may be made to open up that content for students uninterested in the more formal credit and assessment or for organizations interested in repurposing the content for different offerings.

STUDENT SYMMETRY

Throughout this description, we have generally assumed that students select a section and stick with it. However, there certainly may be many instances where a student needs to shift between cells. For example, a student might generally attend as part of the SR classroom but one week may have work-related travel. As a result, that week may mean watching the class in an AR format. In another instance, a student may learn that there exists an S^CR cohort of the class specifically built around one of their own special interests (for example, machine learning for education data) and thus might decide to switch from the SC class to that S^CR section in order to engage in those discussions. International students experiencing a delay in having their visa approved may start a class as an SR student, then switch to SC once these issues are resolved. Students who fall ill, have family emergencies, or otherwise experience significant disturbances to their interaction may similarly find a temporary switch to an alternate cell of the matrix to allow them to continue progressing where historically they would have had to withdraw, fail, or seek onerous accommodation from the teaching staff.

This introduces the idea that we define as symmetry. As a term in this context, *symmetry* could easily take on two different definitions. The natural definition would be "an identical experience between different cells of the matrix." Thus, a student attending in person would have the same experience as a student attending with a synchronous co-located cohort on the other side of the world. This is actually *not* what we mean by *symmetry* in this context; we would argue that specific cells of the matrix lend themselves to specific advantages that should be leveraged. For example, the S^CR cell may be leveraged to create cohorts around shared interests that would be impractical within the SC cell. This makes the experience in the two classrooms different, but specifically because each takes advantage of its classroom's opportunities.

Instead, we define *symmetry* in terms of the type of credential or credit that the different cells can provide. Two different cells of the same class in a distributed classroom are considered symmetrical in our vernacular if they can offer the same credit. This follows closely with the outline of the distributed classroom in the previous sections: students across all versions are grouped into the same asynchronous environments, complete the same assessments, and are evaluated by the same graders, thus justifying the symmetrical credit across the offerings.

The importance of symmetry, however, is primarily to the flexibility that it extends to students. If a distributed classroom is symmetrical across these cells, it may mean students can move around the matrix without affecting what they ultimately may earn or achieve in the class. A class would be said to be symmetrical if students may freely switch between cells without affecting their ability to complete projects, receive grades and feedback, and interact on a course forum, and thus earn course credit. There will of course be differences in the experience; a student switching from a synchronous remote class to an asynchronous remote class loses the ability to interact live with classmates, and this changes the classroom experience. However, these differences may not need to affect whether they can complete and earn credit for the class.

This sort of symmetry may not always be possible across all cells of the matrix. For example, a class that requires building a physical prototype with expensive parts supplied in a lab environment may not be completed in an AR format to the same standard. The class may still be distributed in some fashion to the AR cell as we saw previously with MOOCs and open educational resources that do not carry typical course credit, but it is not symmetrical in that the credential available from participation in that cell is different.

Thus, symmetry (again, from the student perspective) represents an additional level of flexibility for students: not only can they individually select a version of a class that fits within their constraints, but they can shift between those versions as their constraints change because all the versions are tied to the same ultimate credential.

TEACHER SYMMETRY

This symmetry can take on a second form, one that may be even more powerful. The previous section discusses the freedom for individual students to move around cells in the matrix, but what about the teachers themselves? The distributed classroom matrix is defined in many ways in relation to an original cohort and delivery. If you (as a student) are not where the teacher is originally teaching the class, you are in some way remote. If you are not watching while the teacher teaches the class live somewhere, you are in some way asynchronous. You can move among the various distributed classrooms. But can the teacher as well?

In one sense, clearly not. Students are asynchronous if they are not participating at the same time that the teacher is presenting; students are remote if they are not in the same place as the teacher at that time. But teachers cannot be remote and asynchronous relative to themselves. However, the previous section assumed that students were electing to move themselves around the matrix based on their evolving constraints. Could the students instead be moved around the matrix based on the *teacher's* evolving constraints? In some ways we saw this dynamic in fall 2020: even SC classes had to have contingency plans in mind to rapidly shift to SR or AR structures depending on local infection rates. There are far more positive reasons to support the development of teacher symmetry, however.

Georgia Tech's faculty already regularly spend semesters abroad teaching students at its campuses in Lorraine, France, and Shenzhen, China, as well as several other study-abroad programs. Under the distributed classroom arrangement, those classes might instead be distributed versions of classes taught concurrently at the main campus. We have described hypothetical sections of CS4643 existing at the Lorraine and Shenzhen campuses, following along with the section in Atlanta. What if the teacher were to travel to Shenzhen for a couple of weeks, delivering class from there? The behaviors of students in Atlanta and Lorraine could remain largely the same, but their placement in the matrix would shift to the $S^C C^C$ cell based on the teacher's actions; meanwhile, the Shenzhen section would shift to the SC cell even as students continue to attend at the same place and time as they had before. This would allow a teacher to provide a presence to those other campuses without the heavy commitment of spending an entire semester overseas.

For another use case, professors during a term regularly are required to travel for conferences or research tasks, which can pose a significant disturbance to an in-person class. It is common to have teaching assistants cover these classes or offer guest lecturers, but instead, could a professor facing travel prerecord a session to be used as the foundation for all the various versions of the class, similar to how our prerecorded CS6750 material is being used as the foundation for an S^CC^C section of the course at Shenzhen in fall 2020? This similarly repositions the formerly SC class as an S^CC^C class, while the teacher records as if producing an AR class.

Some would argue (including us) that guest lectures are a great opportunity to enhance the typical course; if they are such an asset, this mechanism provides a way to offer them even more frequently. In fall 2019, David offered a guest lecture to a class at Carnegie Mellon. He did not travel there; the professor, Chinmay Kulkarni, instead video-called and put David on screen in front of the class. David gave a presentation, then answered live questions. Under the distributed classroom matrix, this would be viewed as an SC^C class: the class in Pittsburgh was synchronous with David, the guest lecturer, and co-located with one another. In this case, there is no SC class from which it builds; it is developed as a single SC^C class session in the first place. This mechanism lowers the barriers to offering such guest lecturers. No longer is it a matter of opportunistically finding whoever is available on the day a teacher is traveling; rather, it becomes finding the people a teacher may truly want to have offer such a lecture.

As the teacher moves around the distributed classroom matrix, we can see how the remaining cells pivot around the teacher. A teacher visiting different international campuses during the term would see each class take on different forms as the semester progresses: the Atlanta section would begin as an SC class, then transition to an SC^C class when the teacher presents from Lorraine at the same synchronous time, then transition to an S^CC^C class when the teacher presents from Shenzhen. During those travels, the teacher may sometimes even present remotely, which might spark a temporary shift of the Atlanta section to an SR mode if the teacher would prefer to present directly remotely rather than to a remote co-located class. In a more heavily distributed class including multiple S^CR cohorts, the teacher might choose to present from a different cohort each week, temporarily altering them to an SR class and giving each a chance at more direct interaction. Then, if in the subsequent semester the teacher is taking a sabbatical, battling a health issue, or otherwise unable to commit to presenting the course on a weekly basis again, the previous semester's material can be used as the foundation for a new offering of the course when it would otherwise be unavailable.

These modalities all stay within the ecosystem of one large course with shared assessments, forums, and teaching assistants, but it might extend even further. If such a course was being used to support a local high school's survey of the topic, that school could welcome the teacher in person on occasion. A workplace using the course content as the foundation of a training program could support a presentation of a topic more closely aligned with its needs, which may then be integrated as optional content in the course itself for the other students. A researcher in a cutting-edge field could record a class session specifically to be reused by other courses at other universities to teach a truly emerging topic.

In the process, some of these initiatives transcend the classification of the distributed classroom matrix in the first place, which in some ways is the goal. Teacher symmetry indicates that the teacher can move among different locations and teaching modalities while leaving the majority of the course—especially the ultimate credit that it offers—unaffected. If this happens, the classroom is truly distributed to the point where it becomes difficult to determine where the "primary" classroom even is. True symmetry, according to this view, occurs when the shifts among the cells, by both students and teachers, pose relatively little challenge to the overall value and experience of the course itself.

THE DISTRIBUTED CHURCH

As we initially brainstormed this book, David could not shake the feeling that many of the ideas we were describing were familiar. Following our hope earlier that these ideas are underwhelming due to their familiarity, we assumed that he was just passively aware of similar initiatives that he could not name in specific terms.

But at some point, it dawned on him that these ideas are familiar because he has witnessed the same progression in a very different context. Many of the ideas of the distributed classroom—such as deliberately welcoming remote students, replaying the entire classroom experience rather than just a lecture, offering certain in-person classroom structures while streaming others, and accommodating both synchronous remote cohorts and synchronous remote individuals—came from a development he witnessed growing up, one that is continuing to this day. So, to close this chapter on symmetry, and, more broadly, these two chapters on defining the distributed classroom matrix, we are going to trace through a development that already implemented these ideas: the growth of North Point Community Church.

In some ways, this example is very different: church is not school, there are no tests or assessments, and there is no credential to award or protect. There are fewer incremental costs to attend to, but at the same time there is no cost of attendance (although donations are, of course, encouraged). At the same time, however, it is similar in many ways. Attendance (and thus, donations) and enrollment (and thus, tuition) reflect that the institution is providing something attendees or enrollees want. A falling attendance or enrollment suggests that the church or school is no longer offering an experience that is in demand. If it is full (such as full Sunday morning services or turning away qualified applicants), the church or school may be artificially limiting its audience. Lastly, the pastor and leader of North Point Community Church, Andy Stanley, has always been in David's view more of a teacher than a preacher; his sermons more closely resemble Randy Pausch's *Last Lecture* than Billy Graham's "Who Is Jesus?"

We think that both these similarities and these differences reinforce the analogy: the similarities tell us that the lessons learned in the context of organized religion have the potential to transfer to an educational context, and the differences tell us that these trends are more universal than just education. This is not just the way education is moving but the way the world is moving.

THE SC^C CHURCH

North Point Community Church (often abbreviated simply as North Point) started in 1995. Initially, it rented auditorium space at the Cobb Galleria in Cobb County, northwest of Atlanta. It then began meeting on Sunday evenings at a Baptist church in Dunwoody, northeast of Atlanta. Finally, it bought its own property in Alpharetta, about forty-five minutes north of downtown Atlanta. It held its first meeting at the new property in 1997, under a tent in the rain on Easter

Sunday. David was there, ten years old, wanting to go home because he did not like the outdoors much (perhaps they could have guessed he would go on to teach computer science online from his home office).

Within a couple years of its opening, however, North Point had a problem, though the kind of problem other churches at the time longed to have. While a 2002 study found church attendance in America had slipped from 49 percent to 42 percent over the previous seven years,[10] North Point's weekly attendance had grown to over four thousand per week. Notably for the analogy we are drawing, North Point's mission from the beginning was to reach "unchurched" people—those who were not already attending regularly elsewhere. Like the distributed classroom, its goal was to reach people who were not already being reached, not to grow at the expense of other churches. With that attendance, North Point found its weekly services full, despite already offering three services every Sunday.

Therein lay a dilemma: more people wanted the North Point experience than the church could accommodate. How could the church expand its audience? It could offer more services—at one point, five services were offered in a single Sunday. This is analogous to offering more sections of a class, but it poses its own issues: it is draining and expensive for a teacher or pastor to deliver the same content five times in a single day. A class could be offered by more than one instructor, but that creates a differential experience; for North Point, this may have been a nonstarter because it was Andy Stanley's content that was likely the church's largest draw. The solution had to be to offer the same number of services, but each to a larger audience.

They experimented with overflow rooms showing a closed circuit broadcast of the sermon happening in the main auditorium, but some elements of that experience were decidedly subpar. Specifically, the live, contemporary music was one of North Point's early defining features, and watching Todd Fields, one of their original band leaders, perform on screen was not the same as singing along live. This, in our analogy, corresponds to classroom elements that you cannot simply watch on the screen. Watching a live music performance is different from watching a performance on TV and participating in a class discussion is different from watching a recording of others' class discussions. There are elements that can be recorded and replayed, and there are elements that are better recreated live.

In 2001, North Point opened a second auditorium on the same site, the West auditorium. The stage of the West auditorium mirrored the stage of the original (now East) auditorium, allowing them to share a backstage area and letting presenters quickly move between the two rooms to address the different audiences live. Seating capacity with the two auditoriums expanded to five thousand attendees under a normal configuration, but the West auditorium was also configurable to support conferences and other events. Michelle Obama, for instance, delivered a speech as part of her Let's Move! campaign at the church in 2011.[11]

Every Sunday, attendees filled both auditoriums. Each auditorium had its own band, which played at the same time to open each service. After the opening music, Andy often offered an opening prayer in the West auditorium while the bands packed up and left the stage. Then a large screen descended in the West auditorium while Andy went back to the East auditorium to give his sermon. The screen in the West auditorium showed a live video feed of the sermon from the East auditorium. During the sermon, Andy often looked into the camera and referenced the West auditorium as well, reiterating its status as an important part of the congregation. Sometimes there would be music to close the service, where the bands in each auditorium would return.

In the distributed classroom matrix, this is the transition from a strictly SC church to an SC^C church. A second group of people gathered together in a different place. Certain parts of the experience were deemed to need to happen live, such as the live music. Other parts were determined to be shareable via video feed, specifically the sermon. In this instance, the co-located cohort was close to the main cohort, allowing both to share infrastructure, a single bookstore, a single Sunday school program for children, and so on. This came closer to realizing the church's potential reach, but more was possible. Some people from around the Atlanta area drove over an hour to attend the church, and the church's leaders knew there were likely hundreds more who would attend if it could fit within their time and space constraints. So the church set about expanding some more.

THE S^CC^C CHURCH

In 2003, the first satellite campus of North Point Community Church opened: Buckhead Church. The campus originated with an informal group of people who began meeting in 2001, using materials produced by North Point to host their own services, in a model very similar to the local groups using Stanford University's CS Bridge program. North

Point leadership encouraged the endeavor; the new satellite campus grew and went on to move into its own facility in 2007.

For a time Buckhead Church was what we would describe as another SC^C church: the sermon in Alpharetta (where North Point Community Church was located) was broadcast live to the campus in Buckhead. Buckhead had its own band, and it had its own local pastor as well, Jeff Henderson. Jeff offered the opening prayer at Buckhead Church before joining the live broadcast of the sermon from Alpharetta. Once this arrangement started, Andy frequently acknowledged Buckhead Church when he spoke. His sermons often consisted of running through a series of hypothetical examples, like, "Maybe you're here this morning, and you're struggling with a marriage you think is breaking"; during these lists he would often look into the camera and directly acknowledge the other campus—for example, "Or maybe you're at Buckhead Church this morning and you're struggling to find a way to connect with your daughter." These additions again made it clear that the target audience for these sermons was the entirety of the distributed church; attendees at Buckhead Church were part of the broader congregation, not just eavesdroppers watching through a camera in the back of the room.

This broadcast structure meant that Buckhead Church followed the same sermon calendar as North Point, which is important because Andy's sermons typically came in series, just as each lecture in a course may build on the previous one. By sticking to the same schedule, people may alternate which campus they attend on a given Sunday without missing a part or seeing one twice. This is similar to the requirement in our CS4643: Deep Learning example where all students across the matrix must stick to the same weekly calendar because assignments and grading follow that structure. This shared structure also allowed North Point to experiment with what we would describe as "pastor" symmetry; Andy sometimes gave the sermon from Buckhead Church (and later, Browns Bridge Church, another campus, which opened in 2006), while attendees at North Point watched remotely. This could lead to the somewhat funny circumstance where attendees in the West auditorium at North Point, knowing they would be watching a video anyway, did not realize that not only was Andy not in their auditorium, but he was actually twenty miles away.

This structure presented some significant coordination challenges, however; David remembers some awkward moments waiting for the other campuses' bands to catch up so the sermon could begin or joining sermon video feeds several seconds late. Coordinating a live event across that many different locations—including components as unpredictable as live music and prayer—was difficult. So at some point, the arrangement shifted to using recordings. These recordings were still near-live: after all, it was important for all the campuses to receive the same message on the same Sunday. Thus, the alternate campuses became S^CC^C churches: the congregation at each gathered together at their local campus, sang with their own live band, gave their own offering, had an opening prayer from their own local pastor, and then turned on the video of the sermon from minutes or hours earlier in Alpharetta. Sometimes the sermon in Alpharetta was not complete by the time a remote church tuned in, but remote churches no longer had to match perfect synchronicity like a live television broadcast; it was as if every church had its own DVR and could start a few minutes late if need be.

This arrangement expanded over time: a fourth and fifth campus, Gwinnett Church and Woodstock City Church, opened in 2011, and a sixth, Decatur City Church, followed in 2014. All of these campuses are located in the metropolitan Atlanta area and generally follow the same calendar as the main church, albeit with significant leeway left for individual churches to add their own components. Andy often does not preach during summers, and instead the pastors of each church give their own sermons or welcome guest preachers. This allows the distributed churches to build on the foundation of North Point while still tailoring the experience to their local audience, similar to a distributed classroom offering extended discussions in a version with fewer time restrictions or tailoring course topics to the common interests of a particular cohort.

It is particularly important to note the role of additional people at these distributed churches. MOOCs and large classrooms are often criticized for potentially taking jobs away from teachers while also hurting the educational experience; similarly, megachurches are often criticized for losing the intimacy and community associated with smaller local churches. The size of North Point as a distributed church has not diminished the number of pastors it requires, however; individual campuses still have their own dedicated pastors, but these individuals are able to devote more attention to the specific needs of their congregation because they are not also tasked with preparing the week's sermons. Additionally, other church employees are dedicated to specific roles, like premarital counseling, financial mentoring, and divorce recovery, domains that require special expertise but often are instead covered by a single pastor at smaller churches. This has far-reaching benefits: individuals have different skill sets, and it is probable that a compelling speaker may not be a gifted organizer or mentor. By separating out the role of preaching from some of the other responsibilities of a pastor, people may be chosen for those roles who excel at a smaller set of responsibilities. This has a clear analogy in teaching. David, for example, does not consider himself a particularly good in-person speaker—he gets winded, he talks too fast, and he speaks rather quietly. By separating out presenting course content from other elements like organizing the course experience and answering individual questions, he can focus on the responsibilities at which he excels and delegate other responsibilities to those who excel at them.

This is not just about the leadership either: the various campuses of North Point still require the same linear expansion of volunteer staff that they would need if they were independent churches. They still need more people to support child care and children's ministries, offer counseling, run volunteer enterprises, and so on. This is akin to our own programs' need for teaching assistants to support grading, question answering, and integrity verification as enrollment rises.

One final component of the analogy between a distributed church and a distributed classroom is North Point's focus on small groups. Several times a year, pastors at every campus of North Point Community Church emphasize that the large gatherings on Sunday mornings are only one part of the church experience. Small groups are an equally important part. These are cohorts of eight to twelve people from a similar stage of life who meet weekly. They discuss the sermon from that week, have their own separate conversations, and follow activities designed by the church. These are small, intimate, and interactive, and Andy will regularly say that anyone who is not in one of these small groups is not really participating in the church. In our analogy, these small groups are integrated into the distributed classroom; we have frequently discussed how the responsibilities of teaching assistants in distributed sections include facilitating in-class small group discussions.

Megachurches like North Point and large educational programs like MOOCs share a perception that they are large, anonymous, and impersonal. Critics accuse both of fundamentally misunderstanding the goal of their enterprise; both worship and learning are meant to be personal, interactive, and relationship-driven. Those critics are right: many megachurches miss the point, and many large educational programs miss the point. That does not mean that the structure is fundamentally incompatible with the objective; it merely means that intimacy must be deliberately designed into the enterprise at scale. North Point has provided a blueprint for how that can be done in a religious context, and the distributed classroom seeks to realize that potential in an educational context.

THE SR, AR, AND MORE DISTANT S^CC^C CHURCHES

We have covered the SC, SC^C, and S^CC^C church, especially from the more closed context where all these churches follow the same general schedule, akin to multiple sections of CS4643: Deep Learning that group students together into shared forums and grading workflows. We do not know if North Point has made many efforts in the S^CR direction, where groups of people gather online to watch prerecorded sermons. However, the church does exist in the other two cells (SR and AR) and has another variation in the S^CC^C cell, all of them worth exploring for their relevance to the distributed classroom.

The idea of SR and AR churches is not new: church services have been televised for decades. Andy Stanley's father, Charles Stanley, was until recently the senior pastor at First Baptist Church of Atlanta and began a television and radio version of his ministry in 1972. It was a surprise to many that North Point resisted having a recorded broadcast for so many years; when it eventually did, it was via the internet, although a television presence followed later. Along with its physical campuses around Atlanta, North Point Ministries (the collective name of all the churches together, and also colloquially referred to as North Point) offers an online "campus" where attendees can watch the music and sermons live from any of the campuses. The interactive nature of the internet allows these online experiences to be designed more deliberately to welcome the online audience. There are networking mechanisms supplied within the interface to facilitate interaction and connection, unlike the one-to-many mechanism of television and radio. While preaching, Andy often greets the online audience specifically before going onstage and then gives the online audience a specific sign-off after the sermon. During the sermons, Andy has added to his list of examples with comments like, "Or maybe you're watching online because you haven't yet found a local group that you want to attend church with." These steps all bring the synchronous remote audience into the fold as first-class members of the distributed congregation.

These messages are similarly available asynchronously. This has long been true, dating back to CDs and DVDs of sermons available in the church bookshop before it even opened its second auditorium. Today these are available streaming on demand to accommodate those who are not near a campus or cohort of potential congregants, those who have an irregular schedule that prevents attending at the set times, and those who are from a place where such participation must be done in secret rather than in the open. These sets of constraints mirror those facing many potential audiences of our educational offerings as well.

It is this foundation, however, that sets up the ease with which North Point has a network of strategic partners. Strategic partners are similar to satellite churches but more independent and remote. If the satellite churches are like the managed sections of Stanford University's CS Bridge, then its strategic partners are more like the independent groups that pick up the content to use themselves. Unlike their campuses and satellite churches, these strategic partners may not follow the same schedule and are not represented in the central organization of the ministry. Instead, these are small churches that leverage North Point's open resources to offer their own local services. North Point currently has over 170 such strategic partners listed on its website; the closest are only a bit farther out from the six campuses in metropolitan Atlanta, while others are as far as Chile, Venezuela, Australia, and South Africa. Thirty-two states, fourteen countries, and five continents are represented. These strategic partners are more akin to our high school groups, workplace groups, or other informal groups that would not participate in the full, graded, credit-bearing version of CS4643: Deep Learning, but nonetheless may use the fact that the content is recorded and available to support their own learning.

What all this means is that when COVID-19 hit, North Point was in a far better position to survive and thrive than many other churches. Essentially overnight, it switched from operating as an SC church distributed to other campuses and remote audiences to operating as an SR church that broadcast directly to a remote audience from the outset. This rapid transition was a fundamental part of its preexisting structure. This preparation can be seen in its subsequent reaction as well: other churches in the metropolitan Atlanta area rushed to reopen as soon as possible, potentially in the face of dwindling donations[12] or the perceived risk of a drop in relevance after weeks and months apart. Meanwhile, North Point Community Church announced in early July 2020 that it would remain closed through the end of the calendar year, continuing to conduct services online. It remained online into spring 2021, but the key observation is how readily the church announced a six-month hiatus of its in-person meetings rather than waiting to see how conditions changed. The ease with which it made that decision is likely the envy not only of other churches, but also of educational institutions that were forced to grapple with reopening in fall 2020.

In North Point, we see over the past twenty-five years the progression from a single church in a single location to a distributed church across time and space. These varied locations and offerings are still built from their own version of classroom capture, then distributed to other campuses and remote audiences over the internet. Several aspects of the in-person experience—such as live music, small group inter-action, and dedicated children's ministries—are recreated in the distributed locations. The number of people neces-sary to make the whole enterprise run is unchanged, but the responsibilities are shifted; individuals are tasked more with relationship building and interaction. Analogically, we in education are still relatively early in this progression; we have experimented with many of the individual components and found that they are successful, and the time has come to knit those components into a broader, more cohesive vision. The history of North Point Community Church, with its similar challenges, similar criticisms, and similar priorities, shows that such a vision is plausible and desirable.

6

PRACTICAL CONSIDERATIONS

To say our vision is rosy would likely be an understatement. Several times throughout the first five chapters, you may have read a suggested solution and scoffed at how simplistically we described a complex problem. This chapter delves deeper into some of those practical difficulties. We can identify three things that we anticipate you might believe we have oversimplified:

- Technology: We have described technology in many ways as almost a passive afterthought that runs invisibly in the background. It is, of course, not that simple. If it is not that simple, does the feasibility of the idea fall apart?
- Staff: Constantly throughout this ideation, we have referenced the availability of a large body of teaching assistants qualified and willing to help with distributing these classrooms. Does that body really exist? If not, does the scalability of the idea fall apart?

- Applicability: Our emphasis so far has been on classes in high-demand fields where it is difficult to find instructors; again, we teach computer science, and this is our reality. But if we venture outside computer science, does the distributed classroom still solve other problems? Is it solely relevant to the niche of graduate-level classes in computing? If so, does the relevance of the idea fall apart?

In the following three sections, we generally make two arguments. First, the distributed classroom is technologically feasible, realistically scalable, and generally applicable. Second, even if the technology is too complex, if the teaching assistants are not available, and the topics are too narrow, the distributed classroom paradigm is still feasible, scalable, and relevant.

TECHNOLOGY

We are computer scientists. When it comes to describing all the amazing things technology can do, that works against us in two ways. First, we are obviously generally optimistic about the role that technology can play. Second, we have a greater comfort with technology than many others do; what is straightforward for people like us may be overwhelming for others. We actually argue that this is one of the reasons that the OMSCS program has succeeded: because we are computer scientists using computers as our medium to teach computing, we were equipped to build the things we needed to succeed.[1]

That said, our particular niche within computer science is in interactive computing, which places a heavy emphasis on designing with users in mind. We do not assume that any novice will be able to use a complex tool with ease. We believe that tools should be designed with the user's context in mind; that means that if a tool requires significant cognitive load to operate, it is incompatible with a teacher simultaneously teaching a synchronous class. So while we bring to this discussion an optimism about and comfort with technology, we strive not to underestimate the toll additional steps can take on a teacher who should be focused on presenting content. We believe the technology required can be cognitively "invisible" to the presenter (meaning that it can require little to no extra thought) and run with minimal additional human effort.

In this section, we discuss the state of the art in case you are an administrator or technologist who is tasked with making the decisions about what your classrooms should support. We then discuss the (relatively) low-tech, do-it-yourself approach if you are a teacher or learner forced to operate within existing constraints.

STATE OF THE ART

The state of the art in lecture capture and telepresence has come a long way from the single camera at the back of the room. Georgia Tech's Global Learning Center (GLC) is an example of what is possible. The distance-learning classroom at the GLC is equipped with two intelligent video cameras. These cameras are mounted on the wall and can automatically follow a speaker as that person walks around presenting, alternate between panelists who are discussing back and forth, or locate a student asking a question in the audience. Microphones throughout the room capture audio no matter where the speaker is standing; speakers may also wear wireless microphones to capture their own audio consistently. The contents of the screens in the room are automatically captured to add to the video feed. All these input feeds are routed into a central system that merges them into one core experience, while also preserving them separately to allow for future additional editing. For example, while the system attempts to intelligently determine when to focus on the speaker and when to focus on the on-screen visuals, these streams are preserved so that a human may later intelligently select when each is more pertinent.

The result of all of this, at its peak performance, is a classroom where the teacher can walk in, flip a switch, and immediately begin teaching to both the students present in the classroom and the synchronous distributed audience in other classrooms or homes around the world. This system then passively generates a recording of the session that, with minimal editing, is ready to be used as the foundation for asynchronous opportunities.

Of course, the distance-learning classroom at the GLC is exceptional in many ways. To support a distributed classroom of the scale we have in mind, essentially every classroom would need to be equipped with the same sort of technology. Is that reasonable? In 2019, we might have said no; the equipment is expensive and the potential benefits too intangible. The history of educational technology is replete with examples of expensive systems foisted on teachers that only go on to gather dust because the learning curves are too great or the use cases too narrow. But in the wake of COVID-19, this sort of initiative has proven far more feasible; many schools have already rushed to implement systems like these as a way of offering an in-person experience while also accounting for smaller class sizes and the inability of some students to come to campus. Georgia Tech, for instance, incorporated these technologies into every centrally managed classroom on campus to support hybrid courses. This has happened outside higher education, too: a private school in Atlanta implemented essentially the same initiative for its K–12 students as well.[2]

The state of the art accomplishes our use case. If you are involved in purchasing decisions, include your faculty in the discussion, but give a serious look at the potential that these sorts of systems open up.

DO-IT-YOURSELF

It remains the case that most teachers and schools do not have access to that kind of setup. If the distributed classroom approach can be implemented only by the big research universities of the world, then we are well on our way to the mass centralization of higher education that Udacity founder Sebastian Thrun predicted almost a decade ago.[3] Meanwhile, well-funded private elementary schools will be able to continue to improve their reach and product while public schools are left behind. Neither of these outcomes is desirable. If we thought this approach was just a way for the big, well-funded schools to get even bigger, we would not write this book.

For this approach to have a positive impact, we believe it must be implementable with the tools that a teacher may already have or could easily acquire. So, let us look at how a teacher might build this setup from scratch. First, we consider the common classroom setup where a teacher speaks accompanied by prepared visuals, often in the form of slides.

In order to present this way in person, the teacher must have a computer and a projector. The computer and projector take care of the in-person class. When the class starts, the teacher may turn on some videoconferencing tool (Zoom, BlueJeans, Microsoft Teams, Google Meet, YouTube Live, Twitch; any of these will work) and begin screen sharing. Most such tools now allow a presenter to both present the screen and remain on video, so the visuals that the teacher is showing in class are streamed live along with a camera feed of their presentation. Most of those teleconferencing systems similarly offer recording, and so the recording of the classroom experience is accomplished within that system as well. At the conclusion of class, a remote synchronous audience (whether in a single classroom elsewhere or at their individual homes) has been able to watch live, and a recording has been generated for later viewing by students seeking to review the material and those who could not attend live.

What was required for this experience? The computer was already a part of the classroom setup; an additional webcam may have been needed. A high-speed internet connection was necessary. Access to a video-streaming platform was necessary, but some of the ones that would work are already available for free use. A web host for the recorded content was needed, but similarly, file hosting is available with most learning management systems. With minimal additional effort, the content was able to be both streamed live and recorded for later use.

The technical requirements are not the only limiting factors here, of course; the teacher needed to stay in the webcam view, which means either huddling behind a desk or managing to position the computer's webcam to capture their movement and presentation, which might have an impact on the audio capture quality. Some relatively small additions can make a big difference. First, audio quality can be improved tremendously by having a dedicated microphone for the teacher. Fortunately, that can be simple: most computers (especially laptops) accept Bluetooth wireless connections, with microphones as cheap as twenty dollars. Adding such a microphone to the setup can allow the teacher much more freedom to move around without worrying about monitoring the audio quality of the presentation. The camera can still keep the teacher pinned in place, though, and moving an entire laptop just to reposition the camera can be awkward and unwieldy. What about a wireless webcam? Those tend to be significantly more expensive until you remember that you are likely already carrying one with you wherever you go. If you have a smartphone, you already have a wireless camera. Apps like DroidCam for Android and iCam for iOS allow your smartphone to connect to your computer and function as a webcam; or a teacher could separately join their own class teleconference from a phone to provide multiple angles. The camera is thus untethered from the computer: it can be positioned more freely and moved around to follow the teacher or zoom in on demonstrations. These two changes do not affect the original setup: the computer still sees the camera as a webcam and the microphone as an audio input device and passes them through to the teleconferencing system accordingly.

Slight changes to teacher behavior do become necessary. It is important that teachers directly address the camera sometimes to make remote students feel more included. We recommend following the pattern from chapter 5, directly welcoming remote students before class and specifically acknowledging them at the end of class, as well as directing some content and questions to them along the way. It also becomes important for teachers to ensure they remain on camera and repeat in-person questions out loud for the online audience since the audio feed is constructed to focus on the teacher's audio presentation. In the grand scheme of things, these are relatively minor.

What if the teacher's presentation style is not slide based? This will dictate some changes to the experience. If the teacher instead makes heavy use of writing on the whiteboard, it may be feasible to simply aim the camera at the whiteboard; in this case, the writing must be large enough to retain its meaning when transmitted and potentially compressed over a videoconference. If this is the setup, we recommend grabbing a snapshot of the whiteboard before it is erased and making that available after class to resolve any ambiguities there might be in the video feed. Even better may be to make use of a USB document camera. These cameras function just like webcams, except they are set up to record from a physical desktop. The teacher can then write on paper and have that content simultaneously streamed to the remote audience and projected on screen to the in-person audience. Unfortunately, this does mean that there is no longer a camera on the teacher in the classroom, but the feed from the document camera captures live writing instead of just static images, keeping the experience a bit more lively. It can also be possible, depending on the specific tools, to easily switch between video feeds.

There are, of course, many other kinds of in-person presentation styles, and most can be handled by some variation of this approach. For example, a chemistry class with live demonstrations can benefit from the mobility of using a smartphone as the webcam. A software development class that requires using live software can broadcast it just as simply as a slide-based presentation. A class that involves looking at a number of live artifacts or items can pass these under the document camera or take special care to show them directly to the camera feed. There will still be some distance between the in-person audience and the remote audience, but with current technology, it may feel far closer than ever before—close enough to treat remote students as first-class members of the course.

THE STUDENT SIDE

Regardless of whether the state of the art is employed or the more do-it-yourself angle is adopted, the result to the remote students is relatively similar: they receive a live-streamed version of the in-person experience complete with an avenue for interacting with the in-person class, as well as an asynchronous version of the experience to watch later.

It is critical to acknowledge an assumption made in this arrangement, however. We generally assume under this setup that students are available to attend live during the class time, even if remotely. In the rapid shift to remote learning after COVID-19, the argument was that students' schedules were still dictated by their registration, and so it was reasonable to expect them to sign into a live virtual class at the same time as they had previously been attending in person. This assumes, though, that these students' remote arrangement is conducive to that sort of attendance: they must have access to an adequate internet connection for live participation, they must have access to their own device they can use during that time, and they must have a home setup that is conducive to learning. None of these are guaranteed. Students may be remotely attending from areas with poor internet, they may have to share a single device with multiple members of their household, or they may have to attend using a makeshift setup on a couch in the living room while siblings watch TV or parents struggle with their own work-from-home setup.

As long as we are using technology to facilitate this experience, we are putting down a line in the sand dictating who is welcome and who is not. Those who do not have an adequate technological setup are not welcome in our course experience. This is the digital divide: students who have access to good technology are in position to succeed, while students who do not are left behind, typically exacerbating preexisting differences. Of course, this same distinction happens whether technology is in the loop or not: tuition costs, geographic accessibility, local funding, and more already create such divides. We want technology to be an equalizer, though, not to exacerbate these inequities.

This, fortunately, is one of the advantages of designing for a distributed classroom. The various cells by design accommodate audiences with different constraints and opportunities. For example, a student whose internet connection is insufficient to attend class live or one who cannot access the family computer until after work hours can make use of the recorded content to achieve an AR classroom. Teachers who are aware of many such scheduling conflicts can even use their own material to self-administer an S^CR classroom; they can offer, for instance, to be online at 8:00 p.m. to answer live chat questions while students watch the recorded class from earlier in the day. The burden on the teacher is far lower than reteaching the content to students who missed the synchronous section. There is still added work, but it may be diminished enough to be more feasible, especially if teams of teachers or teaching assistants can pool their resources around those responsibilities. The important consideration is to constantly ask how every cell of the matrix can be treated as a deliberate, equivalent experience rather than relegating any to an afterthought: by doing so, students who are constrained away from certain types of interactions may not be left behind.

OTHER TECHNOLOGIES

This section has focused on the technologies involved to make the classroom experience itself distributable. We have taken for granted the idea that those activities that may now happen outside class—such as submitting homework, receiving grades and feedback, and asking questions on a forum—already do. This is not the reality in many places, however. As we were writing this book and soliciting feedback, one of our students shared a since-deleted comment on Reddit from a teacher describing many of the issues she encountered with the rapid shift to online learning in the wake of COVID-19 and her fears for hybrid learning in fall 2020. Most of these fears and problems are not covered by the technologies we have described. The teacher notes, for instance, the difficulty in tasks as simple as administering worksheets to both remote and in-person audiences. In person, students typically do not have access to technology in every class, so the teacher must print worksheets for them to fill out manually;

but at home, students may not have access to printers, and so worksheets must be completed virtually. This means the teacher may have to prepare parallel workflows for these students. This trickles through to other components as well, whether they are lab experiments that cannot be done at home or copyrighted material the teacher may be uncomfortable sharing remotely. Other issues are more deliberately technological. The teacher in that comment notes, "I have 10 Google Classrooms and 10 gradebooks to set up, which is double my workload. And if I post something on Google Classroom and want to attach a new link or change the due date, I have to edit it one by one. Also, you can't schedule an assignment to be posted on multiple classrooms at a time, so now I have to do that on 10 classrooms. And now there are 10 places for me to look on a regular basis to see if any late assignments have been turned in." This is directly counter to our notes about grouping all students regardless of their classroom structure into one giant section.

Numerous other challenges come up as these ideas are implemented at different levels, in different subject matter areas, within different regulatory environments, and so on. We do not mean to trivialize these. Instead, we advocate that decision making deliberately include all stakeholders; for example, in the case of the teacher with the ten Google classrooms, it is preferable for her to be able to organize them into one larger class for certain functions, and that should not be prohibited by artificial external constraints.

But more important, we also feel this model presents a solution to these same challenges. The benefit of the distributed classroom model is in its distributability and scalability. In well-defined fields, every teacher does not need to become an expert in this methodology. If a class is developed well once, that well-developed version may be scaled and reused to accommodate the students who need a remote option. These teachers may then pivot to more student support, answering individual questions, and planning for Individualized Educational Plans (IEPs) and accommodations instead of having to develop complete classroom experiences themselves. Right now, every teacher is asked to play dozens of roles simultaneously; the distributed classroom provides a mechanism to allow teachers to specialize in individual roles, to the overall benefit of teachers and students alike.

STAFF

Throughout chapters 4 and 5, we invoked the existence of these mythical creatures called "teaching assistants" who provide individual support to distributed students. The reason we heavily rely on these individuals in this vision is because we heavily rely on them in our normal roles on our OMSCS program as well.

In our online master's programs, every class receives one head TA and an additional TA for every fifty students who enroll in the course. For example, in the current term, David's CS6750: Human-Computer Interaction class drew 519 students. Our staff for this class, then, is 12 teaching assistants: the head TA plus 519 divided by 50 (rounded up). The head TA, Ronnie Howard—now a faculty member at Georgia Tech—manages the grading workflow, answers routine questions on the course forum, and escalates certain issues up to David. The remaining TAs focus mainly on grading papers: every week, they receive thirty to forty essays to grade. They also answer questions on the forum when they want, although that is mostly because they are awesome people who like to help out, not because they are assigned that responsibility. David, meanwhile, focuses his time on tasks that most heavily demand significant subject matter expertise: designing class assessments and rubrics, answering advanced questions on the course forum, and producing course content. Not only does David still inter-act with students but he interacts even more frequently and substantively than he would otherwise because he may share or delegate those responsibilities that do not require his expertise to teaching assistants. In another class, CS1301, he personally emails students who fall behind, an outreach many students reflect they receive in no other classes; this is not because he cares any more than other faculty members, but rather because the distributed nature of the classes opens up more time to invest in such regular, direct interaction instead of behind-the-scenes management and one-to-many presentations.

All of our classes operate under a similar model. The tasks for specific courses differ; in some courses, TAs write assign-ments, review exam data, write autograders, or provide more one-on-one mentorship, but regardless of their specific role, we could not run our program without these TAs. Without them, we would have to rely on peer review or automated evaluation. These both have important pedagogical roles to fill—peer review is a valuable learning exercise for stu-dents, and autograding can be used to create rapid feedback cycles on certain types of content—but rebuilding the entire program to use them alone would dictate a more dramatic change to the assessments themselves.[4] The distributed classroom follows a similar model: it assumes that when a certain number of new students enroll, a new teaching assistant will be available to support them. This separates the distributed classroom from MOOCs and means that the model follows a linear scale: the only limit to a course's reach is the teaching assistants who are available.

This brings up two questions for this vision: Will they be available? And what if they are not?

CAN WE FIND TEACHING ASSISTANTS?

To explore the feasibility of our reliance on teaching assistants, we must first define this role. Teaching assistants are individuals who have already attained A-level knowledge of the course for which they are now working as a TA. They are not subject matter experts who could teach the class themselves from scratch; rather, they have already reached the ambitious goals we have for current students in the class. As part of this level of ability, they are able to facilitate discussions on course topics, answer many (but not all) questions about course content and assessments, evaluate student work according to a rubric generated by the teacher, and give useful feedback—both positive and negative—on that student work. Depending on the course, these teaching assistants may also be asked to serve other roles that require that same level of experience, potentially equipped with some additional light training; this might involve checking work for signs of plagiarism, debugging student code submissions, or designing alternate presentations of course content.

To make one part of this arrangement clear, we consider the comparatively low level of ability of these teaching assistants to be an asset rather than a liability or a compromise.[5]

Topics from cognitive science like expert blind spot and cognitive load tell us that very often, the subject matter experts who live and breathe the course content are not the best instructors of that content. They may not remember what it is like to not understand the material, and thus may have difficulty identifying student misconceptions or properly scaling course difficulty. This is more of an issue with college-level professors teaching classes related to their research, but even among high school teachers or instructors of early undergraduate classes, the familiarity that comes with teaching the same content year after year may get in the way of mentally adopting the viewpoint of new learners. Teaching assistants who only recently attained knowledge of the subject are well suited to know the plight of students in the class; discussions with these TAs are more akin to peer learning given the relatively close level of experience between the TA and the new student. There are other assets as well: employing a large number of TAs brings multiple viewpoints to the course, each with its own perspective. The TAs themselves benefit as well because teaching the content solidifies their understanding.

We know individuals with these qualifications exist; after all, they are the ones who earned As in the class. Are they interested in the role? Can we afford them? Historically, we know that they do exist, at least in higher education: the position has existed for decades. Paid TA positions are often in high demand (in part because they often carry lucrative tuition waivers), and the supply of positions can be low by comparison. The context was different there, however: class sizes were already going to be capped by classroom capacity. The question then was, "Are there enough TAs available for this seventy-five-person classroom?" Summing the total capacities of such classrooms would also give an estimate for how many students a program could accept, leading to selective admissions. Our paradigm in the OMSCS, and our goal in the distributed classroom, is to accommodate all interested and qualified learners; thus, the question is, "Are there enough TAs for the number of interested students?"

Here, we draw on our experience in the OMSCS program. We recounted the story of our first foray into hiring online students as teaching assistants in chapter 3. To briefly recap, when we started, we knew there were not enough on-campus TAs to support unlimited growth in the online program: the on-campus program draws its TAs from its own student body, and so for the online program to scale, it would need to draw from its own student body as well. We anticipated, however, that online students—older, more experienced, more likely to be working—would not be interested in helping out as teaching assistants. On-campus students are highly incentivized by a tuition waiver and also need roles that are compatible with taking their own classes; TA roles are by far the best option. Online students pay far less in tuition and generally are juggling their own jobs and families along with taking classes; whereas working as a TA would be the second priority for on-campus students (after their own classes), it would be third or fourth for online students (after their own career, their own classes, and likely their family).

So, for the first few semesters, we hired only on-campus students to work as TAs for the online classes. That posed a problem for summer, as we recounted in chapter 3: on-campus students leave campus for internships, leaving us with no teaching assistants, so we began recruiting from the

online student body to see if we could muster enough candidates to offer at least a small section. We ended up with
far more candidates than we needed to accommodate every
student who wanted to enroll, and since then, we have hired
a large number of online students as TAs. Many continue to
work in the role even after graduating. We regularly receive
many more applicants than we have capacity to hire with
our target ratio of students-to-TAs, so our staffing is comfortable. This scale has been achieved also while we are currently
able to hire only US residents; our student body is 35 percent
international, meaning only two-thirds of our student body
is currently even eligible to help as teaching assistants.

The math here gives an optimistic picture. If we need to
continue to find one new TA for every forty students (our
average ratio when factoring in the head TA each class
receives), then we need 2.5 percent of students to be qualified
and willing to work for one semester as a teaching assistant.
Instead, we see about twice that number apply, and the vast
majority stick around for at least three semesters. In spring
2020, David had fifty-five TAs for his online master's classes;
forty-seven of them were still TAs in fall 2020, representing
at least three semesters of work. For many, the actual number
of semesters is significantly higher: our longest-tenured TAs
have logged twenty semesters over six years.

So it appears that people are available and interested—at
least in our field. It may turn out that other fields differ, but
we believe our experience is sufficient to move forward. The
next question is: Can we afford them? Our experience there
has been positive as well. At our tuition ($540 per class),
forty students generate a little over $20,000 in revenue. Our
TAs are generally paid $15 per hour for twenty hours of work

per week; in a seventeen-week semester, that works out to $5,100. The percentage is not small, but it is certainly sustainable. They are supervised by a faculty member, who is paid $12,500 per semester they deliver the course. Put together, any class of at least forty-two students covers its own direct costs; most classes are larger (350 students on average), contributing significant funds to support program advisers and other staff. The math at other schools will vary, of course, but tuition is likely to be higher, meaning that even if the ratio is lowered or the pay is increased, the financial model likely remains feasible.

If it is not, there may be other models to explore; we simply have not needed to. We know from our research that our teaching assistants are largely not motivated by the money in the first place; 53 percent are primarily motivated by what they get out of the role itself (a résumé item, a chance to network with faculty and classmates, greater understanding of the material), and 38 percent are primarily motivated by altruistic factors. Only 9 percent of online applicants for TA positions cited financial incentives as their main reason to apply; by comparison, 54 percent of on-campus applicants cited financial reasons as their primary incentive.[6] A model built around volunteer teaching assistants might be feasible if needed.

What is perhaps most notable, though, is that many of the same benefits that draw students into this program are at work drawing teaching assistants as well. Just as students are distributed, remote, and asynchronous, so are teaching assistants. For those who are motivated by the compensation, this makes the position far easier to balance with other work obligations for extra income; for those motivated intrinsically or altruistically, the role becomes far easier to rationalize because the sacrifice is more minimal. We are not describing an unpaid internship that requires physical presence in an office for twenty hours a week; we are describing a role that can be performed at night after the kids are in bed or on weekends more as a hobby. This not only increases the number of possible applicants but also their match for the role: they know what it is like to be a remote student and can tailor their support accordingly.

We can see similar patterns at work with other organizations. Coursera has had success with volunteer mentors supporting students, albeit with less pressure on responsibilities like consistent grading and rapid assignment feedback. Udacity, which often emphasizes its project-based assessments, relies on human project reviewers to deliver feedback and grant credentials; through this mechanism, they are able to evaluate hundreds of projects every day, although the amount they pay for those reviews may exceed that paid to teaching assistants in our program.[7]

WHAT IF WE CAN'T?

These trends provide some reassurance that a capless linear scale can be achieved by hiring additional teaching assistants to support increasing enrollment in a distributed classroom arrangement. It has worked for us, it has worked for others in different contexts, and the numbers are comfortable enough to suggest that even if the specifics differ, the overall picture should be relatively durable.

But what if it isn't? There are reasons that this model may not generalize. Computer science itself is famously pursued by hobbyists more passionate about the career than you might find in other fields; these types of individuals may be dramatically more willing to help out. Or, we may be seeing an early-adopter effect: these are still relatively new programs, drawing the types of people who embrace new initiatives and may be more likely to want to give back. As these programs become more mainstream, the percentage of students willing to help out as teaching assistants may dwindle.

These threats are part of why we feel it is important to focus on low-cost approaches to building up a distributed classroom. A distributed classroom built around classroom capture using relatively accessible equipment means that a failure does not incur a massive financial cost. Growth can be pursued slowly. Even in our program, we typically cap classes the first semester or two that they are offered so we can build up a pool of qualified TA candidates to support future growth.

If such an audience of TA candidates is not available for a particular program or field, there are options nonetheless to offer a form of the distributed classroom. We may find that it is more difficult to attach the same credit-worthiness to these asynchronous and remote audiences if we cannot attach the same rigorous assessment evaluation to their work, but some form of the experience may still be offered that is more credential-worthy than merely making the material openly accessible.

First, we might consider how this distributed classroom setup offers to reframe the system as a whole. We have noted that one of the potential pitfalls of this approach is central-ization: if one teacher can teach ten thousand instead of one hundred students, does that put ninety-nine other teach-ers out of their jobs? In fields like machine learning, the answer is no because ninety-nine other teachers likely were not available in the first place. But what about in more well-established fields like calculus? We would argue the answer there is still no; there are numerous tasks those other teachers need to perform, including those that we are assigning to teaching assistants. In smaller classes, teachers regularly perform their own grading tasks; for these sorts of fields, the distributed classroom merely offloads the pressure to deliver the content, allowing teachers to focus more on individual feedback and support. In other words, one potential source for this audience of "teaching assistants" may be teachers themselves, empowered by this arrangement to focus more on personalized aid. Here, the result would be improved outcomes rather than increased access or reduced cost.

For other fields, the mechanism instead may seek more contribution from students themselves. In the analogy to North Point Community Church, we noted that the church puts heavy emphasis on small group meetings, which correspond to our cohorts of classmates who engage in their own discussions and group work. North Point's small groups do not have teaching assistants, however; instead one member of the small group is typically designated the leader and is responsible for administering the group's activities. A similar model may be used to extend some structure to distributed cohorts; a particular student (perhaps rotating) may be designated responsible for following clear instructions to administer the experience for their own cohort. This individual would not be able to answer questions like a teaching assistant would, but by assigning responsibility to an individual and giving instructions on how to carry out the session, some version of the class experience may remain distributed.

This covers issues of classroom experience, but it does not venture into concerns regarding assessment and integrity verification. Technological tools may support these. Although we are generally skeptical about peer grading, studies have shown that it can be reliable under certain circumstances[8] and approaches to augmenting it with artificial intelligence are gaining momentum.[9] Automated evaluation may also support some scaling. With technology, this can go far beyond the multiple-choice tests of the past. Students can instead be automatically evaluated through participation with simulations for a more authentic learning experience. Stealth assessment attempts to generate an assessment of students' ability based on actions performed when they are not even aware they are being assessed, which may further offer a scalable approach.

In all these cases, the question goes back to the trade-offs we discussed in previous chapters. What does it take to argue that the distributed experience is worth the same credit or credential as the synchronous co-located experience? The focus of the distributed classroom has been on distributing the full experience as much as possible: same content, same class interactions, same assessments, same graders, same expectations. Symmetry was all about offering the same credit or credential across multiple cells of the distributed classroom matrix. Reality may sometimes stand in the way of distributing some of these factors, and in those cases we must return to the question of compromise: What can be removed while still offering the same incentives for course completion? What incentives can be removed while still offering an experience that students want? If a distributed workforce of teaching assistants is available, then very little may need to be removed; if it is not, other compromises may be possible to continue to expand access, potentially without the same assurances of individual learning outcomes and integrity.

APPLICABILITY

As we have noted, we work in graduate-level computer science, and our biggest problem is often teacher availability; the sorts of cutting-edge fields we want to be able to teach are also those where it may be far more lucrative to work in industry. Our focus has been on how to expand the reach of a particular individual through technology and a network of teaching assistants. We thus identified that we were able to reach an audience of learners who were not otherwise able to participate in higher education.[10]

In this context, however, we are sort of an exception. The majority of college classes are in fields that are more well established, and K–12 education with its national standards is even more so. Is this idea applicable only to cutting-edge fields like computer science? In this section, we argue for the relevance of this approach to better-established fields and other levels of learning. Then we will note that even if our other arguments are wrong, this philosophy still is highly relevant given the rapid rate of change characterizing the world today.

OTHER FIELDS

We start by looking at other—particularly more established—fields. We dedicate the next section to other levels of education (especially K–12), and so here we stay at the college level. Instead of upper-level or graduate classes that can only be taught by a rare expert in the field, what about lower-level classes? These are typically classes with well-established canons of course content such that there exist documented "exchange" programs where credit earned at one place can cover a requirement at another—for example, students receiving a 5 on the AP Chemistry exam are exempted from taking CHEM1310 at Georgia Tech. Teachers already may share instructional duties over these large introductory-level classes. At Georgia Tech, CS1371, our largest variant of CS1, is taught by three instructors each term to address the large demand.

These fields are far better staffed in terms of teachers. Is the distributed classroom relevant here? We argue an emphatic yes. It is easy to focus on the teacher shortage when trying to scale up computer science education, but that is only one of the many different factors that have played into our OMSCS program's success. Traditional structures still did not meet the needs of working professionals. Demand for computer science may be particularly high, but the same obstacles exist to prevent students from pursuing other fields as well. The distributed classroom is about expanding access regardless of why access was limited in the first place.

For example, degrees in accounting are well established at hundreds of universities, and while the field does undergo changes, those changes are not quite as rapid as those we see in computer science. As a result, evening programs and other flexible programs are more common for this subject matter. Nonetheless, Indiana University launched (in partnership with edX) an online master's in accounting with lower tuition and an asynchronous, remote design. Although the content is more generally available from other universities, the program has found significant success by reaching an audience that would or could not commit to all the additional requirements of face-to-face programs. Demands for this access are not restricted to rapidly developing fields like computer science. There is a need for distributed classrooms to expand access to more well-established fields as well.

That does not necessarily mean that every similar program will reach enrollments of ten thousand active students in five years; computing is uniquely in high demand. Aspirations for other fields may be more modest. That is why we emphasize the low effort and cost involved in distributing a classroom. Readily available equipment and services can be used to perform the classroom-capture portion of the framework, and the incremental cost introduced by adding instructional support may fall well within tuition prices. Thus, efforts to open up more accessible pathways need not be high-risk endeavors. The upfront costs may be kept low, and the incremental costs may be directly mapped to tuition to ensure financial sustainability. We see little reason that many classes already on the books to be offered next semester could not quickly be extended to accommodate more distributed student bodies. Most important, we have seen how these sorts of efforts can be performed at affordable tuition costs, further expanding access to audiences for whom financial constraints are particularly significant.

The other major outcome of this approach in other fields is the role it may play in improving pedagogy itself. In chapter 4, we described how online material may be used to create a flipped classroom. Flipped classes—where students consume content outside class and use class time for synchronous activities, discussions, and so on—are not exactly what we are striving for here. After all, we are putting specific emphasis on distributing the in-person classroom experience, which quite likely would include teaching the content itself.

However, many of the advantages of the flipped classroom apply here as well. The work involved in preparing a classroom session, including creating visuals, scripting out examples to do on a whiteboard, or outlining content to present verbally, is nontrivial. Delivering it similarly requires a significant investment of time. PHYS2211 at Georgia Tech is offered six times a day Monday, Wednesday, and Friday by multiple instructors. If more of the original presentation could be used to support the other sections, then significant teacher time could be opened up for more individual support—and instructors could specialize more in those individual support responsibilities instead of having to serve all roles at once.

There are risks here, of course. Many would see the opportunity to reuse more labor as a chance to cut costs while preserving outcomes rather than maintaining costs while improving outcomes. Our model for CS1301 is somewhat dangerous in that regard. We built a class where outcomes improve despite significantly less mandatory human effort. The ongoing effort of the teacher and teaching assistants is still the same as the traditional class, but that effort is focused solely on improving outcomes rather than what must be accomplished to deliver the class, such as grading work and authoring assignments. We would argue that CS1301 is an exception, though; the course content in CS1 is uniquely suited to automated evaluation and feedback in a way nearly no other field is—not even fields with objective answers. In nearly every domain, teachers continue to play necessary roles even if they are not tasked with conducting the traditional classroom. The key under this paradigm is that they may focus more narrowly on those roles that truly require a teacher to be present and responsive for a set of students rather than those that just require someone to disseminate the content.

To summarize, in fields that do not struggle to find teachers, the distributed classroom paradigm has several other benefits. First, its focus on asynchronicity and remote access may still be used to expand access to audiences unable to participate in traditional synchronous co-located programs. Second, through its scalable model, it may be used to drive down tuition prices, increasing access by reducing financial obstacles. Third, following the principles of flipped classrooms, it may be used to improve learning outcomes by opening up more time for individual assistance and support rather than one-to-many content dissemination.

OTHER LEVELS

It might be sufficient to attach these ideas solely to higher education. We are greedy, however, and we believe that these ideas are applicable at the K–12 level as well—and not only in examples like offering otherwise-inaccessible classes at smaller schools. We recently witnessed the need for these ideas. In the wake of COVID-19, schools were forced to rapidly shift to remote learning. The approaches to this shift were wide and varied. Some attempted to keep things as normal as possible, replacing in-person meetings with synchronous teleconference classes. Others shifted more dramatically, adopting entirely asynchronous remote models. We could find no pattern to what types of schools adopted which approach. Two expensive private schools in the Atlanta area, similar in many other ways, fell on opposite ends of this spectrum; one emailed students their instructional videos and work to complete at the start of the day, while the other ran synchronous meetings matching their original schedule. Two large public school districts near Atlanta similarly took dramatically different approaches, one favoring asynchronicity and the other synchronicity. For all schools, however, the shift was seismic, in contrast with the principle of symmetry from chapter 5 advocating class designs where shifts between cells in the matrix are minimally disruptive.

On its surface, K–12 education, at least in the United States, may not seem like a clear candidate for a distributed classroom approach. Massive efforts already aim to make it universally accessible and publicly funded. It is not only freely available, but mandatory in every state. Access and outcomes, however, are two different things. Academic achievement in the United States is average compared to peer countries.[11] A 2013 report found that class sizes in the United States are larger than average as well.[12] Dozens of books and articles have been written about this phenomenon. Some people blame our focus on testing and standards; others point to the underfunded schools; others attribute it to mismanagement and bureaucracy. The question is, What can the distributed classroom offer to improve this situation? Or, in other countries, what can the distributed classroom do to improve outcomes in general? We focus on four potential benefits.

First, although access to K–12 education (or local analogues) is already high in many countries, all such education
is not created equal. The quality of instruction varies enormously from district to district and state to state. This is not
a critique of teachers. Teachers are asked to play far too many
simultaneous functional roles to be effective in all of them.
Teachers who can deliver a compelling live class session may
not write quality assessments; teachers who can deal with
psychological issues like students' self-confidence may not
be the best at clearly organizing course content. Part of the
distributed classroom calls for taking high-quality material
and distributing it across a greater number of audiences and
classrooms. What that means in this context is that teachers
who excel at delivering a good live classroom can focus on
that skill, knowing that it will be used to support a much
larger number of students. Then other teachers—freed from
the demand to be the original source of content knowledge—
can focus more narrowly on giving quality feedback, supporting individual students, and other responsibilities that
require greater closeness to individuals. In his work on mas-
tery learning, Benjamin Bloom famously used the one-on-
one tutorial as the gold standard against which to compare
group instructional approaches.[13] By freeing teachers from
the responsibility to teach groups together, it may be possible to introduce more one-on-one tutorials back into traditional education environments.

Second, as a natural product of the distributed class
approach, a greater number of persistent learning materials
are generated. The content presented in the classroom is no
longer scarce. This is a boon for everyone: students may con-
sult the full breadth of content that was previously restricted

to live attention in the classroom. We should not forget that learning takes place in a social environment, and thus there will be distractions in the live classroom experience; making these materials available persistently means a student no longer risks missing a key concept because they are reeling from a confusing interpersonal interaction or a bad grade in another class. This can play a major equalizing role as well for students with health issues that make in-person attendance difficult, or for students with behavioral disorders who may not always find they can focus at the exact time when they are required to do so. Even if the distributed classroom is used only to allow the existing SC students to "replay" the class in an AR environment, that alone can have significant advantages.

Third, this dynamic can lead to much greater flexibility for individual students. For instance, a student who misses three or four weeks of school due to a health issue would currently need to retake the entire class; catching up with so much missed course content is not feasible. The teacher cannot devote the time to reteaching four weeks of content to a single student. But if the content is captured, then recovery becomes far more plausible. We saw this in the wake of COVID-19. David announced a blanket policy that any student who could not complete the course material during the semester could fill out a single form; they would be given an Incomplete grade (a placeholder in our system) and could finish the course work later. This was trivial for him to do: the course videos were all persistently available, and his grading team stuck around over the summer as well. The options for flexibility introduced by this mechanism are tremendous: students going through tough times at home, students who simply need more time to learn the content, students unexpectedly affected by natural disasters or local unrest, and more would benefit from the flexibility this mechanism can offer.

Finally, we have described previously some K–12-specific advantages to this approach that should be reiterated here as well. Larger schools in more populated areas can often offer more classes and opportunities because a critical mass of students is seeking that content. This risks increasing existing divides as students residing in more affluent areas have greater opportunities. A distributed classroom approach can take these opportunities at larger, better-funded schools and extend them to areas that are unable to offer such classes themselves. This approach is already at work in the various virtual school initiatives around the country, where students can choose to enroll in an online class to fill out their schedule, but these online classes are often designed deliberately for the AR cell. The distributed classroom paradigm calls for designing these classes to function more like typical classes, distributing the entire experience rather than just access to the content itself.

EMERGING FIELDS

But maybe we are wrong. We may be dramatically oversimplifying the constraints on K–12 schools or overestimating the extent to which this mechanism could improve experiences and outcomes in commonly offered college classes. Maybe the distributed classroom is a solution only to material that is scarcely available. Would that be such a bad thing?

For all the good that we believe the distributed classroom approach can do for existing populations, the ultimate goal and focus for much of the remainder of the book will be on how it can be used to create lifelong learners: people who would not have otherwise continued their education, but because of the access offered by the distributed classroom can do so. So while we think it would be great for this to have a positive impact on outcomes at the K–12 and undergraduate levels, that is not the main goal. The goal is to increase the number of learners in the world in the first place.

Lifelong learning is critical in this area because the world is changing far faster than ever before. Various studies and think tanks estimate that as many as 85 percent of the jobs of 2030 do not exist yet today.[14] While specific numbers are highly speculative, the overall message that people need to upskill and retool far faster than in the past is undeniable. According to research and advisory firm Gartner, which publishes an annual report on emerging technologies and their progress through their hype cycle, numerous fields across a multitude of industries are due to enter their productive phase over the next several years. Computing fields are highly represented, including areas like mixed reality, quantum computing, and smart fabrics, but there are many others. More established fields are changing rapidly as well; battery technology today bears little resemblance to that of a decade ago. Increasing computing power, increased communication, and increased education are all leading to rapid change.

To keep up, classes are going to need to be developed far more quickly than they have been in the past. It is not uncommon for textbooks to take years to produce or for new classes to take a year to receive approval to be offered in a university context. We will need to teach people new content long before it is formalized into a textbook. People who can teach these fields will continue to be in demand within the fields themselves, making it infeasible for them to leave their industry roles to teach full time, and yet we will need the capacity opened up by full-time teachers to meet the demand for these skills. The distributed classroom offers an avenue to this reality: a highly qualified individual may develop and teach a course one time in person, then have that be used as the foundation for hundreds of thousands of students to learn that content over the next few years—students who themselves are still able to continue to work and advance in their career rather than take expensive years off to update their skill set. Three years later, when the demands have sufficiently shifted, a new class may take its place, taught by another of the world's leaders in the field. MOOCs are already capitalizing on this model, with visionaries like Andrew Ng and Sebastian Thrun teaching tens of thousands of students today despite having not recorded new content in months or years, but these classes need not be MOOCs; they can be rigorous courses offering strong credentials and credit options, accompanied by authentic assessments and human feedback, powering both faster, better learning and stronger endorsements of student ability.

Just as critical, this is also not just about job skills. The world is an increasingly noisy, confusing place. We do not only need people who know how to program a quantum computer or design a carbon nanotube; we also need citizens who can think critically, can evaluate media representations, and can understand complex interweaving narratives throughout history. We need a well-educated human race, especially in the face of rapidly changing technology and unprecedented societal challenges. We need everyone to always be learning.

So, even if the worlds of calculus I and English literature stick to familiar models, the distributed classroom offers a pathway to lifelong learning of emerging topics—whether they are needed for the jobs of tomorrow or just the citizenry of tomorrow. For these reasons, while we believe the distributed classroom can be applied to any content at any ability level, we also believe it has enormous potential even if it applies to only a narrower set of levels and fields.

III

THE PLACES WE'LL GO

7

FROM STOPGAP TO SNOWBALL

When we talk about our OMSCS program, we usually describe three barriers to an MSCS degree that we help our students circumvent: place barriers, time barriers, and cost barriers. There is, of course, a fourth major barrier: lack of prerequisite knowledge to gain admittance to and succeed in the program. What prevents students from achieving that prerequisite knowledge? Place barriers, time barriers, and cost barriers to that earlier content. So, we focus on place, time, and cost, knowing that if we can resolve these barriers, we can extend those solutions to building greater pathways for those who lack the prerequisite knowledge we require.

Early research showed that our incoming students would not have pursued an MSCS degree elsewhere if our program did not exist.[1] Why not? Perhaps no university nearby offered such a program, or perhaps they could not take time from work and family to attend synchronously, or perhaps the cost was prohibitive. We usually think of this third element, cost, as the most defining feature—articles about the program typically focus on the cost.[2] We often poll our classes, though, and ask what they think, and interestingly just as many students say that place and time would be the more significant barriers. Some students say that they would have paid the normal price for the program if it meant being able to attend remotely and asynchronously. Other online programs take advantage of this fact, charging a premium for online access rather than using the online mechanism to scale enrollment and drive down costs.

The relationship between these efforts and the COVID-19 crisis is relatively clear. COVID-19 made accommodating remote learners—that is, addressing the place barrier—not just desirable but imperative. Initially that came in the form of a wholesale transition to remote learning, then the focus shifted to more hybrid approaches as the pandemic dragged on into the 2020–2021 school year. Looming over these discussions were concerns about safety and the risk of another rapid shift to remote learning in the event of a local outbreak.

The distributed classroom provides a stopgap against this uncertainty. It advocates a design of educational experiences that is more agnostic to the existence of the original physical classroom in the first place. The goal of symmetry as outlined in chapter 5 strives for an architecture that allows for a natural transition from a live classroom to a remote or asynchronous classroom. What is important is that once this stopgap is implemented, the additional benefits may start to build. A distributed classroom solves several immediate problems, and from there, it snowballs through the remaining barriers to create a revolutionarily different model. Implementing a distributed classroom model has been technologically feasible for some time, but the benefits were too vague to invest in it heavily. Due to COVID-19, however, that investment has already been made in many places, and it can now be leveraged for dramatic improvements.

This chapter predicts this snowball. It starts by looking at how elements of the distributed classroom will be needed for the foreseeable future. It then examines how these new designs demolish existing geographic barriers for populations that have long lacked full access to educational offerings. This, then, provides solutions to financial barriers accomplished through economies of scale and a more distributed instructional team. Based on this scale, synchronicity barriers may be resolved: a larger population of students means greater likelihood of finding a synchronous, similar cohort.

POST–COVID-19

In many ways, the transition to fall 2020 was an even more difficult one for schools than the rapid shift to remote learning in spring 2020. Spring 2020 brought a wholesale shift to remote-only learning; fall 2020 saw many schools trying to offer some form of in-person experience. Students in spring 2020 could be reasonably expected to be relatively patient as teachers were asked to shift on a moment's notice; in fall 2020, schools were expected to have had more time to prepare for the term. In higher education, students in spring 2020 had already paid tuition and fees; fall 2020 put universities in the difficult position of either justifying normal tuition costs during an uncertain semester or cutting tuition at a time when revenues were already plummeting.

Above all, universities were tasked with an uncertain landscape in fall 2020 with regard to ensuring consistent access for students. Some students were unable to travel to campus at all. All faculty and students were at risk of needing to self-quarantine for two weeks after a potential exposure, during which time they would still need to continue with either teaching or taking the class. Entire schools had to be prepared to shift to remote education in case of a local outbreak. All of these concerns required accommodations and contingency plans, which we will look at first.

TRAVEL RESTRICTIONS

One of the biggest concerns to emerge in the wake of COVID-19 was travel restrictions. With visa offices shuttered and travel bans in place to contain the spread of the virus, international students—both new and returning ones—risked being unable to come to campus. Without remote options, these students would be forced to take the semester off, slowing their progress to their degree. Skipping a semester could also carry financial aid implications as well as cut into university revenues. The only option to accommodate these students would be remote learning.

For schools that opted for fully remote learning from the outset, these students were somewhat naturally accommodated, albeit with more minor problems to solve like selecting class times when students may be dispersed across several time zones. For schools that strove to include in-person components, however, accommodating purely remote students required additional effort. Remote students could be offered dedicated remote sections to keep them progressing toward their degree, but this added work to faculty members who were already struggling to prepare socially distanced hybrid classes.

Instead, hybrid classes could be designed specifically to accommodate remote students as well. This was ultimately the guidance that Georgia Tech's Office of International Education put out, that all hybrid courses should be available to remote international students: "If the academic unit offers the hybrid mode courses to these students, then the instructors should allow for remote engagement such as no in-person attendance requirement, asynchronous lectures, and submission of assignments online." Reframed in terms of the distributed classroom, this essentially calls for the creation of an AR course experience for all hybrid classes. Unlike offering a parallel online experience, this leverages the existing hybrid course to accommodate this distributed body, but it also requires thinking about this distributed classroom structure from the outset.

ABSENCES

These international students (and anyone else unable to return to campus) generally fell into one modality for the entire semester, which in some ways made planning for them easier. That was not the case with students who were physically present for a hybrid semester. First, most hybrid models to accommodate COVID-19 called for only a portion of students to attend class on any particular day to allow room for social distancing; that meant that a significant portion of the class would be "absent"—at least physically—for most classes. Even if a large enough classroom was available to accommodate everyone enrolled, there would nonetheless be students who must self-quarantine due to exposure who needed to be able to keep up with the course content. There also would be students who themselves get sick, likely more than in a typical semester; they needed a mechanism to catch up with the course content.

Taken altogether, the situation was more complex than simply accommodating remote international students: some students are guaranteed to be remote part of the time, whether on a predictable cadence due to social distancing measures or unpredictably due to unforeseen exposure or illness. A course experience must be designed to allow students to rapidly shift between these modalities. This may be accomplished through a classroom distributed among the SC, SR, and AR cells: synchronous and co-located for students fortunate enough to be present on a particular day; synchronous and remote for students who cannot physically attend but are available at the same time (such as those self-quarantining or those who are not in the socially distanced class's in-person cohort for that day); and asynchronous remote for those who must catch up with the material later due to illness or incompatible time zones. For classes at universities that are entirely remote from the outset, we might see this instead just as SR and AR depending on whether the course opts to include a synchronous component.

Complicating matters still further, it is also likely that a teacher may need to stay away from the classroom due to quarantine or illness. Under this situation, teachers may need to teach remotely, or a substitute may need to be found; both are significantly easier if the roles can be performed remotely. In summer 2020, for instance, the teacher of one of our on-campus machine learning classes had to withdraw midsemester; the online nature of the term meant that we could quickly recruit an alumnus from Colorado to work with a campus faculty member and finish out the term—in a normal term, an alumnus in Colorado could not teach a class in Atlanta. So not only was it the case that some students would be remote for the full term, but also that many students and teachers would need to be remote on an unpredictable week-to-week basis.

COMPLETE TRANSITION

Finally, the specter of an emergency transition to online-only instruction loomed over the fall 2020 semester. Some schools asked teachers to create contingency plans for how they would rapidly shift to a remote setup if needed during the semester. The easiest way this is accomplished—especially in light of the demands above—is to nest a large part of the classroom online in the first place. If class meetings are already streamed and recorded for later viewing, then substituting remote instruction for in-person instruction minimizes the shift that is actually being made: content exists in the remote medium either way. The shift becomes about where it originates, but the structure and distribution of the classroom remain relatively unchanged.

Other schools reacted to this specter by starting with remote classes or by preemptively committing to remain remote at least through the end of 2020. This solved many issues, mostly relating to student and faculty safety, and it also avoided inequity between in-person and remote audiences by removing in-person audiences altogether. However, some issues remained under this setup. Student access to technology when they are separated from a campus environment can vary tremendously. The requirements of a synchronous remote class—such as high-bandwidth internet, reliable access to technology, and a consistent, comfortable place from which to attend—may not be feasible for many remote students. Schools with many international students will still run into scheduling issues: If 15 percent of a class has returned to Asia for a semester, when are those synchronous lectures scheduled? Other problems remained as well: while students may not need to miss a remote class in order to enforce social distancing or protect their classmates after a potential exposure, they still may need to miss class due to being sick themselves.

The other issue raised by a shift to all-remote learning is cost: Should students be expected to pay the same tuition for an online experience? This is a veritable Pandora's box because if we open the idea that the online experience is inferior (and thus warrants lower tuition), we may then ask questions like whether it deserves the same number of credit hours, the same accreditation, or the same diploma. We have seen these questions raised about our OMSCS tuition; some have speculated the tuition is lower because we know the product is inferior, when in reality, the tuition is lower because we are able to take advantage of economies of scale and front-loaded development costs. There are synchronous and co-located features we would like to introduce in large part because students desire those components, but the instruction and assessment are found to be equal to the face-to-face experience.[3] To make a shift to all-remote instruction practical without raising numerous other issues, remote education must be comparably good.

Taking this all into consideration, fall 2020 represented a massive push to distribute the classroom across SC, SR, and AR cells to accommodate students able to attend in person, students able to attend synchronously but remotely, and students who need the extra flexibility to attend asynchronously and remotely. The mechanisms described in chapter 5 provide an avenue to doing this with relatively little additional work by using the traditional classroom as a foundation and building distributed experiences from there.

PLACE BARRIERS

Due to COVID-19, efforts were made to create what we are describing as a distributed classroom. We are certainly not suggesting that that is what people would describe themselves as having done, but the work fits squarely into the distributed classroom matrix. The question now becomes: Once the work has already been done to implement a distributed classroom, what other impact can it have? We see these barriers falling like dominoes, each helping to topple the next, but there is likely more parallelism to them. We'll tackle them one by one: first place, then cost, then time.

For what other populations has distance from a college environment been an obstacle? Distance in this context does not just mean geographic distance: it can also be other obstacles to attending in person even if the student is located near the university. Obstacles may not be strictly physical either; they may be other issues introduced by physical presence on a university campus. We'll run through some of the audiences who may be affected by greater remote access to the same curriculum and credit.

NONLOCAL STUDENTS

The first and most obvious group of students aided by this setup are nonlocal students; we use this term to differentiate them from remote students, who may actually live near the university but are completing their studies remotely rather than physically on campus. Many OMSCS students, for instance, live in the Atlanta area, but are still remote as a way to resolve time and cost barriers. The category of nonlocal students includes international students, but it also includes students who live in the same country as the university but not close enough to attend in person.

This audience of students is not superficially any different from the on-campus students forced to switch to remote learning in the first place, with one key exception. On-campus students who transitioned to remote learning had applied, been accepted, and intended to start as in-person learners. On its own, this is a massive filter. Even if we set aside tuition costs for a moment (we will return to those in the next section), moving to another city to pursue a college education presents massive obstacles. There are moving costs, which increase with distance from the student's destination. There is the emotional cost of separating from one's family. Some students may have significant care responsibilities at home, and moving to another city to pursue a college education may leave siblings or elderly parents with weaker support structures. There are many people who do not apply to universities because they know they cannot move near them even if they are accepted. These are also often the people who would benefit the most from the education. The distributed classroom makes the content and class experience available to students unable to attend in person, but that same effort also makes it accessible to students who never would have been able to attend in person in the first place.

STUDENTS WITH DISABILITIES

In the United States, the Americans with Disabilities Act ensures that students with disabilities can still access the same educational resources as others. However, equivalence of access does not mean equivalence of ease of access. Ramps and elevators may mean that students who rely on a wheelchair can access all the same areas, but significant additional effort may be required. Students with balance disorders may be able to walk around campus with the aid of assistive devices, but the energy required to do so is far higher. The sum total of these and other difficulties is a significant barrier to entry for students with physical difficulties navigating campus. Other disabilities or chronic conditions may manifest themselves in frequent absences. These students may consider themselves unable to attend college because they know they cannot commit to the amount of regular and physical attendance that the courses require.

Mental disabilities and behavioral disorders may similarly provide significant friction to traditional campus attendance. Students with focus disorders, for instance, may find it extremely difficult to focus in class surrounded by a herd of noisy classmates. Students with anxiety disorders may find it difficult to stay on task when they find the environment uncomfortable.

Online education also intersects with identity and self-perception in interesting ways. In our years working in online education, we have had dozens of conversations about what makes the context uniquely convenient for different students. For many, it is the usual factors: flexibility to plan around work, around family, and so on. There have been surprising factors raised as well, though. One student once told us that she was grateful for the program because she always felt that people did not take her seriously when interacting in person due to elements of her appearance and behavior outside of her control; online, she did not have to interact through the filter of her physical appearance. We met another student at a graduation event who had a severe speech impediment, which he later disclosed had been one factor in his decision to withdraw from another graduate program; in the online program, it never affected perceptions of his performance as he felt it had in a face-to-face program. These issues do not present literal physical obstacles to attendance of the kind the Americans with Disabilities Act (and analogous international regulations) seeks to address, but they affect the students' experience so much that they become obstacles.

For all these students, remote access removes a major source of friction to their course experience. It is not a perfect solution, of course: students with focus disorders may similarly find audio issues or background conversations more extremely distracting, and students concerned with physical appearance may still find it intimidating to interact in synchronous classroom environments. Still, for numerous individuals, the remote environment is an option when the in-person alternative is not.

UNDERREPRESENTED GROUPS

In narratives of successful women in engineering or computing (or medicine or law before those fields achieved more balanced gender ratios), a common trope is that a student succeeded "despite being the only woman in her classroom." While these success stories should be celebrated, we must acknowledge that knowing you might be the only one of your gender or race in a program can be a powerful deterrent against joining it in the first place. When a field has pervasive stereotypes of the kinds of people who "belong" in that field, it is intimidating for those who do not meet those stereotypes to attempt to enter.[4]

The asynchronous environment may provide some mitigation against this: students have much more control over how they appear to their classmates. An African American woman aware of how rare students like her are in a computer science class may select an avatar and an appearance for her name that do not give away elements of her identity that she does not want to share. In some tools, she may go even further, appearing as fully anonymous to her classmates. Thus, students concerned about being perceived as not belonging due to some element of their demographic profile may control whether that information is revealed to classmates with more granularity and effectiveness than in-person students.

Is this effect hypothetical or genuine? It is hard to say. In our OMSCS program, we do see twice the fraction of underrepresented minority students enroll as on-campus program, but we also see half the fraction of women as our on-campus program.[5] These trends intersect with many other effects, and it is hard to attribute them to any one cause. It may be that our underrepresented minority students are more likely to enroll in the program because it is online and therefore allows them to avoid the "only one in the room" effect, but it could just as well be that that audience disproportionately benefits from the program's flexibility or the inclusive admissions policies. For women, it could be that awareness that online communities, especially in the tech sector, are often more hostile toward women, and that acts as a deterrent to enrollment.[6] But we also observe that our online student body is more domestic while our on-campus program is paradoxically more international, and the gender divide is larger domestically than internationally; thus, the online program's greater gender divide may just be a side effect of its larger domestic audience.

This dynamic comes with its own pitfalls. It is also the case that in order to combat these stereotypes, we need to visualize how inaccurate they are. We see this effect in our CS1301 class: although the class has an even gender split in both enrollment and forum posting volume, women select to appear anonymous when posting on the class forum far more often than men do. Thus, from each individual student's perspective, the class appears male dominated, which can actually reinforce those stereotypes. Nevertheless, it remains the case that individuals may feel more comfortable enrolling in an online program specifically because they may feel less like the odd person out.

ADULT LEARNERS

Facilitating lifelong learning is one of the ultimate goals of the distributed classroom, and adult learners are one of the key audiences for this approach. Adult learners are often nonlocal learners, subject to the same barriers: they cannot move their families to a new city to attend a graduate program for a couple of years. Adult learners experience some additional barriers that start to blur the line between place and time. For example, it is often infeasible for a working adult to take a year off work and give up a year's worth of salary in addition to the cost of tuition. Is that a place barrier or a time barrier? Both, really; their job requires them to be in a certain place at a certain time, and an alternative educational option would need to resolve both of those to be feasible.

Adult learners represent a massive audience that for the most part are not currently students. The groups in the previous sections are critical to reach from an equity perspective, but they are not likely to move the needle enormously on enrollment itself. Over half of the US population, though, is between the ages of twenty-five and sixty-four, after the typical college age but before the typical retirement age (not that lifelong learning should end at retirement either); and yet in 2018, there were only around 20 million college students in the United States. Similar numbers can be observed around the world.

This is how colleges can radically expand their reach without inadvertently bringing about the predicted centralization of higher education. By turning every adult into a potential learner, colleges can double, triple, and quadruple in size without so significantly competing with one another for students. This audience is ready and waiting, and the work to compensate for the demands of COVID-19 perfectly sets up the platform they need to jump in.

COST BARRIERS

Tuition for our OMSCS program is $180 per credit hour, and thirty credit hours are required to graduate. Each semester students also pay $300 in student fees. The total cost of the program thus varies from $6,900 (two classes per semester, five semesters) to $8,400 (one class per semester, ten semesters) for a student who does not repeat any classes. For comparison, our own in-person MSCS program costs more than three times as much ($586/credit hour) for in-state students and over six times as much ($1,215/credit hour) for out-of-state students, with student fees three times as high per semester as well. At the University of Washington, students pay $1,015 per credit and must complete forty credits, a total tuition cost over seven times higher than OMSCS.[7] At Princeton University, students pay $53,890 per year for the two-year program, a total tuition cost twenty times higher than OMSCS.[8] The University of Washington and Princeton University are ranked on either side of Georgia Tech in the most recent (2018) *US News & World Report* ranking of computer science programs.

How is this discrepancy possible? It can partially be attributed to economies of scale. In spring 2021, we enrolled over eleven thousand students, taking an average of 1.3 classes each. With these resources, we can fund the development of sophisticated autograding frameworks and work with industry partners to streamline grading, proctoring, assignment submission, and more. The cost savings are about more than just economies of scale, however; the other significant criterion of the online environment is that far more costs are incremental rather than fixed. While fixed costs may become insignificant when spread out over a large number of students, they presuppose that large number of students. Our focus on a linear scale instead ties the resources that students bring into the program directly to the costs that they incur. We may compute the per student costs in terms of teaching assistants, academic advisers, software licenses, and so on and ensure that the math works out for students to cover their own individual expenses. This reduces the need to achieve scale in the first place: the program is as viable at a smaller size as it is at a larger size.

This, combined with earlier observations, gives us a three-pronged approach for reducing financial costs in a distributed program. First, we leverage as much of the existing classroom experience as possible through initiatives like classroom capture; this lowers the flat cost associated with producing course content in the first place, while also allowing the online course experience to feel more like a classroom. Second, we carefully note the incremental cost introduced by each additional student and ensure that the resources they contribute cover the costs that they incur. Third, we invest the surplus into initiatives or tools that we may not be able to justify without the scale of their impact. We see this at work with how we produce course material, although this is not the model we are advocating here: a single course takes over $100,000 to produce, an enormous sum, but it is well justified if that course is then able to enroll as few as two hundred students per semester for two or three years.

This is where we begin to see this snowball effect emerge. By removing the place barrier, we radically increased the number of students interested in our courses. With that increase, we were able to cut tuition costs due in part to economies of scale. With cheaper tuition, demand rises even more. There is, of course, a limit to economies of scale, which is represented by ensuring that students' tuition dollars cover the costs they incur, but the design of online programs allow us to strive for that goal more directly because more of the costs are incremental rather than fixed. Of course, this is a bit of revisionist history: our program resolved all three barriers at once, and it is not clear what would have happened if we had started with higher tuition and scaled it down as enrollment rose. But the prototype our program provides gives some reassurance that resolving location constraints can help resolve cost constraints and vice versa, a symbiotic cycle that can lead to a sustainable program.

What is further notable in our design is that we adopt a one-size-fits-all approach to tuition: all students pay $540 per class. This makes sense as our cost model is such that all students incur the same costs as well. Does it have to be that way, though? In Nigeria, for instance, tuition for a year of school is about US$160.[9] This is not only far below our tuition; it is even far below the "affordable" MOOCs, given the scope of a year of undergraduate education compared to a single MOOC. But the content available through OMSCS is likely not available from a university in Nigeria. Are these students saddled with paying a disproportionately large relative price for their education? Not necessarily; some incremental costs could diminish due to local conditions as well. Hiring local teaching assistants in Nigeria would not only lower the amount students need to pay to cover their expenses, but also inject a local context into the course material. Local teaching assistants may tailor discussions to local issues. Local universities in Nigeria may even partner to launch courses in these in-demand fields for which faculty are unavailable but attach their own credit and degrees. The material is already available, after all; allowing a new school to reuse it does not incur an additional cost.

Throughout this model, one effect ought to remain clear: nowhere in this equation do we assume that students now attending one university will opt instead to attend a different one. Rather, we assume there are potential students who can be converted to actual students if only the right material were available at the right price with the right flexibility, and we argue that the balance of right content, right price, and right flexibility is achievable.

TIME BARRIERS

The third barrier, time, is already resolved in some ways by the same solutions to the place barrier. Making content remotely accessible happens automatically when making it persistently available through streaming services, file uploads, and so on. If a class is already being delivered to the SR cell (either directly in a teleconference or live-streamed from an SC class), then all we must do is click Record to set up the foundation for a subsequent AR version. But to go back to one of the definitions set up in chapter 2, the distributed classroom is about the classroom as much as the distribution. The classroom entails live interaction, and students thirst for it even while they need asynchronicity to be able to enroll in the first place.[10] While the designs we have explored may have resolved the problem in terms of access, they have created a new problem in terms of equivalence. The asynchronous classroom lacks the synchronous interaction of the classroom we are striving to expand.

The scale achieved by removing these barriers, however, supplies a solution for this problem. As more students enroll in a class, the likelihood of being able to form cohorts out of shared availability rises tremendously. According to a student-run course review site, CS7641: Machine Learning, requires about 21 hours per week of work. There are 168 hours in a week. If eight hundred students are in the class, then on average one hundred will working on the class at any given time, and that is if participation is evenly distributed across all hours of the day. Equipped with the knowledge that most students work evenings and weekdays, we can narrow down relatively small time slots where hundreds of students will already be working on the course.

We think of this approach as emergent synchronicity; it is synchronicity that arises not because we tell everyone, "Be here at 9:30 a.m.," but because the numbers guarantee that a cohort of students *will* be available at the same time. Our task is to create the environment to allow this emergent synchronicity to become evident and useful.

This is not merely a hypothetical. In one of the studies where we identified a synchronicity paradox, we recruited students to commit to participating in synchronous events. We recruited 120 volunteers and asked them to select what times they would be available for these sessions. We only needed five times to accommodate the schedules of all 120 volunteers: four weekday evenings and one weekend day. Thus, the time barrier may be resolved in a different way from the place and cost barriers—not by removing the constraint, but rather by finding enough other people who share the same constraint that it is no longer nearly as limiting.

There are a lot of possible models for how this might work in practice, ranging from light to heavy in how much commitment they expect from the student. On the lightweight side, we might draw an analogy to movie theaters:

class sessions may begin on a regular time interval, and students may jump in and join whichever they want. Cohorts of students who prefer to stick together may plan what time to attend as a group, similar to friends selecting a showtime at a local theater. Or we might borrow the model used by Pokemon Go or other online games: at any time there is a lobby of students, and once a critical mass is reached, the class may begin for that group. On the more formal side, perhaps this does not need to be as different from a traditional model as we assume: the same course can be offered at multiple times, and students commit at the beginning of a semester to attend at the times listed in the registration system.

Through the sum of these initiatives, we may build a program such that anyone with the prerequisite knowledge and with access to the technological requirements may enroll, participate in live classroom sessions with real classmates, complete authentic assessments, receive grades and feedback from human teaching assistants, and ultimately earn credit toward a degree. And students without the prerequisite knowledge? There is no reason this model cannot be applied to distributing that knowledge as well. As the place barriers fall, more students may have access; as more students access, the more economies of scale allow for price to be matched to incremental cost; as price falls, even more students may have access; and as more students join, the likelihood of finding a synchronous cohort rises and the authenticity of the classroom experience returns. Efforts like classroom capture and hybrid courses that were initially put in place as a stopgap against COVID-19 quickly snowball into a new model for delivering education to anyone, anywhere, at scale.

8

THE DISTRIBUTED CAMPUS

A key component of the previous chapter's argument is that we are focused on expanding certain components of the educational experience. We want to expand access to an authentic classroom experience covering the same content and carrying the same credential. That carries with it components of assessment and integrity verification. Education is about much more than just what happens in the classroom, however: Where do the other components fit into this model?

The prophecy that has been thrown around for years has been that higher education is on its way to becoming "unbundled." In simple terms, "unbundling" in this context refers to breaking higher education into its constituent parts and then selecting and recombining them individually. It often refers to credits, allowing students to assemble a degree more easily from classes taken across multiple schools, but it can also refer to unbundling other peripheral services. Students who do not need certain components would no longer be required to participate in and pay for those components. In some places, this removes a cost: students who are not on campus, for instance, would not need to pay for on-campus facilities unless those facilities are supporting the distributed classroom. This especially applies to lifelong adult learners who do not live on campus the way traditional undergraduate students do. Changes in this direction are already taking place: it is estimated that 75 percent of undergraduates meet one of several criteria that we would likely consider nontraditional, such as being a single caregiver, maintaining full-time employment while enrolled, or having delayed postsecondary enrollment.[1] In other places, unbundling might support the greater treatment of distributed students as part of the student body: campus services are often structured with full-time students in mind, but by unbundling them from the broader campus context, they can be more directly tailored and reopened to remote students as well.

Unbundling brings many exciting prospects. An unbundled higher education experience could allow students to more dynamically construct their own curriculum from classes offered by different universities. At the K–12 level, unbundling may help extend more robust supplementary programs to school districts that cannot afford them independently. But unbundling brings with it significant risks as well: sometimes, efforts to unbundle are driven by efforts to privatize, which do not always hold students' best interests as their main motivation. Charter schools across the country represent an effort to unbundle individual schools from broader school systems; that can have positive effects, like more local involvement and greater license to experiment and innovate, but it can also be used as an excuse to outsource instruction to distant companies with poor track records.[2]

We bring up unbundling here because in some ways, it is a natural consequence of efforts toward a distributed classroom. By spreading students out in space and time, many of the other components attached to the education enterprise become untenable, infeasible, or irrelevant. In one way, the idea of pulling out the learning experience from all these other programs is desirable: Why should students feel that they are "real" students only if they are living in a dorm and attending football games on weekends? Why should students have access to networking events only if they are also coming to campus five times a week? Why should students who never visit campus be saddled with fees dedicated to paying for campus transportation and technology they will never use?

But philosophically, this is actually somewhat counter to the goals we have had all along in designing the distributed classroom. We have frequently referenced the in-person classroom experience as worth keeping for any number of reasons. We have designed the different cells to instantiate many different possible compromises, forcing students to give up as little as possible to retain as much as possible of the original experience. Should this same philosophy not apply to the campus as well? There are students, of course, for whom the campus experience is relatively insignificant, but these efforts may risk diminishing the campus experience for those for whom it *is* a major part of their education. Even for those for whom campus as a whole is irrelevant, there likely exist services on campus that have relevance if they are extended to the distributed audience. In keeping with the distributed classroom philosophy, we ought to ask students to give up only the components of a campus environment they do not need rather than forcing them to choose between two extremes.

To be sure, many components of the modern education complex solve problems that themselves disappear when students are no longer synchronous and co-located. For example, from kindergarten to graduate school, schools and universities have to put considerable attention into dining services; this problem likely needs not be solved for a distributed student body. But for a great many of these components, the need persists (or even grows) when students are remote and asynchronous; the mechanism by which that need has been met in the past, however, may not. Many on-campus organizations—fraternities and sororities, service organizations, student clubs, and others—serve a valuable social role but do not translate naturally to a distributed audience. That does not mean that a distributed audience does not still have the need for academically grounded social connection, only that the existing mechanisms—which are heavily embedded in the synchronous, co-located campus context—do not easily transfer.

We can look at this in a number of ways. We could see this as unbundling, which absolves us of responsibility. Services that are left behind when we unbundle instruction from the rest of educational institutions should have been independent anyway, and others will move in to fill the void we are leaving behind. (If you want to read about this view, we invite you to read any of the other number of books and articles about unbundling in education; this is not the view we will take here.) Alternatively, we can look through a more one-to-one lens, piecemeal replacing each component we still deem necessary with the nearest analogue we can design for an online audience. This is, in many ways, what we have done with the OMSCS program: we have attempted to keep things as similar as possible, using the same workflows and departments for many processes.

In this chapter, though, we adopt a third viewpoint: we ask in general, What happens if we extend the distributed classroom analogy to the distributed campus? What would it mean to ask students to make the minimum compromise not just for their classroom experience but for their overall campus experience?

We cannot claim to have a lot of concrete answers here. The distributed classroom grew out of witnessing a large number of small, existing initiatives and observing that they could perhaps be unified into a cohesive vision. The distributed campus is a bit more of a thought experiment: there may be efforts in many of these areas already underway with which we are unfamiliar due to our focus on instruction or our own school. Rather than answering what a distributed campus may be, our goal here is instead twofold: first, to reassure you that the other positive features of the campus environment *can* be preserved if we distribute the classroom, and second, to urge you to consider these factors if you pursue a distributed classroom design of your own.

To explore this idea, we look at three different general visions of how to create distributed campuses that go beyond simply offering remote classes. These visions are not meant to be as prescriptive as the distributed classroom framework, but rather general directions in which we might move to create distributed campus-like environments. We will use Georgia Tech as our running example, assuming that we continue to operate as normal in Atlanta while seeking to distribute that local experience to new places.

THE REMOTE CAMPUS

The first approach to a distributed campus should be familiar. In many ways, it is already similar to universities that span multiple campuses or offer study-abroad programs with dedicated facilities. These approaches have been called satellite campuses or branch campuses and have been growing significantly over the past two decades as technology has made it far easier for many different departments—financial aid, admissions, registration, and others—to be administered remotely.[3] The major growth for these campuses has been in the realm of local satellites for regional universities, such as the sixty-four campuses of the State University of New York, although farther-removed campuses have been catching on as well, such as Carnegie Mellon's West Coast Campus in Mountain View, California.

Many of these approaches do not actually implement a distributed classroom; instead, they distribute those auxiliary services, as well as the accreditation and curricular requirements of the core university. This expands the reach of the university but may not resolve the challenges associated with offering certain courses across different locations. Opening a new campus becomes a significant endeavor not only to recreate campus services but also to recreate local delivery of course content. That is not to say that campuses focusing more on delivering remote course content do not exist, but they have not been the focus of many of these efforts.

Instead, let us ideate campuses built from the ground up to support the distributed classroom while accomplishing the roles of the campus we have outlined. We describe this as a "remote" campus rather than satellite or branch to emphasize the potential independence of these campuses even in light of their instructional connection to the original experience.

FULL-SERVICE REMOTE CAMPUS

First, we may imagine a full-service remote campus that offers all the facilities associated with the original campus: local student housing and dining, local recreational facilities, local meeting facilities, local student groups and social organizations, and so on. Academic advisers and career counselors would be available on site. These provide not only a crucial service, but because they are present in the local context, they are able to imbue the advice they give with awareness of local constraints and opportunities.

Classrooms under this arrangement may be set up with strong connections to classes in Atlanta; projectors may turn entire walls of the classroom into live feeds of remote classes, making the class feel more like an extension of the classroom in Atlanta. Presentation responsibilities could alternate between the campuses, reflecting the notion of symmetry from chapter 5: an instructor could feasibly move from one campus to another without radically changing the course experience for the cohort in either location. Student tuition may be commensurate with these local costs: advisers, counselors, teaching assistants, and facilities are all local, and many of the efforts toward distributing content were already underway, limiting the direct costs to the new campus. Thus, the costs of this education may be attainable by local audiences.

Most important, the heavy presence of local individuals may ensure that the content is presented through the lens of local culture and needs; this is especially important in the case of international campuses. Under this design, the distributed campus should supply only the minimum content necessary to let the local campus handle the remaining implementation. In this way, the focus of the distributed campus is on outreach and access, not imperialistically adding international students to its sphere of influence.

LEAN REMOTE CAMPUS

Full-service remote campuses are well suited to large population centers. What about smaller locales? For these, we might see instead a lean remote campus that especially targets the social side of campus life, as well as the physical environment for implementing a high-fidelity distributed classroom. It is thus likely most appropriate for undergraduate audiences, where personal independence and growth are as much a part of the college experience as the content.

Under one implementation, an apartment building could be turned into a distributed campus for a cohort of a couple hundred students. Four or five on-site classrooms would support remote attendance with a synchronous or asynchronous class taking place at the main campus, as well as some lightweight on-site recreational facilities of the sort you might typically find in an apartment complex (for example, an exercise room or a recreational room). Common areas would supply space for students to meet up socially and work on team projects.

Beyond these features, the majority of other support structures may remain delivered online. A central team of academic and career advisers could support students at multiple such lean campuses, and teaching assistants may not even need to be local for all classes. Certain expensive equipment may not be feasible to deploy to all such campuses, especially as the smaller student body may lead to more limited shared interests, but such campuses could also be designed with closer ties to specific programs. A campus, for instance, might specifically be for students interested in robotics, justifying equipment for those classes without worrying about other technology.

PRIVATE REMOTE CAMPUS

Taking a step away from the core campus, it is also not infeasible to imagine this generalizing to another remote model: a private remote campus. This campus would retain some element of central administration, but the university would not have to supply it on its own. Instead, other entities may buy facilities, rent rooms, and market to students investigating particular remote programs.

In many ways, this model is like typical private campus housing, the large complexes that often spring up in college towns or areas with large concentrations of universities. Georgia Tech, for instance, has no fewer than half a dozen student-targeted private housing facilities within a few blocks of campus. But with a remote campus, these no longer need to be tied to the university's local context. An organization could, for instance, market to students a private, lean college campus located somewhere highly scenic with a low local cost of living.[4] Students could thus keep their living costs down while attending an affordable remote degree program. From the perspective of the program, these could be typical remote students, but the organization offering the experience could supply its own advisers and instructional support staff. It would not have an official role with the university itself but would be part of the package offered to students. This model is the most similar to the unbundling of higher education: it sees private organizations stepping in to take on the responsibilities that are far removed from the stated mission of a university like campus dining and housing.

EMERGENT REMOTE CAMPUS

What may be particularly notable about this model is that central administration may not even be necessary. The full-service, lean, and private models all assume a central entity is arranging facilities and recruiting students. If instead students could self-organize their own local campuses, we would have what we describe as an emergent campus: students may be admitted to a remote program that itself carries no assumption about where they are, and then themselves group together into communities that choose to live together and adopt elements of the traditional college experience.

In some ways, this may resemble fraternity or sorority houses that collectively share a home near a campus, but a campus is not required. The cohorts may be small, and from the perspective of the university, they may be treated the same as any other remote student, but they are then able to instantiate the social elements of a campus on their own. This phenomenon occurred among Georgia Tech students in fall 2020: a large number of students in China who would have otherwise moved to campus in Atlanta were unable to do so due to COVID-19. These students petitioned the university to open up the Georgia Tech-Shenzhen campus so that they could retain the peer interactions and social connections they might have otherwise had on campus. However, Georgia Tech-Shenzhen had already reached its maximum capacity, so it partnered with Tianjin University to allow Georgia Tech sophomores, juniors, seniors, and graduate students unable to return to Atlanta to live for the semester in that campus environment. Although top-down coordination helped to realize this initiative, the demand itself was entirely organic and student-driven. Some students even noted that if neither the Shenzhen campus nor Tianjin University could accommodate them, they would rent a space on their own to stay close to one another during the semester.

SPONSORED REMOTE CAMPUS

This initiative at Tianjin University may more closely resemble yet another remote campus model, which we might call a sponsored remote campus. Under this design, existing schools seeking to augment their course offerings and options may offer to allow students to take advantage of the campus infrastructure while enrolling in another school's academic program. For example, many schools offer BS/MS programs; a school could offer to allow graduating seniors who are going on to enroll in a program like OMSCS to remain in campus housing, use campus facilities, and retain their status as active students at their local campus while enrolling in a remote master's program. While the school would gain no tuition, it would also incur no educational costs; instead, it enhances its own collective campus knowledge by adding in students pursuing an alternate advanced course of study that the university cannot supply on its own.

These models of a remote campus—full service, lean, private, emergent, sponsored—are by no means exhaustive and do not address all of the possible use cases. For example, these models all assume the social role of campus in offering students an independent experience; this is an important feature to traditional undergraduate audiences but is likely irrelevant to graduate students or nontraditional students. Does a campus have no role for these students? In all likelihood it still would; the environment for collaboration, the tools for certain projects, and the infrastructure for high-fidelity remote attendance all require some local investment and would still be relevant to their own nearby commuter students.

The point of this section is to suggest that even in the absence of a significant local instruction component, the campus still retains its draw and function. A shift to a distributed classroom does not mean that undergraduate students will instead live at home until they are twenty-two years old, missing out on all the social roles that college plays. Instead, the distributed classroom may serve to further expand access to campus in general.

THE ONLINE CAMPUS

The remote campus by nature targets replicating some of the social rites of passage of the traditional college campus. Its target audience is students who would physically live at the campus. While this is interesting, it does not represent the majority of the audiences opened up by this distributed campus approach. For adult learners, their individual lack of mobility is one of the appeals of the online program. To this audience, a remote campus could offer centralized resources and higher-fidelity classrooms, which might warrant commuting to the remote campus. In fact, many of the existing branch or satellite campuses target precisely this arrangement. For many adult learners, however, we would certainly expect the fully remote classroom options to be preferable, whether synchronous or asynchronous. Even if a campus is geographically close by, leaving the house requires additional time and may require arrangement for child care or other practical considerations.

The challenge with a fully remote experience is, of course, that it can be isolating. A number of factors can play into this, but we would argue that a significant part of this isolation is that online programs lack the feel of a "campus." We replace lecture halls with websites, classrooms with internet forums, and offices with email, and while functionally these replacements can handle the same use cases, we lose the periphery. Walking onto a college campus feels like entering a physically different place, with its own geography, architecture, and history. Attending online classes can feel like visiting a website: the "campus" is categorically the same as Reddit or Facebook in the next tab.

In some ways, this is acceptable. The function of the experience is still preserved. We have scaled our OMSCS program to eleven thousand students with this approach. Other virtual schools and online colleges have achieved far greater scale with similar approaches. But do these environments accomplish the roles of a campus? We would argue generally not. This turns our attention to the question: How would we build an actual, virtual campus rather than just a website? What would that entail? Based on conversations with students and brainstorming with other faculty, we see a continuum stretching from simple improvements for existing websites to a wholly immersive experience as possible avenues for building virtual campus-like environments.

INTEGRATED ONLINE CAMPUS

One of the key factors of a campus environment resides in its integratedness: in a physical space, it unifies a multitude of functions including instruction, socializing, studying, and advising. Perhaps a campus environment can be arranged simply by having a single, integrated campus that handles all elements of a student's college experience rather than forcing them across a multitude of different tools and sites.

Learning management systems (LMSs), for all their strengths, potentially present one of the reasons this issue is pervasive: the LMS is in many ways the hub of the student experience, but most such systems are very closely tied to individual classes rather than the experience that exists beyond classes. In our LMS, for instance, a student's home page lists their courses, a to-do list derived from the assignments in those courses, and a calendar derived from the calendars of those courses; nothing exists that is not part of a course. Contacting academic advisers or career counselors, viewing upcoming social events or seminars, or socializing with other students outside individual classes all require other tools. It is possible that if a single tool integrated all these elements, the site may feel more like a virtual campus than a decentralized collection of tools.

VISUALIZED ONLINE CAMPUS

We are skeptical, though. An integrated campus might be more usable, but would it really feel more campus-like? Our suspicion is that to truly make a virtual campus feel like a campus, it should leverage the visual metaphor of a campus in some ways. This visual campus may functionally be the same as the integrated campus, but visually embedding the tools in the metaphor of a virtual campus may introduce a greater sense of a community.

For example, imagine that an SC class is taking place in Klaus 2456 (one of the large classrooms on Georgia Tech's campus) and that the class has been distributed to an SR variant as well with students watching live from around the world. This could be accomplished by sending students in the SR section a teleconference link to click when the time comes, but this loses the connection to the physical space where the SC class is taking place. Instead, this same interaction could be visualized as virtually joining Klaus 2456 by name by selecting the room on a map of campus.

Meetings with advisers may be enabled in the same way; the process may be functionally identical, but the visualization of the process could instead suggest clicking to enter an office rather than clicking to join a videoconference. Social areas could thus be implemented as general areas a student can go to and join without the typical targeted use case. The goal here would be to create the impression that students may be "on campus" even if there is no particular task they are completing, such as attending a class or meeting with an adviser. In this way, students could be available for impromptu interactions with classmates based on their virtual presence on campus rather than all such interactions emerging entirely intentionally. The goal of all of these subtle modifications is to drive home a stronger analogy between virtual presence and physical presence on campus, connecting remote interaction to a representation of where that interaction would take place face-to-face.

VIRTUAL ONLINE CAMPUS

Under this metaphor, we are approaching the idea of a campus as a virtual world, the next stage of development of this spectrum. The lightweight approach, which we call a virtual online campus, would be to borrow the metaphor used by tools like Gatherly.io, Gather.town, and Sococo. In these tools, remote attendees see an actual two-dimensional floorplan and move their virtual presence around within it. When people are in the same physical vicinity as one another, they may talk using chat or video.

Such an arrangement could be developed for a virtual campus as well: students could always reside in a particular location in a two-dimensional campus, moving their virtual presence around within it to attend class, visit advisers' offices, participate in group study sessions, and so on. This could contribute to a feeling of peripheral community as well: even if they are not interacting with classmates, simply knowing that there are other people on the same "campus" as they are can create a peripheral sense of social connectedness. Thus, this serves two purposes: like the visualized online campus, it anchors interaction more strongly to a visual metaphor of a campus, and it also provides more peripheral awareness of classmates along with more emergent opportunities to connect with them.

IMMERSIVE ONLINE CAMPUS

Finally, to take this idea to the extreme, we might even conceive of a fully immersive three-dimensional campus that could be attended in virtual reality. This does present some obvious challenges: many people take notes while attending classes, which is difficult to do if the class is meeting in virtual reality. Some immersive interfaces, such as Second Life and Mozilla Hubs, allow for three-dimensional immersive environments that nonetheless run via a typical on-screen interface, preserving the student's physical capabilities while maintaining the three-dimensional metaphor. Under this idea, we might conceive of actually constructing a fully three-dimensional virtual campus through which a student can virtually walk. To attend classes, they might virtually go (with fast travel, of course) to those classes' locations, then receive a view of the course as recorded within that same room. To meet with classmates, they might arrange to meet in the same space within the immersive campus.

It is entirely possible, and even probable, that this metaphor takes this idea too far. One of the benefits of the virtual environment is that it avoids some of the constraints of the physical environment. How frustratingly silly would it be to meet with teammates in virtual reality, only to find that all the virtual study rooms are occupied? Or to be late to class because your virtual avatar cannot walk across the virtual campus fast enough? But the important contribution of these potential virtual campus environments—integrated, visual, virtual, and immersive—is that they introduce features of the physical campus that do not automatically persist in the transition to an online environment. An online program can be implemented with little attention paid to facilitating serendipitous or peripheral meetings among classmates or developing students' personal identities as members of the campus community. While we can attempt to implement those deliberately in other ways, implementing the campus metaphor raises the likelihood we might recapture campus dynamics we did not even fully appreciate in the first place.

THE CONNECTED CAMPUS

In chapter 3, we discussed the idea of the Georgia Tech atrium, and while these atria would clearly be a part of the distributed campus, they have not come up so far in this section. Where do these fit in? The most obvious place is as the leanest of the remote campuses, a small environment solely dedicated to providing a set of services that benefit from an in-person component. This could include high-fidelity classrooms to attend remote classes, maker spaces for completing authentic projects, and meet-up areas for local team projects.

A key part of all these remote campus initiatives, however, has been a more durable, ongoing student presence. Under current online arrangements, students generally log in only when they have specific, directed tasks to accomplish; this is different from campus environments where students interact more consistently and peripherally. The remote campuses attempt to recreate that presence literally by getting students back into a persistent environment, a physical campus where they live, work, and collaborate. The online campuses attempt to recreate that presence more metaphorically by embedding it in some way on a screen, so that students need not leave their home to attend campus.

How do initiatives like the Georgia Tech atrium work into this metaphor? We would argue that they actually present a third approach, qualitatively different from the above two, hinging on the idea that the various such environments around the world would be connected with both each other and the larger campus environments. In this way, the atria form one, global, connected campus. The connected campus would remain physical in a way the online campuses would not: it would still generally expect students to visit a physical space. That physical space would be linked live to spaces around the world. One wall in the atrium in New York, for instance, might show a live feed of the environment in San Francisco, creating an impression that although the two cities are thousands of miles apart, they are part of a connected whole.

This connected campus would include more individual options for remote meetings. A high-fidelity classroom could allow virtual attendance with a remote class, but smaller rooms (borrowing the metaphor of a phone booth) may be equipped with similar environments to connect students to remote advisers, teaching assistants, and counselors. Although functionally no different from a teleconference, these borrow a metaphor that recaptures the in-person experience: instead of emailing someone to set up a time to have a formal meeting, students may instead drop by virtual offices to interact more casually. Similar social areas may be set up to put students peripherally in contact with others, allowing casual, emergent conversations to occur rather than the directed and deliberate conversation more characteristic of online interactions. The arrangement may also be leveraged to more easily allow authentic remote participation in on-campus events. For example, the main lobby of Georgia Tech's Klaus Advanced Computing Building is often used for poster sessions, job fairs, and seminar presentations. How do these transfer online? With a connected campus, a two-way feed may be set up as part of the event. Students in the remote Georgia Tech atrium may interact directly with people attending the event in person.

The key function of the connected campus, however, is the notion of peripheral interaction. Such an arrangement is built primarily to help students recognize they are part of a greater whole. Witnessing the similar activity of students from all over the world in virtual environments just like one's own presents a global view of the campus. This may be reciprocal as well: views of the various remote environments could be installed around the main campus to give students attending that campus a view of the global reach of their university.

This idea is ambitious and expensive, as are the remote and online campus ideas. They are not necessary to scale access: existing programs have shown that even without a cohesive campus, online programs can grow tremendously. This is one of the fears about online education: that it represents a misunderstanding of the holistic education process and that in the transition, we will lose other functions of the campus. It is tempting to move forward quickly with virtual class experiences, leaving behind some of the functions that the campus serves, but college is more than the classes that it offers. Building a distributed campus surrounding the distributed classroom preserves these benefits.

The blueprints in this chapter may be the way to offer a distributed campus, or there may be many others; the main thrust here is that preserving the campus experience is possible, and it must be pursued deliberately.

9

FEARS, RISKS, AND OTHER SCARY WORDS

Despite our rosy view of the potential of this medium, we are aware of all the ways it may go wrong. In chapters 6 and 8, we sought to get ahead of some of these issues: chapter 6 focused on some of the obstacles and emphasized the approach's feasibility, and chapter 8 looked at fears about what might be lost in the way of a campus experience in a transition to a distributed classroom.

Moreover, the distributed classroom on its own is an answer to some of the drawbacks of other initiatives, such as MOOCs: it reintroduces social interaction, classroom community, the campus experience, authentic assessment, human feedback, and so on. It focuses on the ability of modern technology to adapt to the way we teach rather than the need for teachers to adapt to the constraints of technology. It shows there is very little that we do in person that is not possible now with a remote, distributed audience.

The fear we have heard in the wake of COVID-19 is that universities will rush to remote learning due to its potential to cut costs and preserve enrollments, and that these incentives will be sufficient to disregard or leave unexplored whether the same learning outcomes are still being achieved. The distributed classroom is an answer to this as well: it provides a blueprint for pursuing remote learning while preserving as much of the typical experience as possible, keeping both the benefits we know about and the subtle ones we may never have noticed. That is not to say that outcomes will not suffer but rather that they do not *have* to suffer. The outcomes suffer if students are just watching prerecorded lectures with no interaction. The outcomes suffer if we water down assessments to be more easily deliverable online. The outcomes suffer if we focus only on material that can be assessed easily at scale. The outcomes suffer if we ignore the immeasurable social outcomes. But remote learning need not entail any of these drawbacks.

Thus, the distributed classroom as a whole is a counterpoint to one fear about remote education: that even if the outcomes are worse, it will be embraced due to its ability to cut costs. The goal of this paradigm is to preserve the experience and outcomes even as more remote options enter the fold. Success in this approach, however, may come with its own risks. If the distributed classroom were to take off in a large way, would it cause more issues than it would resolve? Would it be a net improvement or a net loss when considering other effects?

For example, this paradigm is deeply compatible with efforts to unbundle higher education, and yet those efforts on their own have significant critics who argue it risks losing

the freedom and independence academia has sought to preserve at a time when those are more important than ever. For
another, when discussing expanding the number of students
a single teacher can reasonably teach, are we not promoting
a plan that will leave many teachers without jobs?

This chapter does not argue that these developments will
not happen. Left unchecked, it is highly likely that they
would. The pressures to reduce costs are too high for that
potential benefit to be ignored. The distributed classroom
could be used to standardize curricula to fit certain political
agendas, relying less on individual adoption of content and
more on the distribution of centrally managed information.
These are real risks.

Instead, this chapter argues that these negative repercussions are avoidable. It further provides some plans for
avoiding these negative effects, whether they emerge due to
complacency, incompetence, or malice.

TEACHER EMPLOYMENT

The extended example of a distributed classroom in chapter 5 looked at a machine learning class. This was particularly relevant because in machine learning (as with much of
computer science), teachers can be hard to find: extending
the number of people a single teacher can teach can open
access to the course to people who could not have otherwise
enrolled.

Under the "Applicability" section in chapter 6, we discussed the idea that this paradigm might only be relevant
to classes for which it is hard to find instructors. We argued
there that it was not: it could be applied to common classes

as well, but the benefits would be felt in a different way. The fear here is that we may be right: the distributed classroom could be used to let one teacher teach ten thousand calculus students at a time instead of one hundred, and as a result ninety-nine calculus teachers may be fired. This would lead to widespread centralization around a small number of teachers and universities, which we discuss in the next section; instead, here the threat is that this will be used as a mechanism to thin the ranks of teachers.

CONTINUATION OF EXISTING TRENDS

In response to this fear, it is first worth noting that in many ways, the distributed classroom for a well-defined field is the next evolution of years of efforts to collect reusable, distributable materials. Textbooks themselves are an instance of this effort: they collect together curriculum design, instruction (at least as far as it can be done on static paper), and practice problems. Absent a textbook, teachers have to design their course content, author all instruction, and write all individual work themselves; textbooks give a reusable resource that multiple teachers can leverage, allowing them to focus instead on in-person content delivery, individual feedback, and assessment. More recent developments with virtual textbooks further allow some of these functions to be played by the book. In McGraw-Hill's Smartbook platform (which we have used in our CS1301 class), textbooks can be augmented with adaptive visualizations, automatically evaluated practice questions, and embedded videos. The book on its own thus plays a stronger instructional role, assessing students and giving them guidance on their own areas of strength and weakness while also teaching with higher-fidelity video content. ZyBooks, another recent innovation, embeds more animations and walk-throughs into its content, allowing the textbook to play a more instructional role.

Textbooks are just one of many other trends that serve a similar purpose. Schools and districts often heavily manage the delivery of individual classes in order to ensure consistency across teachers, exchangeability across schools, and adherence to standards. As part of this, they issue day-by-day schedules, minute-by-minute lesson plans, and shared assessments to use across dozens of classes. These already function as a sort of distributed classroom, but rather than distributing the product, they distribute the blueprint. Teachers we have spoken to generally dislike this practice: it takes much of the individual control and improvisation out of the teachers' hands, like asking a chef to follow a recipe rather apply their own knowledge to designing a dish. Part of this, however, is the disconnect between lesson design and the individual teacher's strengths and weaknesses. If the teacher was responsible not for carrying out the lesson design, but rather for designing complementary elements (such as facilitating discussions and group work), we might see some improvement. Either way, there have long been many initiatives that can be thought of as shifting teaching roles around to central individuals or groups, reducing the number of responsibilities carried by in-person teachers (albeit while also reducing how much total control they have over their classes).

Do these diminish the demand for in-person teachers? Absolutely not. Instead, they aim to give teachers another tool to improve outcomes for their students. Their success in this regard is debatable, but the approach to offloading certain responsibilities onto textbooks, lesson plans, and so on has a clear appeal given the number of different demands teachers are asked to juggle anyway. With more instructional roles played by the book (as in the case of zyBooks or Smartbooks), teachers can focus on guidance and individual feedback in the class. The distributed classroom is yet another evolution in this direction: it gives teachers well-designed classroom instruction designed deliberately to be used with a live audience. This reduces the number of roles in which a teacher must excel to be effective. It was already a tremendous demand to expect a teacher to simultaneously administer a compelling live classroom, give quality feedback and reliable grades on assignments, work with students individually to overcome their misconceptions, and handle all the other elements of administering a credit-bearing class. The distributed classroom allows more specialization.

GUIDELINES FOR FOCUSING ON OUTCOMES

The key focal point in this regard is outcomes. If student outcomes were already as good as they could possibly get, then allowing one teacher to teach more students would pose a threat to the number of available teaching roles. In this case, however, outcomes could be significantly better; the savings from moving toward a distributed classroom may be implicitly reinvested into the actual student experience. Like giving a lumberjack a chainsaw rather than an axe, the product may be greater results rather than fewer individuals.

This is not to say that the alternative—cutting costs with consistent outcomes rather than preserving costs with greater outcomes—will not be tempting. Especially in times of budget crisis, like those following COVID-19, there will be efforts to reduce costs; but when budgets recover, there is rarely a push to increase spending to match the preceding push to cut costs. Thus, it will still be important to be vigilant about the way these ideas are used. We offer three guidelines to ensure that the distributed classroom benefits students.

First, the ratio of students-per-faculty should rise only if the total number of students also rises. One goal of the distributed classroom is to open access to students who would not have otherwise had access to content; to accomplish this, there almost inherently must be more students per faculty member, especially in in-demand fields. For more well-established fields, however, the student-to-faculty ratio should remain consistent if the number of students is remaining consistent. This ensures that the benefits of a distributed classroom are being used to reduce teachers' load, allowing them to reinvest the saved time into students.

Second, delivery of feedback and assessment should stay local. There are significant benefits to centralizing the design of assessments. Designing a good assessment is incredibly difficult, and teachers are busy. Moreover, it is unreasonable to expect every individual teacher to be an expert on assessment design, much less to put that expertise into practice regularly on top of their other responsibilities. But while the assessments (meaning the instructions, rubrics, and interfaces) may be distributable, their delivery should stay local. Students should continue to receive their grades and feedback from someone they know and someone to whom they have access. This allows for follow-up questions, and the feedback may become the basis for conversation rather than a summative result.

Third, classroom time should be clearly devoted to letting teachers contextualize the current content. As we referenced earlier and will discuss in the next two sections, teachers often (rightfully) resist being simplified to a cog in a machine carrying out some far-removed lesson plan. At the same time, there are clear benefits to offloading some teaching responsibilities onto centralized resources or individuals. How do we balance the two? The key here would be to deliberately leave room in the design of classrooms for local tailoring. Teachers may have room to contextualize current content to the interests of their students, the nearby historical context, the teacher's individual strengths, and so on. This serves two purposes: it pushes back against the temptation of widespread standardization, and it preserves a clear local role a teacher must play. The classroom is not complete without a local teacher.

In the context of these guidelines, a distributed classroom may be pursued where the advantages of offloading class delivery and instruction may be reinvested in teachers' ability to interact individually with students, devote significant time to giving quality feedback, and find the natural connections between the content and the issues most pertinent to the current cohort of students. It is also important that this shift in role does not diminish the importance we attach to these teachers: this shift is about specialization, not promotion. The teachers to whom classroom delivery is assigned are the ones for whom that is their strength, and the teachers to whom individual feedback and assessment are assigned are those that specialize in that sort of personal interaction. Both are equally necessary; this model just removes the demand that every teacher excel at every role.

This is the paradigm we use in our classes. Across our online MSCS classes, we have dozens of teaching assistants each term. Nearly 100 percent of their responsibilities are directly student facing: they answer questions on the course forum, interact with students in office hours, and grade students' assignments, including providing detailed feedback. Similarly for us as instructors, our main in-semester responsibilities are answering questions, leading discussions, and handling edge cases; we have front-loaded all other responsibilities, including delivering course content, writing assignments and rubrics, and even posting weekly (which similarly can be scripted in advance). By front-loading all these responsibilities, our entire course delivery time is spent on direct, regular, and significant student interaction in one way or another.

Our undergraduate CS1 class takes this even a step further: all the assessments are autograded. We would not advocate this approach in most other subjects, but it is uniquely useful and authentic in computer science. We still hire a teaching assistant for every twenty-five students, though, just as regular on-campus undergraduate classes do.[1] Thus, 100 percent of our TAs' time is spent helping students directly. Could we survive with fewer TAs? Absolutely; in fact, the MOOC version of the course shows that we do not actually *need* any TAs to endorse students' success in the course. Five times more students have completed the MOOC version of the course than the for-credit section, showing the course's scale. The instruction and assessment are the same. For students paying tuition and receiving course credit, however, we reinvest the time saved by front-loading content into helping them individually succeed.

THE MEGA-UNIVERSITY

Sebastian Thrun, architect of one of the first MOOCs and founder of Udacity, one of the major MOOC companies, once predicted that in the future, there will be only ten universities in the world.[2] There is certainly precedent for the idea: the past few decades have seen a dramatic centralization in many other industries as well, such as news media.[3] Our own analogy to North Point Community Church applies here. If we argue that its trajectory to become a megachurch is similar to our own trajectory in higher education, then how does that trajectory not also lead to mega-universities? Technology may lower barriers to entry, allowing new entrants into markets that were relatively impervious to challenge (such as Udacity entering the education marketplace in the first place), but it also allows organizations to exert much greater control at much greater distances, allowing savvy existing behemoths to grow ever more powerful.

There are some that actually view the "threat" of a mega-university as promising. One argument is that the massive repetition of work present in modern education is duplicative and wasteful: every semester, tens of thousands of students take a calculus class that covers roughly the same material, but with a student experience that varies significantly based on the individual instructor. Would it not be more efficient to produce one ultimate calculus course for them all to use?[4] This sort of arrangement is exactly the type of structure we have advocated for throughout this book. Is the distributed classroom not just a mechanism toward a mega-university?

Without a doubt, it could be used that way. If Georgia Tech and other universities decided to scale up their curriculum across all majors the way we have done with OMSCS, it is feasible that we might see the mass centralization that Thrun predicted. This may carry massive repercussions. The decentralized nature of higher education allows the pursuit of multiple research agendas, which would likely be squashed with fewer players in the market. Universities are critically embedded in local contexts; the social contract between universities and society discussed in Rich DeMillo's *Revolution in Higher Education* relies on a close connection between local populations and their higher education systems in a way that likely would not exist if the university was instead far less connected to a local context.[5]

You may disagree, of course; we have colleagues who see potential in the growth of individual universities to improve student outcomes, reduce costs, improve efficiency, and so on, even if it comes at the expense of some other schools. The distributed classroom could clearly be used as a mechanism to realize this. However, it does not inherently guarantee this outcome.

There are at least two ways in which the distributed classroom may be used not to forward this centralization, but rather to combat it. There are certainly more, but in light of present trends, these two approaches strike us as the most immediately important.

GREATER CONTENT EXCHANGE

First, as we noted in chapter 8, the distributed classroom has a deep compatibility with movements to unbundle higher education. We often describe this in terms of separating out housing and dining from teaching from career services and so on, but it also applies across the curriculum: if you are an engineering student, should you really need to take your

English and history classes from the same university that specializes in engineering? Or should you instead be able to compile a curriculum from the strengths of individual schools? This already exists in some ways via transfer credit, but the obstacles are usually high enough that most students do not embrace the opportunity beyond taking the occasional summer class at their local community college.

Under this paradigm, the distributed classroom becomes a way for universities to exchange content with one another far more easily. Multiple approaches are possible, from students at one university actively enrolling in a class at another with an advanced guarantee that the credit will transfer, to universities sharing content with one another for reimplementation with their own local teaching assistants.

As one example, we are in the process of creating a dual-degree program with a college that does not offer its own graduate degrees. Students would complete their bachelor's degree at the other college, and while finishing the degree, they would begin taking classes in our OMSCS program. The other college grants them credit for enrollment in our courses, and once they complete their undergraduate work, they may continue with the master's degree while remaining on the other college's campus, using its infrastructure, and interacting with the rest of its student body. In this way, the other college is able to open access to something—a graduate degree in computer science—that it cannot offer on its own by forming a relationship with an existing entity. This provides a model by which universities may leverage the distributed classroom to increase their own offerings without needing to build them up entirely from scratch. Universities continue to play valuable roles within their local contexts, so using this mechanism to expand their offerings allows their existing value to persist.

Of course, this approach need not go this far. Under this approach, the "borrowing" university is essentially building a pathway for its students to go on to send resources to another school and using the presence of such a pathway as a feature to preserve interest in its own programs. Instead, the distributed classroom that the borrowing university leverages could be further removed from its original context. Just like buying a textbook to use to offer a new class, the university could instead license the entirety of the content but handle all delivery itself. Under this model, the borrowing university would still have its own course numbers, give its own credit, hire its own teaching assistants, and so on, making the product more local to the university itself. It would merely use the existing content from another school as the foundation. This already happens in an ad hoc way: every month we receive emails from professors asking if they can use the content we have made public for our courses to offer their own sections of Human-Computer Interaction or Introduction to Computing. This merely formalizes this mechanism.

The lesson of all of this is that the distributed classroom focuses on making the course experience more available to a greater number of students, and part of that audience may be students already present at other colleges and universities— not by stealing those students away but by letting those other universities leverage the content. Those institutions can then embrace the newly available materials in one of multiple ways, incorporating it into their portfolio while adding their own local context. The distributed classroom thus is a tool for colleges to fight against obsolescence from a small number of growing mega-universities: they can offer what the mega-universities offer while still providing their individual attention, local connections, and campus experience.

MORE LEARNERS

An assumption embedded in the fear of the emergence of a small number of mega-universities is that there exists a stable audience of potential students, and that audience will be divided up among a smaller and smaller number of higher education institutions. One of the goals of the distributed classroom, however, is to increase access to content: it aims to accommodate people who were not otherwise students. We discuss this idea in chapter 6 (in the "Applicability" section) and in chapter 7 (in the "Adult Learners" section). The demands of emerging technologies and the rapid shifts underway in the world will require far more frequent retooling. Not only does technology make lifelong learning more possible, but it also makes it more necessary. It is no longer feasible to go to school for four years and then have a forty-year career in the field you chose; people must continue learning.

Thus, mega-universities are bound to emerge. Some would argue they already exist. How can universities of the size of the State University of New York or the University of Phoenix not already be considered "mega"? Their emergence, however, does not need to come at the expense of other schools if the focus is on reaching potential lifelong learners, not other schools' current students. Instead of attending school for four years to set up a forty-year career, a student entering their freshman year in college now is likely looking at a lifetime of education in one form or another. The initial bachelor's degree still has a role to play in fostering independence, supplying a foundation, and teaching students how to be adult learners, but from there, a student may be looking at returning to the classroom five or six years after graduation, and again a half-decade after that, as the skills they need have changed rapidly. The classroom, of course, can take on various forms: workplace training, informal online courses, boot camps, and so on. The intellectual independence, reputation, and generalizability of a college education, however, can certainly be a rich part of filling this need.

Pundits for years have forecast that workers in the future will change careers many more times than in the past, and each of those changes comes with the need to learn new skills and content. We must find ways to support the need for that education that are affordable and flexible enough for career professionals to pursue; the distributed classroom gives a model for realizing that, making only the minimal trade-off regarding the learning experience for each individual student's cost, place, and time constraints.

CENTRALIZATION, STANDARDIZATION, AND IMPERIALISM

Much of the discussion in the areas we have addressed have touched on fears of centralization and standardization. The implicit belief is that something will be lost if a small number of teachers or universities exert much greater control over the learning experience for a much larger audience of learners. Not everyone shares these fears of more centralized control: those who see educational data as a treasure trove to mine for novel insights and improvements likely embrace the idea that a central system could be much more quickly improved and disseminated. What if you could upgrade learning the same way you upgrade software?

But there are many reasons to be fearful of these movements. We have seen how education can be a political battleground. George Orwell's *1984* includes the slogan, "Who controls the past controls the future. Who controls the present controls the past," a reference to how controlling individuals' perceptions of the past can allow one to exert control over the future. These perceptions of the past are often developed via K–12 history classes; central control over these curricula leaves them more susceptible to political agendas, especially for public education. We have already seen this with differences in how evolution, the causes of the US Civil War, and sex education are taught from state to state (and country to country, with a local analogue in place of the US Civil War).

Similarly, standardization has vocal detractors: programs like No Child Left Behind and the Common Core State Standards Initiative have good intentions, but their implementations have many critics. Tying funding to test scores carries fundamental issues. In addition to the concerns with central control, efforts to create formal standards risk only prioritizing that which can be measured; this is Justin Reich's Trap of Routine Assessment, which we discuss at length in the next section.

Finally, when we start talking about initiatives like US universities opening campuses in developing countries, we risk comparisons to colonialist pursuits. On the one hand, it is easy to see an argument that it is toward the betterment of the world for a US institution to open a branch in a developing country in order to help its local populace gain the skills necessary to be employable and competitive in today's global marketplace. On the other hand, does this not inherently undermine local universities? If students could choose between their local college and a branch of Georgia Tech for the same price, could the local college remain competitive? And if not, are we not weakening local culture and local control with our efforts? This is just one of many possible faults people may find with well-intentioned efforts to expand a school's sphere of influence into areas in need.

As with the above risks, these outcomes are possible: the distributed classroom framework could be used to undermine local control of curriculum, educating a population in an area with lower cost of living and fewer employment regulations in order to give multinational corporations an opportunity for cheaper labor. There are two trends that must be preserved in tandem to avoid this result.

DEMOCRATIZATION

We tend to distrust the term *democratization*—not the idea, but the way it is often used. We find every start-up has some argument for how its business plan democratizes some existing industry. That is not to say it is not used authentically in many places. Robinhood, for instance, clearly democratizes investing, giving control more directly to the people, but we find many initiatives that claim to pursue democratization are really seeking to shift power from existing institutions to themselves, not to individuals.

That said, part of the way in which the distributed classroom can be leveraged against this centralization is through
its compatibility with democratizing the classroom. In chapter 6, one of our points of emphasis was how a distributed
classroom could be created without a heavy investment into
infrastructure; for example, although AI-driven cameras
and distributed microphones are nice, they are not necessary. This is critical to leveraging the distributed classroom
for more democratic purposes: it means that pursuing a distributed audience of learners is plausible not only for well-
funded institutions but also for any individual teacher with
access to a relatively limited set of technology.

As with other trends in this book, this one is already
underway as well. Southern New Hampshire University
(SNHU) is a private university in New Hampshire, one of
the ten least-populous US states. It pivoted to focusing on
online education in the wake of the 2008 recession and
now is one of the largest universities in the world: it enrolls
ninety thousand students, over 90 percent of them entirely
online. What was once a small, regional university pivoted
to having national significance by leveraging technology to
distribute its classroom.

By keeping the technological demands low, this direction is available for other institutions as well. Not only can
it push back against the tendency toward centralization
that may be carried by these distributed efforts; it may even
attack the underlying power structures already present. A
private, distributed school system in a state with controversial standards regarding some topic may be competitive with
local public school systems due to these economies of scale
and low distribution costs. Of course, this carries risks of its

own: in the post-truth era, it may be dangerous to allow individuals to select their school based on which truth it teaches,
but it is arguably even more dangerous to allow a centralized
set of individuals to select the truth that will be taught to
all students.

CONTEXTUALIZATION

We referenced the second approach to finding the best balance between increasing access and supporting local control
in the "Teacher Employment" section under its third guideline: allowing local contextualization. If we were to form a
campus of Georgia Tech in an emerging area using faculty
who reside in Atlanta, teaching assistants who reside in
Atlanta, advisers who reside in Atlanta, and so on, then we
would not be able to cater significantly at all to the local
student context. This might be seen as a latter-day type of
colonialism or imperialism, seeking to conquer a local educational context and subsume it within our existing structures. Instead, any such effort should hold as one of its first
priorities to integrate the local context into the offering.
Anything that can be done locally should be done locally.
Advisers and teaching assistants thousands of miles away in
a dramatically different cultural context cannot understand
what a new student body is encountering, and thus cannot
be expected to adequately tailor the content and communication to that local audience.

Two of our initiatives have followed this same sort of
guideline. First, in the OMSCS program, our critical point
was the discovery that online students were available to
work as teaching assistants to support their classes. This was

critical from a numeric point of view in terms of scaling, but even more important, we discovered that these students made better teaching assistants because they understood the plight of the other online students. They matched their schedules, their backgrounds, and their expectations more closely than on-campus graduate students working as TAs for a very different audience of people. Since then, we have extended this to our academic advisers as well: our advisers now work from home most of the time, and while that comes first from space constraints on campus, it is also a valuable way of making the advisers' experience more like that of the students they are advising.

Second, in our efforts to use our online CS1 to expand access to CS education in Atlanta Public Schools, we will not simply give the students access to the online course and augment them with a Georgia Tech teaching assistant. Instead, our Constellations Center for Equity in Computing trains local fellows to work in the classrooms. They may still use our online material, but because they are physically present in the classroom and getting to know the individual students, they are able to imbue the course with local relevance, context, and pacing to match their own audience.

Thus, when pursuing these efforts, two types of contextualization must be preserved. First, we must start by asking how many roles in our distributed classroom can be served by people most similar to the students we are trying to reach; these sorts of individuals should be selected whenever possible. As a general principle, an online student should be selected over an on-campus student to be a teaching assistant for an online class; a potential teaching assistant in Nigeria should be selected for a class in Lagos over a remote teaching assistant in Atlanta; and a local teacher should be selected for a class in the Atlanta Public Schools over an undergraduate student at Georgia Tech. If such individuals are not available, we may fall back on those that we do have, with an eye as well toward training such individuals to be available in the future. Second, these distributed courses should be built with deliberate flexibility to allow such individuals to tailor the experience to the particular student body. Local individuals might be given the freedom to select discussion topics. Instructors might give options for projects that are most relevant to a particular local context. Courses might let local instructors selectively prioritize and reorder course content based on their students' needs, a feature zyBooks offers with its interactive textbooks. Our goal throughout should be to select the people best positioned to help a particular student body and augment them with quality materials rather than controlling them through centrally managed structures and standards.

REICH'S INTRACTABLE DILEMMAS

In his book *Failure to Disrupt: Why Technology Alone Can't Transform Education*, Justin Reich presents four as-yet intractable dilemmas facing learning at scale.[6] These dilemmas limit the impact that technology can have in scaling learning. Given that the distributed classroom is heavily related to scale, to what extent do these dilemmas threaten this paradigm?

We are, quite obviously, a proponent of the distributed classroom, and so it is not surprising that we find that the distributed classroom is viable despite these dilemmas. However, this viability goes beyond the benefits outweighing the drawbacks: in many ways, the distributed classroom is the antidote to these dilemmas. This is apparent in the ways in which technology has been invoked throughout this book. We have devoted very little time to common topics in learning at scale like automated evaluation (which will come in Reich's Trap of Routine Assessment). We have not allowed data analytics or A/B experiments to play any role in our design, despite the potential treasure trove provided by online classes' inherent tracking of student behavior (which will come up in Reich's Toxic Power of Data and Experiments).

The primary, and almost exclusive, role of technology throughout the distributed classroom has been not to replace existing experiences, but rather to distribute across space and time what has typically been synchronous and co-located. During this distribution, it has strived to alter the experience as little as possible, only when necessary or when improvement is possible, and with attention to what else must be altered as a result. Thus, the distributed classroom paradigm is in complete agreement with the premise of *Failure to Disrupt*: technology alone cannot transform education. Its role should be to distribute, extend, and support people, not replace them. To explore that, we examine how the distributed classroom addresses each of Reich's four dilemmas: the Curse of the Familiar, the Trap of Routine Assessment, the Toxic Power of Data and Experiments, and the EdTech Matthew Effect.

THE CURSE OF THE FAMILIAR

The first dilemma we address is Reich's Curse of the Familiar. Reich writes, "People tend to teach how they were taught, and new technologies are far more likely to be bent to fit into existing systems than they are to lead to major reorganizations." The dilemma here is that for new technologies to have their maximum impact, they must be part of major reorganizations, which is often infeasible. As examples, Reich gives MOOCs and Quizlet. MOOCs now heavily resemble traditional classes even when they are no longer subject to the same constraints that dictated those designs in the first place. Quizlet, one of the most popular educational technology platforms in the world, directly recreates the same kinds of flash cards students have been making for decades, if not centuries. Its advantages are efficiency and distributability. When new technologies do not fit into old systems, they are less likely to be adopted—or if adopted, they are likely to lose some of what they were designed to do in the first place. The creators of the kid-friendly programming language Scratch observed this when Scratch was used in classrooms: teachers often gave students very specific assignments instead of allowing them to interact creatively, even though the language was designed with open-ended creative exploration in mind.

The other part of this is that even if new technologies are adopted, they are more likely to be confusing to students if they do not fit into old systems and structures. We have witnessed this in several ways through our work, even though a large percentage of our course experience exactly mirrors the on-campus design. Our CS1 class is delivered on edX, which employs a novel approach to grades: grades are cumulative rather than rolling, meaning that they only ever go up as you earn more points. Students are more familiar with rolling grading schemes that support questions like, "I have an

83 percent now. What do I need to keep a B?" We spend a significant amount of our time helping students understand how well they are doing even though the metaphor of cumulative grading more closely resembles more familiar systems like saving money or earning points in a game. In our master's classes, students accustomed to peer grading systems often need to be reminded several times that our peer review system does not determine their actual score on an assignment; its purpose is purely pedagogical, which is unfamiliar for many.

It is not that the distributed classroom is impervious to this dilemma: instead, the classroom uses this dilemma to its advantage. This description has sought to preserve much of the traditional experience and sacrifice only those parts that are incompatible with certain potential audiences and their constraints. When those sacrifices must be made, it seeks to sacrifice as little as possible and identify what else must be lost as a result. In short, the distributed classroom strives to leverage familiar technologies and structures in order to preserve the experience and minimize the additional work required.

The relevance of this dilemma to the distributed classroom, then, is that it may not fully leverage the possible advantages we can derive from emerging technologies. Rather than a reason why the distributed classroom will not change education, it is a reason the distributed classroom may not change it *enough*. Reich goes on to say, however, that the path through this dilemma is community. He writes that the solution "involves scaling community rather than scaling distribution channels." We place significant influence on building a network of teachers and teaching assistants around a distributed classroom and on facilitating content exchange between teachers and schools. Thus, we optimistically provide an infrastructure for new, more novel technologies to inject themselves more efficiently into the course experience. The risk of centralization may have a silver lining as well: a more centralized structure, at least for a single course, may allow a new technology to move through the community more efficiently and have impact more quickly.

THE TRAP OF ROUTINE ASSESSMENT

The trap of routine assessment arises from the best intentions. We know that frequent assessment, typically formative but also summative,[7] leads to improved learning outcomes. Thus, we should assess students frequently. But assessments create work on the teacher to review the results and provide feedback. Assessments can only be given as quickly as they can be evaluated. To give more frequent assessment, we thus have to give assessments that are easier to evaluate, so we find those things that can be graded easily: correctness in math problems, multiple-choice questions, straightforward fill-in-the-blank, and so on can all be evaluated automatically. We then focus on them in designing our assessments in order to support that frequent assessment we know is beneficial. Then, in order to give our students the best chance to succeed on our assessments, we tailor our instruction to the questions we know we will be asking. Before long, despite our best intentions, we are trapped in teaching only what we can routinely assess. We can see this at many levels of education, from multiplication tables in lower school mathematics to quizzes on countries and capitals in middle school geography to free-body diagrams in high school physics.

These skills are all easily assessed, and so they take on a high importance in assessments. But an enormous number of skills we want to teach are not so easily assessable, such as explaining how a country's borders came to be where they are or putting free-body diagrams into practice in an authentic problem. These sorts of complex reasoning skills require more hands-on human evaluation, which is difficult to scale.

The distributed classroom addresses the trap of routine assessment in two ways. First, it strives to preserve as much of the existing structure of a classroom as possible. When describing the various versions of a class spread across space and time, we have noted that these students would still do the same assessments and be graded by the same graders. MOOCs, with their pursuit of essentially infinite scalability, rely on assignments that can be routinely assessed; the distributed classroom not only does not require that compromise for the majority of students, but it actively pushes back against making any such changes without a clear reason.

On its own, that does not mean that the other forces incentivizing routine evaluation will not affect the distributed classroom; it does not instantiate those other forces, but that does not mean it protects against them either. In one way, though, it does provide some resistance. We have noted that one of the goals of the distributed classroom, especially in more well-defined subject matter areas, is to allow teachers to focus more of their time on giving individual feedback and assessment. Those who teach five classes a day do not have time during the day to grade and write high-quality feedback; they are forced into either offering fewer assessments with slow turnaround times or assessments that focus on more routinely evaluated skills. If components of the real-time experience are offloaded onto a distributed class-room, however, it may open up additional time for teachers to devote to that individual feedback. For instance, if the distributed classroom is used in a flipped model, then much of the feedback that would usually be delivered asynchronously on paper might be delivered synchronously during live class activities.

Our classes in the OMSCS program invoke this design. The vast majority of our teaching assistants' time is spent giving students feedback on their work. As a result, we require a considerable amount of work—sometimes more than analogous on-campus classes because we have more resources to devote to generating grades and feedback. Part of this is to compensate for implicit learning outcomes we might derive from knowing students attended, but part of this is because we have reduced the responsibilities of our teaching assistants down to only tasks that cannot be done in advance.

THE TOXIC POWER OF DATA AND EXPERIMENTS

The third of Reich's dilemmas we discuss is what he deems the Toxic Power of Data and Experiments, referring to the complex ecosystem around data gathering in our increasingly online environment. To allow students to participate in learning at scale, how many compromises are we asking them to make with regard to their personal data? For example, he describes the increasing use of online proctoring, which requires invasive webcam, microphone, and screen capture. Is it fair to require students to give up so much privacy to participate in these systems? What students do we exclude by issuing these requirements?

In some ways, it is worth noting that the distributed class-room poses no greater a risk of this than any other online initiative, including the already-prevalent use of learning management systems and web forums in on-campus classes. No part of our designs has fundamentally relied on students giving up their rights to privacy; we advocate recording in-person class sessions, but part of the relevance of the editing phase is to edit out questions by students who may not feel comfortable having their query recorded. When recording in a remote environment from the outset, we recommend recording only the presenter or some preselected students and teaching assistants who have agreed (without any coercion or incentive) to participate in such a recording.

Similarly, although the distributed classroom represents an effort toward distributing content and digitizing elements of participation and performance, we have never discussed the potential for data analytics in education. There could be enormous applications: in a digital at-scale environment, we could find significant relationships when we combine personal demographics with class performance and interaction data. Admittedly, we are skeptical; Reich's Law, articulated elsewhere in *Failure to Disrupt*, states, "People who do stuff, do more stuff, and people who do stuff do better than people who don't do stuff." These massive data sets may help us uncover what kinds of people do stuff and how doing that stuff makes them more likely to succeed, but it does not give us any natural ability to intervene. Perhaps it is due to this skepticism that we have devoted nearly no attention to data analytics in this book; the potential impact of the distributed classroom is in no way reliant on the analytics that may be possible.

Still, is it sufficient to simply say that we do not need analytics for the distributed classroom to succeed? Much of the Toxic Power of Data and Experiments is not about how analytics can be positive, but about how the very existence of the data poses a risk to students. The distributed classroom is a move toward more data, in part because more interaction is digitized (and thus persistent) and in part because there are more students from whom to get data. How can students' privacy be preserved?

To address this dilemma, we invoke the European Union's General Data Protection Regulation (GDPR). We believe, especially when we are making major movements toward digitizing more and more of the educational experience, that institutions should adopt GDPR-like policies on their own. GDPR is built on six pillars: data minimization; data retention; lawfulness, fairness, and transparency; integrity and confidentiality; accuracy; and purpose limitations. Some of these are already covered by many existing laws. In the United States, for example, confidentiality is covered by the Family Educational Rights and Privacy Act (FERPA). But to address the amount of data aggregated passively in online education contexts, policies regarding data minimization, data retention, and purpose limitations should also be adopted.

First, regarding data minimization, only the data necessary to complete a task should be gathered. Certain examples are obvious: assessments must be gathered to give grades. Proctoring data must be gathered to ensure integrity. These only scratch the surface of what technological systems can aggregate, however; for example, many learning management systems give comprehensive access logs so that a teacher may know if a student has not logged in for several weeks. These data can play a key role in intervening with at-risk students or holding students accountable for their effort; if it is not to be used in this fashion, though, it should not be gathered in the first place. Every item of data that is gathered should be examined to determine whether it should ever be gathered, and if so, under what circumstances. For access logs, if the school actively intervenes when students are not digitally present to try to help, they may be gathered at the school level. If not, then it may be that individual instructors wish to use these data to assign participation credit or monitor progress; if so, then data should be gathered only at the course level. If neither will use the data, the data should not be retained; it provides no benefit and poses only unnecessary risks.

Second, regarding data retention, schools need to be able to revisit and defend grades and integrity violations for a set period of time. Thus, it is important to retain artifacts like student assignments and exam recordings for some number of months or years. Once this time has lapsed, these data should be purged. Any data that will not need to be reviewed once the semester is over should be removed immediately. For example, if the only function played by access logs is to allow teachers or administrators to actively intervene with students who appear to be falling behind, then those data are no longer needed once the semester is over and should be purged immediately; continued retention again provides no benefit, and thus any risk, no matter how small, is unnecessary.

Third, purpose limitation notes that we should gather data only for specific purposes and that data should be used only for those specific purposes. This requires us to be very clear about the purpose of various pieces of data that we gather. For example, based on the classes David teaches, he and Alex Duncan wrote a paper titled, "Eroding Investment in Repeated Peer Review: A Reaction to Unrequited Aid?"[8] In the paper, they investigate trends in courses that require peer review and observe that students tend to give less and less feedback as the semester progresses. Was this sort of research part of the purpose of gathering these data? In our case, certainly; the study was covered under an institutional review board protocol that noted that part of the purpose of gathering these data is to better understand peer review as a social activity in online education. The study could just as easily have been performed without that approval, however, for the purpose of improving the peer review activity in the courses. Would that have been acceptable? What if it was conducted not by David as the instructor of the class for the purpose of ensuring the activity is useful, but another researcher at Georgia Tech for the purpose of informing other classes' peer review designs? What if it was conducted by a researcher at the company developing the product? All of these entities would have access to the data. Is it acceptable for them to use the data that way? For these reasons, a clear policy on purpose limitation should be available for all data, including for what purposes the data may be used and by whom.

THE EDTECH MATTHEW EFFECT

There is an elephant in the room regarding the distributed classroom, and it falls under the umbrella of Reich's EdTech Matthew Effect. The name of the effect comes from Matthew

25:29 in the Christian Bible, which states (in one transla-
tion), "For whoever has will be given more, and they will
have an abundance. Whoever does not have, even what they
have will be taken from them." Reich summarizes the effect
in the context of learning at scale, stating, "For many years,
educators, designers, and policymakers have hoped that free
and low-cost online technologies could bridge the chasm of
opportunity that separates more and less affluent students.
This dream has proven elusive." Elsewhere, he elaborates,
saying, "New technologies disproportionately benefit learners with the financial, social, and technical capital to take
advantage of new innovations."

Part of the goal of the distributed classroom is to expand
access, which can come in different ways, many of them
compatible with increasing equity in education. For example, in the OMSCS program, we observe that we enroll twice
the rate of underrepresented minorities as the on-campus
program.[9] There are many potential reasons for this: our
program's flexible structure accepts students who can less
afford to take time off work or compromise their career
progression; our low tuition cost means students can enroll
who have not already found as much career success; and
our inclusive admissions allow students to enter who were
not already able to attend the most prestigious undergraduate university. Any of these effects may be correlated with
increasing equity of access.

But when we discuss the potential of the distributed classroom to expand access in the K–12 space, we run directly into
issues of equitable access to technology. In his book, Reich
describes three myths that lead to the emergence of this Matthew effect, and the third is the myth that the digital divide

can be closed simply through providing access to technology. This runs into two issues. First, providing access to technology in the first place is immensely difficult. This became an enormous issue in the wake of COVID-19. As schools shifted online, students who did not have home access to technology were left behind.[10] Second, even if access is technologically provided, it still runs into complex sociocultural issues regarding how underprivileged audiences understand, use, and trust it.

It is tempting to regard this as a moot issue. After all, as described in the "Applicability" section of chapter 6, perhaps the distributed classroom is exclusively relevant to emerging fields where training is sparse and in high demand. These audiences are far removed from the K–12 students for whom internet access is an issue. But upon further investigation, Matthew effects crop up everywhere due to technology access as well as other issues.

First, regarding technology access, one of the key components of how rapidly technology changes is that no one is ever as far behind in the workplace as they might have been in previous decades. Many popular programming languages, libraries, and technologies of 2030 have not even been invented yet. This can mean that underprivileged audiences should be better suited to move up in the world in technological fields because past inequities in access are less relevant. A career as a medical doctor may be out of reach for a thirty-six-year-old cashier who cannot commit to eight years of medical school, but a career as a software developer may be plausible because even existing developers need to retrain. However, this audience may be just as likely to still lack access to broadband technology as the K–12 audience referenced before. They may be the parents or neighbors of that audience falling behind in elementary school due to lack of internet connectivity, and their lack of access to these opportunities is the precise reason why their children and grandchildren may find themselves in the same position. There must be a mechanism for access to break this cycle, and if the mechanism relies on rich connectivity, then audiences will continue to be excluded. This, of course, applies just as much to international audiences where local internet connectivity is subject to even more obstacles than cost and infrastructure, including power outages, local unrest, and authoritarian control.

Even setting aside technology access, however, other equity issues abound that risk a Matthew effect. Let us imagine for a moment that a new technology has been developed and needs developers. Due to the specifics of the technology, very few prior languages or frameworks provide any one person with an advantage over another in preparation; it is so new and novel that based on the skills required alone, a twenty-year veteran software developer is equally prepared as the cashier, who recently received broadband access to her apartment as part of a new program offered by a local internet service provider. Despite their equal levels of preparedness for the content itself, the software developer still has incredible advantages. He may have an employer who is supportive of his upskilling, allowing him to devote work time to taking classes. He may have regular working hours, allowing him to better plan for tests or other assessments. He may have the means to pay for childcare in the evening to give himself additional time to prepare. He may have a network of colleagues also interested in this new field who are available for discussions or questions. The cashier, meanwhile, must find a way to work on the course outside of work hours while she is not taking care of her family, and she is largely on her own when she needs support.

The distributed classroom does provide a framework for exploring these issues, however. Throughout this book, we have discussed the notion of the minimum necessary compromise. We can use this to investigate these use cases. The software developer does not need to compromise on synchronous attendance or class pace: he has his employer's endorsement to work on the material during work hours, which are sufficiently predictable that he can likely commit to a shared class schedule. The cashier needs additional compromises: she cannot attend synchronously and may even struggle to attend synchronously with a cohort due to inconsistent work and childcare demands. As a result, she may not be able to keep up with the same class schedule as others. The question then becomes: What is the maximum portion of the experience we can provide to her given these constraints? Can we offer a version of the class that is no less rigorous, that still deserves the same credit and recognition, without requiring her to adhere to the same deadlines or attend class at the same time?

The distributed classroom does not provide general answers to these questions, but rather provides a framework for organizing and exploring them. Who are the potential audiences, and what compromises do they need? In some places, compromises may be possible that preserve the full weight and rigor of the course. In the wake of COVID-19, we gave a record number of Incomplete grades in our classes, which are essentially placeholder grades allowing students to work through the material on their own time rather than adhere to our schedule. In the process, we discovered there is relatively little about our pedagogical design that precludes students from moving through the material more slowly if need be due to external constraints: they are more isolated because they no longer have a true cohort surrounding them on a shared schedule, but no element of the credit or credential is affected. In other classes, such compromises may be more difficult if access to expensive shared resources is required or the synchronous experience is more fundamentally necessary. In still others, we might find that it is theoretically feasible to distribute a classroom, but teachers need more support to actually carry it out; identifying this obstacle lets us brainstorm technological solutions like Coursera's Live2Coursera, which helps teachers make their video content more directly accessible to students with weaker internet connectivity.[11] The distributed classroom provides a mechanism for exploring and organizing these questions to identify what the minimum necessary trade-offs might be, and it encourages us to think about these diverse audiences in considering how to minimize these compromises. It does not resolve the EdTech Matthew effect on its own, but it provides a framework for exploring how it might be mitigated for specific fields and learners.

10

LIFELONG LEARNING FOR ALL

Throughout this book, we have examined the distributed classroom from multiple angles, including the improvements it can support and the mechanisms that might be employed to realize it. In this final chapter, we take inventory of these different goals and mechanisms and then briefly reflect on the relevance this paradigm could have if adopted widely.

To restate the paradigm itself, a distributed classroom is a class experience distributed across time and space, preserving as many of the traditional synchronous co-located dynamics as possible. The traditional experience may include (depending on the course) classroom interactions, course assessments, grades and feedback, Q&A with the teacher, group work, team projects, and anything else that takes place in a classical offering of the course. Where elements of the traditional experience are incompatible with a particular student's needs—for example, if a student cannot commit to any co-located meetings because they do not live near the school—that student is asked only to sacrifice those portions of the experience that are absolutely dependent on those incompatible elements. The inability to attend in person would not demand sacrificing synchronous attendance if the student is able to commit to the latter without the former.

GOALS

The goals of the distributed classroom can be stated at several levels, from the immediate impact on specific students to the broad, societal impact on education as a whole. At the most immediate level, the goal of this paradigm is to open up complete educational opportunities to learners who would otherwise not have access to them due to their location, availability, or financial resources—lifelong learners especially. The term *complete* here has special relevance in differentiating the distributed classroom from other initiatives with similar aspirations. MOOCs, for instance, open educational opportunities to learners who would not have access to them; in the process, however, MOOCs sacrifice many elements of the authentic experience for the sake of scale, such as open-ended assessments, synchronous peer interactions, human feedback, and well-recognized credentials.

The distributed classroom, by contrast, strives to provide the complete educational opportunity, including those elements sacrificed by MOOCs and many other online learning environments. For example, in our online MSCS program, we have scaled human evaluation, feedback, and support and, with them, a recognized credential. In the process, though, we sacrifice other elements, such as synchronous interaction with classmates. This is a bold, necessary, and popular first step: it addresses both end points of the spectrum, creating opportunities for students who cannot commit to synchronous co-location, who are not competitive with selective, capped-enrollment programs, and who cannot or will not pay typical tuition costs. However, it may force some students to sacrifice more elements of the traditional experience than they need to based on their unique constraints; the distributed classroom aims to reintroduce these elements for students willing and able to invest into them.

This introduces another way to state the goal of the distributed classroom: the goal of the distributed classroom is to ask students to make the minimum necessary trade-off to fit the educational opportunity into their life. This involves offering multiple possible trade-offs that students may select depending on their own individual needs; thus, the classroom is distributed across multiple possible constraints regarding synchronicity and co-locatedness. If a student is unable to move to campus, we ask that person only to forgo those things that rely entirely on a presence on campus; this may mean interacting in real time with local cohorts instead of the original cohort or with remote cohorts instead of co-located cohorts. If the student remains able to commit to synchronous interactions at times when other students are similarly available, they may retain synchronous interaction as part of the experience. If the total compromise the student needs to make justifies awarding a credential, they receive that credential. If it does not, the student may still have access to a learning opportunity they did not have otherwise, albeit without the promise of course credit or a degree.

This relates to the more philosophical aspiration of the distributed classroom, with which we opened this book: to diminish the distinction between the online and traditional classrooms in the first place. If students are asked to make the minimal possible trade-off, where does the experience flip from traditional to online? Are students who share a classroom with a synchronous cohort watching a live remote class "online" students? What if the class is prerecorded, but the students still have a synchronous co-located cohort of their own? Thus, the distributed classroom may accomplish its goal of opening access to complete educational opportunities in a separate way: if it reduces the distinction between online and traditional classes, it may also reduce any perceived inferiority among remote experiences. Not only do new students have access to educational opportunities, but those opportunities may be considered more equivalent.

These initiatives all relate to broadening access; however, the distributed classroom paradigm has a relevance to content that is already generally accessible. For classes that are already offered at most universities (as well as classes offered at the K–12 level), the goal of the distributed classroom shifts to using the same mechanisms to improve pedagogy and student outcomes. Here, the mechanism focuses on producing strong content—not just instructional materials, but lesson plans, activities, and guidelines for interaction—that can be used in multiple classrooms. This serves two purposes: it reduces the pressure on individual teachers to excel at so many different functional roles, and it frees up more time for teachers to work with individual students, give specific feedback, and facilitate classroom collaboration rather than one-to-many lectures and presentations.

Within these broader objectives, the distributed classroom offers solutions to smaller problems as well. For instance, a problem with some approaches to online education—seen most prominently in MOOCs and MOOC-based degree programs—is that the high cost of content production can make it difficult and expensive to keep content regularly updated, let alone to be produced in the first place. In contrast, a traditional experience sees content tacitly updated every term as it must be redelivered. By making it easier to build distributed experiences on top of traditional classrooms, the distributed classroom aims to make achieving MOOC-like access a trivial additional effort and cost. In the process, it again makes the distributed experience more authentic because it presents the most up-to-date version of the course, just as an in-person student would receive.

METHODS

To accomplish those goals, the distributed classroom paradigm offers a number of possible methods. First, it notes that many of the components of the traditional experience that need to be distributed are actually already well suited for that change. Modern learning management systems have already distributed many components that used to be reserved for the physical classroom, such as assignment submission and Q&A. What remains to be distributed is largely the physical classroom experience.

The default approach to distributing the class experience that we offer here is classroom capture: record the class as it happens in person and use that as the foundation to build other distributed classrooms, in other places at either the same time or at different times. By using classroom capture, the content remains fresh and the workload remains relatively low compared to developing material from scratch. Classroom capture also preserves classroom interactions and in fact may expand them: students may benefit from the questions and discussions from the original recorded class but may also inject discussions and group work of their own at the corresponding points. These recorded classroom experiences are then combined with live support through teaching assistants to create new classroom experiences with other cohorts in other locations and at other times. Meanwhile, elements that were already distributed—such as asynchronous discussions on a course forum and assignment delivery and feedback through a learning management system—remain accessible to all cohorts, preserving both the remainder of the class experience and its credential-worthiness, if those are desired.

This is not the only method that needs to be used, of course. Custom-filmed material can have many strengths, such as taking greater advantage of the medium in which the material will be presented and avoiding constraints present in the physical classroom. Filming new material outside a classroom allows teachers to script experiences that allow much more time for individual practice embedded within lessons because it is not demanding scarce synchronous class time. It also allows teachers to rethink the underlying structure of their material as they are not forced into a certain scheduling slot. Custom-filmed material can be used to create a distributed classroom through the creation of local cohorts who interact with the material together, participate in their own TA-led discussions and group exercises, and form their own social learning community, as we saw with David's CS1301 course in Shenzhen, China in fall 2020.

Whether content is captured from a live presentation, produced from scratch for use in distributed environments, or created some other way (curated from existing content, perhaps?), the distributed classroom remains feasible so long as we focus on producing reusable artifacts and scaling individual interactions.

OUTCOMES

The goals are the immediate aspirations that the distributed classroom paradigm seeks to accomplish: expanding access, enhancing experiences, improving outcomes, and resolving existing challenges with remote learning. The methods provide the mechanisms to accomplish those goals. But if those methods are used to accomplish those goals, what then are the broader outcomes that may emerge?

The broader outcome of this paradigm would be access to complete educational opportunities for students around the world for whom the existing obstacles are too great. Their obstacle to access may be geographic; they may not be able to commit to physically moving closer to the location where the content is offered. This obstacle is addressed by the remote flexibility offered by the distributed classroom. Their obstacle may be synchronicity; they may not be able to commit to attendance at the time of day when the opportunity is available, or even to any regular time or schedule, due to their individual circumstances. This obstacle is addressed by the potential for asynchronous options. Their obstacle may be financial; education is expensive, and often only those who have already found some success can afford to invest in opportunities for more success (the Matthew effect). This obstacle is addressed by economies of scale: because more students are able to access the experience, the cost per student may drop tremendously. The remote nature of the program may also make it far easier to isolate expenses and ensure that each student is paying for their incremental costs, preserving scalability and sustainability while still dramatically reducing the cost to the student.

This access has the potential to benefit numerous people, but the largest audience is likely adult learners. With the speed at which the world is changing, everyone will need to become a lifelong learner. Learning that requires learners to return to a college campus, take time off from work, and pay tens of thousands of dollars in tuition is not feasible for the vast majority of potential students. When such learning can be pursued as part of life with a job and family living anywhere with internet access, then nearly anyone can become a lifelong learner. That may happen anyway through informal programs like MOOCs and boot camps, but if that learning can take place as an extension of higher education with its existing reach, connection to cutting-edge research, and trustworthy credentials, its impact may be far larger, far sooner.

Most important, this effort is not a zero-sum game. Universities may grow tremendously in size through online audiences, but that growth may come largely from learners who would not have otherwise been students in the first place. In a student's educational career, they may earn credentials from a half-dozen different universities rather than one or two, in addition to students newly able to attend college in the first place. This paradigm does not assign a static number of learners to a decreasing number of mega-universities, but rather radically increases the number of learners in the world in the first place.

This is where we are going twenty-five years from now. There are risks and pitfalls along the way: it is easy to see how these trends could lead to widespread conglomeration as we have seen with the emergence of megachurches and mega-media companies. These trends could lead to widespread centralization, putting curricula even more at the mercy of political agendas. Scale could lead to a self-defeating allegiance to routine assessment or dystopian evaluation through widespread data harvesting and monitoring.

But we can resist these efforts. We can push for a student-centric view on the future of online learning. We can continually see technological advancement as an opportunity to reinvest human time into improving outcomes. We can create authentic learning experiences that accommodate students with any combination of individual constraints. We can expand the diversity of content and perspectives available to learners around the globe.

In the process, we can change the world for the better. We can create lifelong learning for all.

ACKNOWLEDGMENTS

The ideas contained in this book have been developed over the course of a combined three decades of experience in higher education, and, more directly, over the past six-plus years of developing our online Master of Science in Computer Science program. The number of folks who have directly influenced the development of these ideas is thus far too high to list every significant person individually—and we know because we initially tried, but the full list would rival the length of this book itself. In addition to our friends and family who have put up with our rantings, we are especially grateful to the program's original visionaries Zvi Galil and Sebastian Thrun; to the dozens of faculty members, advisers, and other staff who work tirelessly to deliver a great experience; to the hundreds of teaching assistants who devote their precious time to helping their classmates; and to the tens of thousands of students who have been a part of this long journey. The ideas expressed in this book are the distillation of hundreds of conversations via email, chat, forum, and in person. We have learned so, so much from y'all; we are only convinced of the potential of these ideas because we have seen first-hand how y'all have embraced these opportunities and made them your own.

More specifically to this publication, we are eternally grateful to a large number of pre-readers and reviewers sharing feedback and pointing out dozens of typos in early drafts of this book, including Amber Felt, Amanda Madden, Jim Lohse, Cason Cherry, Erin Cherry, Alex Duncan, Jace van Auken, Eric Gregori, Stella Biderman, Ludwik Trammer, and Bobbie Eicher. We are also grateful to our publishing partners at the MIT Press for their diligent work shepherding us through this publication process, for their comprehensive notes and suggestions on earlier drafts, and for giving us the opportunity to share these ideas with the world in the first place. Finally, we are also grateful to Justin Reich and Nichole Pinkard for editing the Learning in Large-Scale Environments series, and for the downright incredible foresight they had to initiate this series a year before online learning became one of the most significant issues in the world in the wake of the COVID-19 pandemic.

NOTES

PREFACE

1. Peter C. Herman, "Online Learning Is Not the Future," *Inside Higher Ed*, June 10, 2020, http://bit.ly/IHE-Herman.

2. Rachel Hall, "'We Shouldn't Go Back to Lectures': Why Future Students Will Learn Online," *Guardian*, July 3, 2020, http://bit.ly/Guardian-Hall.

3. David Jesse, "Judge: Lawsuit against U-M for Switching to Online Classes Can Continue," *Detroit Free Press*, July 28, 2020, http://bit.ly/DFP-Jesse.

4. The Learning Network, "What Students Are Saying about Remote Learning," *New York Times*, April 20, 2020, http://bit.ly/NYT-TLN.

5. For more on Zvi Galil's visionary work in launching OMSCS, we recommend reading the *Wall Street Journal's* profile "The Man Who Made Online College Work" at https://on.wsj.com/3cWZ0JV, as well as the Marconi Society's profile "Forging an Accessible Path for Higher Education: Dr. Zvi Galil on Georgia Tech's Online Master's Program" at https://bit.ly/39LvPYb.

6. HyFlex is a model of teaching in which the classroom experience is broken up by three audiences: synchronous, co-located students;

synchronous, remote students; and asynchronous, remote students. For more on the HyFlex model, see, see Brian Beatty's ebook: https://edtechbooks.org/hyflex.

Flipped classrooms are a classroom model where content delivery and individual activities are "flipped": students consume course content prior to the synchronous class meeting through recorded lecture videos or textbooks, and synchronous class time is then spent on class discussions, groupwork, or assignments that historically may have been assigned as homework.

7. For more on the application of mRNA-based vaccines to older viruses, see: http://bit.ly/mRNAVaccine.

CHAPTER 1

1. Data from the National Center for Education Statistics, available at bit.ly/NCES18-19.

2. Articles and opinion pieces from students, teachers, and employers skeptical of online learning are abundant, especially in the wake of COVID-19. For more academic explorations of this skepticism, see Katherine J. Roberto and Andrew F. Johnson, "Employer Perceptions of Online versus Face-to-Face Degree Programs," *Journal of Employment Counseling* 56, no. 4 (2019): 180–189; Jennifer Willett, Chris Brown, and Leigh Ann Danzy-Bussell, "An Exploratory Study: Faculty Perceptions of Online Learning in Undergraduate Sport Management Programs," *Journal of Hospitality, Leisure, Sport and Tourism Education* 25 (2019): 100206; and Alicia Marie Godoy and Rebecca Pfeffer, "Student Perceptions of Online vs. Face-to-Face Learning in Criminal Justice: Considering the Ethical Implications of Disparities," in *Emerging Trends in Cyber Ethics and Education*, ed. A. Blackburn, I. Chen, and R. Pfeffer, 164–182 (Hershey, PA: IGI Global, 2019).

3. Lindsay McKenzie and Mark Lieberman, "Online Education Rules under the Microscope," *Inside Higher Ed*, January 16, 2019, http://bit.ly/IHE-McKenzie-Lieberman.

4. Details on PHEAASG's grants can be found here: http://bit.ly/PHEAASG.

5. The rules regarding international students, online classes, and campus closures changed frequently throughout 2020. One of the most controversial (and most quickly rescinded) rules is found here: http://bit.ly/2KTsflp.

6. Scot Jaschik, "Illinois Will End Residential M.B.A," *Inside Higher Ed*, May 28, 2019, http://bit.ly/IHE-Jaschik.

7. One of the main selling points of our online MSCS program is that the degree granted contains no such caveat; it is the same MSCS degree that on-campus students earn. This expresses our confidence that the program's learning outcomes will equal the residential program; we are willing to put the degree's full reputation behind the online delivery.

8. For a full exploration of the learning outcomes of the two versions of the class, see David Joyner, "Toward CS1 at Scale: Building and Testing a MOOC-for-Credit Candidate," in *Proceedings of the Fifth Annual ACM Conference on Learning at Scale* (New York: ACM, 2018); and David Joyner and Melinda McDaniel, "Replicating and Unraveling Performance and Behavioral Differences between an Online and a Traditional CS Course," in *Proceedings of the ACM Conference on Global Computing Education*, 157–163 (New York: ACM, 2019).

9. For information on Carnegie Mellon's results, see: M. Lovett, O. Meyer, and C. Thille, "The Open Learning Initiative: Measuring the Effectiveness of the OLI Statistics Course in Accelerating Student Learning," *Journal of Interactive Media in Education* (2008). Results from MIT's similar exploration can be found at Piotr F. Mitros, Khurram K. Afridi, Gerald J. Sussman, Chris J. Terman, Jacob K. White, Lyla Fischer, and Anant Agarwal, "Teaching Electronic Circuits Online: Lessons from MITx's 6.002 x on edX," in *Proceedings of the 2013 IEEE International Symposium on Circuits and Systems*, 2763–2766 (Piscataway, NJ: IEEE, 2013).

10. For more on the relationship between self-regulation and success in online classes, see Richard Lynch and Myron Dembo, "The Relationship between Self-Regulation and Online Learning in a Blended Learning Context," *International Review of Research in Open and Distributed Learning* 5, no. 2 (2004); Rachel L. Bradley, Blaine L. Browne, and Heather M. Kelley, "Examining the Influence of Self-Efficacy and Self-Regulation in Online Learning," *College Student Journal* 51, no. 4 (2017): 518–530; and Heather Kauffman, "A Review of Predictive Factors of Student Success in and Satisfaction with Online Learning," *Research in Learning Technology* 23 (2015).

11. For more on HBX, see http://bit.ly/Boston-Tucker.

12. For more on the Minerva Project and Forum, see http://bit.ly /MinervaProject.

13. For more on Peer Feedback, see http://www.peerfeedback.io.

14. For more on Peerceptiv, see http://peerceptiv.com.

15. For more on the idea of peripheral community, see David A. Joyner, "Peripheral and Semi-Peripheral Community: A New Design Challenge for Learning at Scale," in *Proceedings of the Seventh ACM Conference on Learning @ Scale*, 313–316 (New York: ACM, 2020).

16. Albert Mehrabian, *Nonverbal Communication* (New Brunswick, NJ: Transaction, 1972).

17. For more on the push toward hybrid classrooms in fall 2020, see http://nyti.ms/3cgH4K8.

18. For more on the HyFlex model, see Brian Beatty's ebook: https:// edtechbooks.org/hyflex.

19. The volume as a whole is: Amanda G. Madden, Lauren Margulieux, Robert S. Kadel, Richard A. Demillo, and Ashok K. Goel, eds., *Blended Learning in Practice: A Guide for Practitioners and Researchers* (Cambridge, MA: MIT Press, 2019). The specific chapters about CS1301: Introduction to Computing and one of our OMSCS classes are, respectively: David A. Joyner, "Building Purposeful Online Learning: Outcomes from Blending CS1," in *Blended Learning in Practice*, ed. Amanda G. Madden, Lauren Margulieux, Robert S. Kadel, Richard A. Demillo, and Ashok K. Goel, 45–68 (Cambridge, MA: MIT Press, 2019); and Ashok K. Goel, "Preliminary Evidence for the Benefits of Online Education and Blended Learning in a Large Artificial Intelligence Class," in *Blended Learning in Practice*, ed. Amanda G. Madden, Lauren Margulieux, Robert S. Kadel, Richard A. Demillo, and Ashok K. Goel, 69–96 (Cambridge, MA: MIT Press, 2019)

20. For more on Anant Agarwal's view on blended learning, see https://blog.edx.org/blended-learning-new-normal/.

21. For more on how HyFlex addressed hybrid learning, see http:// bit.ly/IHE-Lederman.

22. This article can be found here: http://bit.ly/AJC-Joyner.

23. For more on the resurgence of MOOCs after COVID-19, see http://nyti.ms/3iRe3WP.

24. For a snapshot of these criticisms, see Fred Martin, "Fight the MOOC-opalypse! and Reflections on the Aporia of Learning," *Journal of Computing Sciences in Colleges* 28, no. 6 (2013): 5–6; Ry Rivard, "Citing Disappointing Student Outcomes, San Jose State Pauses Work with Udacity," *Inside Higher Ed*, July 18, 2013, http://bit.ly/IHE-Rivard; René F. Kizilcec and Sherif Halawa, "Attrition and Achievement Gaps in Online Learning," in *Proceedings of the Second ACM Conference on Learning @ Scale*, 57–66 (New York: ACM, 2015); and Patrick McGhee, "Why Online Courses Can Never Totally Replace the Campus Experience," *Guardian*, November 19, 2012, http://bit.ly/Guardian-McGhee.

25. For more on the growth of MOOCs in the wake of the COVID-19 pandemic, see D. Shah, "By the Numbers: MOOCs During the Pandemic," *Class Central*, August 2020, https://www.classcentral.com/report/mooc-stats-pandemic/.

26. For more on Georgia Tech's OMSCS program, see David A. Joyner and Charles Isbell, "Master's at Scale: Five Years in a Scalable Online Graduate Degree," in *Proceedings of the Sixth ACM Conference on Learning @ Scale* (New York: ACM, 2019); David A. Joyner, Charles Isbell, Thad Starner, and Ashok Goel, "Five Years of Graduate CS Education Online and at Scale," in *Proceedings of the ACM Conference on Global Computing Education*, 16–22 (New York: ACM, 2019); and David A. Joyner, "Squeezing the Limeade: Policies and Workflows for Scalable Online Degrees," in *Proceedings of the Fifth Annual ACM Conference on Learning at Scale* (New York: ACM, 2018).

27. Massive college closings in the United States were predicted even before the COVID-19 pandemic; for more, see: Abigail Johnson Hess, "Harvard Business School Professor: Half of American Colleges Will Be Bankrupt in 10 to 15 Years," CNBC, August 30, 2018, http://bit.ly/CNBC-Hess; George Anders, "Sebastian Thrun's Online Goal: Act Where College Isn't Working," *Forbes*, April 3, 2013, http://bit.ly/Forbes-Anders; and Kellie Woodhouse, "Closures to Triple," *Inside Higher Ed*, September 28, 2015, http://bit.ly/IHE-Woodhouse.

28. There are dozens great books on how to teach online. Of the sample that we have read, we recommend *The Online Teaching Survival Guide: Simple and Practical Pedagogical Tips* by Judith V. Boettcher and Rita-Marie Conrad for guidance on how to teach online, and we recommend *Thrive Online: A New Approach to Building Expertise and Confidence as an Online Educator* by Shannon Riggs for a fantastic look at why teaching online can be so fun and impactful.

CHAPTER 2

1. Robert Johansen, *Groupware: Computer Support for Business Teams* (New York: Free Press, 1988).

CHAPTER 3

1. Mark Katz, *Capturing Sound: How Technology Has Changed Music* (Berkeley: University of California Press, 2010).

2. Dwayne D. Cox and William J. Morison, *The University of Louisville* (Lexington: University Press of Kentucky, 2014).

3. Joshua Goodman, Julia Melkers, and Amanda Pallais, "Can Online Delivery Increase Access to Education?" *Journal of Labor Economics* 37, no. 1 (2019): 1–34.

4. For more on the tuition discrepancy between online and face-to-face programs, see http://bit.ly/Forbes-Newton.

5. Phil Hill, "State of Higher Ed LMS Market for US and Canada: 2019 Mid-Year Edition," Phil on EdTech, August 15, 2019, http://bit.ly/PoE-Hill.

6. David A. Joyner, Wade Ashby, Liam Irish, Yeeling Lam, Jacob Langston, Isabel Lupiani, Mike Lustig, Paige Pettoruto, Dana Sheahen, Angela Smiley, Amy Bruckman, and Ashok Goel, "Graders as Meta-Reviewers: Simultaneously Scaling and Improving Expert Evaluation for Large Online Classrooms," in *Proceedings of the Third Annual ACM Conference on Learning at Scale* (New York: ACM, 2016).

7. David A. Joyner, "Scaling Expert Feedback: Two Case Studies," in *Proceedings of the Fourth ACM Conference on Learning @ Scale*, 71–80 (New York: ACM, 2017).

8. Alecia J. Carter, Alyssa Croft, Dieter Lukas, and Gillian M. Sandstrom, "Women's Visibility in Academic Seminars: Women Ask Fewer Questions Than Men," *PLoS One* 13, no. 9 (2018): e0202743.

9. Clifton A. Casteel, "Teacher–Student Interactions and Race in Integrated Classrooms," *Journal of Educational Research* 92, no. 2 (1998): 115–120.

10. Pooja Sankar, "Our Story," Piazza, 2014, https://piazza.com/about/story.

11. David A. Joyner, Ashok K. Goel, and Charles Isbell, "The Unexpected Pedagogical Benefits of Making Higher Education Accessible,"

in *Proceedings of the Third ACM Conference on Learning @ Scale*, 117–120 (New York: ACM, 2016).

12. Nathan Kling, Denny McCorkle, Chip Miller, and James Reardon, "The Impact of Testing Frequency on Student Performance in a Marketing Course," *Journal of Education for Business* 81, no. 2 (2005): 67–72; Daniel P. Murphy and Keith G. Stanga, "The Effects of Frequent Testing in an Income Tax Course: An Experiment," *Journal of Accounting Education* 12, no. 1 (1994): 27–41.

13. David's "Remote Teaching: Designing Trustworthy Assessments" can be downloaded from the On Teaching and Learning @ Georgia Tech blog here: https://blog.ctl.gatech.edu/2020/05/05/remote-teaching -designing-trustworthy-assessments.

14. For more on the types of assessments used in classes in the OMSCS program, see Bobbie Eicher and David A. Joyner, "Components of Assessments and Grading at Scale," in *Proceedings of the Eighth Annual ACM Conference on Learning at Scale* (New York: ACM, 2021).

15. For more on the benefits of peer learning, see David Boud, Ruth Cohen, and Jane Sampson, eds., *Peer Learning in Higher Education: Learning from and with Each Other* (London: Routledge, 2014); Chinmay E. Kulkarni, Michael S. Bernstein, and Scott R. Klemmer, "PeerStudio: Rapid Peer Feedback Emphasizes Revision and Improves Performance," in *Proceedings of the Second ACM Conference on Learning @ Scale*, 75–84 (New York: ACM, 2015); and Keith Topping, "Peer Assessment between Students in Colleges and Universities," *Review of Educational Research* 68, no. 3 (1998): 249–276.

16. Nancy Falchikov and Judy Goldfinch, "Student Peer Assessment in Higher Education: A Meta-Analysis Comparing Peer and Teacher Marks," *Review of Educational Research* 70, no. 3 (2000): 287–322.

17. Ashok Goel and David A. Joyner, "An Experiment in Teaching Cognitive Systems Online," *International Journal for Scholarship of Technology-Enhanced Learning*, no. 1 (2016).

18. Chris Piech, Lisa Yan, Lisa Einstein, Ana Saavedra, Baris Bozkurt, Eliska Sestakova, Ondrej Guth, and Nick McKeown, "Co-Teaching Computer Science across Borders: Human-Centric Learning at Scale," in *Proceedings of the Seventh ACM Conference on Learning @ Scale*, 103–113 (New York: ACM, 2020).

19. Thanaporn Patikorn and Neil T. Heffernan, "Effectiveness of Crowd-Sourcing On-Demand Assistance from Teachers in Online Learning Platforms," in *Proceedings of the Seventh ACM Conference on Learning @ Scale*, 115–124 (New York: ACM, 2020).

20. Margery Mayer and Vicki L. Phillips, *Primary Sources 2012: America's Teachers on the Teaching Profession*, (New York: Scholastic and Bill & Melinda Gates Foundation, 2012).

21. Rachel Krantz-Kent, "Teachers' Work Patterns: When, Where, and How Much Do US Teachers Work?" *Monthly Labor Review* 131 (2008): 52.

22. https://c21u.gatech.edu/cne/events-projects.

23. We have experimented with this idea in the form of virtual lecture halls in immersive virtual environments. For more on this, see: David A. Joyner, Akhil Mavilakandy, Ishaani Mittal, Denise Kutnick, and Blair MacIntyre, "Content-Neutral Immersive Environments for Cultivating Scalable Camaraderie," in *Proceedings of the Eighth Annual ACM Conference on Learning at Scale* (New York: ACM, 2021).

24. For more on Coursera Learning Hubs, see https://blog.coursera .org/introducing-coursera-learning-hubs-global/.

25. For more on Udacity Connect, see https://blog.udacity.com/2017 /08/udacity-connect-bay-area.html.

26. Michael E. Goldberg, "MOOCs and Meetups Together Make for Better Learning," *Conversation*, January 22, 2015http://bit.ly/ Conversation-Goldberg

27. For more about CopyrightX, see http://copyx.org.

28. For more on the wide variety of rigor, scope, and trustworthiness present in MOOCs, see James J. Lohse, Filipe Altoe, Jasmine Jose, Andrew M. Nowotarski, Farruhk Rahman, Robert C. Tuck, and David A. Joyner, "The Search for the MOOC Credit Hour," in *Proceedings of Learning with MOOCs VII*, 124–130 (Piscataway, NJ: IEEE, 2020), https://doi.org/10.1109/LWMOOCS50143.2020.9234379.

29. For more on the Georgia Tech atrium, see http://b.gatech.edu /3ppI4iT.

30. Kristen Fox, Gates Bryant, Nandini Srinivasan, Nicole Lin, and Anh Nguyen, "Time for Class—COVID-19 Edition Part 2: Planning for a Fall Like No Other," Tyton Partners, October 5, 2020, http://bit.ly /2MzUi9V.

CHAPTER 4

1. Philip J. Guo, Juho Kim, and Rob Rubin, "How Video Production Affects Student Engagement: An Empirical Study of MOOC Videos," in *Proceedings of the First ACM Conference on Learning @ Scale*, 41–50 (New York: ACM, 2014).

2. David A. Joyner, Qiaosi Wang, Suyash Thakare, Shan Jing, Ashok Goel, and Blair MacIntyre, "The Synchronicity Paradox in Online Education," in *Proceedings of the Seventh ACM Conference on Learning @ Scale*, 15–24 (New York: ACM, 2020).

3. For more on the Civil War and Reconstruction XSeries, see https:// www.edx.org/xseries/civil-war-reconstruction.

4. Ashok Goel, "Preliminary Evidence for the Benefits of Online Education and Blended Learning in a Large Artificial Intelligence Class," in *Blended Learning in Practice: A Guide for Practitioners and Researchers*, ed. Amanda G. Madden, Lauren Margulieux, Robert S. Kadel, Richard A. Demillo, and Ashok K. Goel (Cambridge, MA: MIT Press, 2018).

5. In the United States, high school is typically a four-year education for students from ages fourteen to eighteen, divided into grades 9 through 12.

6. In the United States, counties are a subdivision of states. Georgia has 159 counties; 29 make up the metropolitan Atlanta area surrounding the state's capital.

7. David A. Joyner, Qiaosi Wang, Suyash Thakare, Shan Jing, Ashok Goel, and Blair MacIntyre, "The Synchronicity Paradox in Online Education," in *Proceedings of the Seventh ACM Conference on Learning @ Scale*, 15–24 (New York: ACM, 2020).

8. Azad Ali and David Smith, "Comparing Social Isolation Effects on Students' Attrition in Online versus Face-to-Face Courses in Computer Literacy," *Issues in Informing Science and Information Technology* 12, no. 1 (2015): 11–20; Shelley Bibeau, "Social Presence, Isolation, and Connectedness in Online Teaching and Learning: From the Literature to Real Life," *Journal of Instruction Delivery Systems* 15, no. 3 (2001): 35–39; Karen Frankola, "Why Online Learners Drop Out," *Workforce* 80, no. 10 (2001): 52–61; Kyungbin Kwon, Daehoon Han, Eun-Jun Bang, and Satara Armstrong, "Feelings of Isolation and Coping Mechanism in Online Learning Environments: A Case Study of Asian International Students," *International Journal of Learning* 17,

no. 2 (2010); Alfred P. Rovai and Mervyn J. Wighting, "Feelings of Alienation and Community among Higher Education Students in a Virtual Classroom," *Internet and Higher Education* 8, no. 2 (2005): 97–110; and Pedro A. Willging and Scott D. Johnson, "Factors That Influence Students' Decision to Drop Out of Online Courses," *Journal of Asynchronous Learning Networks* 13, no. 3 (2009): 115–127.

9. Barbara Ericson, Michal Armoni, Judith Gal-Ezer, Deborah Seehorn, Chris Stephenson, and Fran Trees, "Ensuring Exemplary Teaching in an Essential Discipline: Addressing the Crisis in Computer Science Teacher Certification," *Final Report of the CSTA Teacher Certification Task Force* (New York: ACM, 2008); and Miranda C. Parker, "An Analysis of Supports and Barriers to Offering Computer Science in Georgia Public High Schools," PhD diss., Georgia Institute of Technology, 2019.

10. David A. Joyner, Qiaosi Wang, Suyash Thakare, Shan Jing, Ashok Goel, and Blair MacIntyre, "The Synchronicity Paradox in Online Education," in *Proceedings of the Seventh ACM Conference on Learning @ Scale*, 15–24 (New York: ACM, 2020).

11. David A. Joyner, Ashok K. Goel, and Charles Isbell, "The Unexpected Pedagogical Benefits of Making Higher Education Accessible," in *Proceedings of the Third ACM Conference on Learning @ Scale*, 117–120 (New York: ACM, 2016).

12. For a full exploration of student motivations for enrolling, see David A. Joyner, "Building Purposeful Online Learning: Outcomes from Blending CS1," in *Blended Learning in Practice: A Guide for Practitioners and Researchers*, ed. Amanda Madden, Lauren Margulieux, Robert S. Kadel, Richard A. Demillo, and Ashok K. Goel (Cambridge, MA: MIT Press, 2018).

13. For more on Michael Schatz's Introductory Physics I with Laboratory MOOC, see the following article in *Nature*: M. Mitchell Waldrop, "Education Online: The Virtual Lab," *Nature News* 499, no. 7458 (2013): 268.

14. David A. Joyner, Qiaosi Wang, Suyash Thakare, Shan Jing, Ashok Goel, and Blair MacIntyre, "The Synchronicity Paradox in Online Education," in *Proceedings of the Seventh ACM Conference on Learning @ Scale*, 15–24 (New York: ACM, 2020).

CHAPTER 5

1. For public access to this course content, see http://omscs.gatech .edu/current-courses.

2. Philip J. Guo, Juho Kim, and Rob Rubin, "How Video Production Affects Student Engagement: An Empirical Study of MOOC Videos," in *Proceedings of the First ACM Conference on Learning @ Scale*, 41–50 (New York: ACM, 2014).

3. Fiona M. Hollands and Devayani Tirthali, "Resource Requirements and Costs of Developing and Delivering MOOCs," *International Review of Research in Open and Distributed Learning* 15, no. 5 (2014): 113–133; Jeffrey M. Stanton and S. Suzan J. Harkness, "Got MOOC? Labor Costs for the Development and Delivery of an Open Online Course," *Information Resources Management Journal* 27, no. 2 (2014): 14–26; and Paul M. Nissenson and Angela C. Shih, "MOOC on a Budget: Development and Implementation of a Low-Cost MOOC at a State University," *ASEE Computers in Education Journal* 7, no. 1 (2016): 8.

4. For more on peer instruction, see Catherine H. Crouch and Eric Mazur, "Peer Instruction: Ten Years of Experience and Results," *American Journal of Physics* 69, no. 9 (2001): 970–977.

5. David A. Joyner, Ashok K. Goel, and Charles Isbell, "The Unexpected Pedagogical Benefits of Making Higher Education Accessible," in *Proceedings of the Third ACM Conference on Learning @ Scale*, 117–120 (New York: ACM, 2016).

6. For more on Coursera for Campus, see https://www.coursera.org /campus/.

7. For more on edX Online Campus, see https://campus.edx.org/.

8. For more on Coursera's CourseMatch, see https://blog.coursera .org/coursera-launches-coursematch/.

9. For more on Universal Design for Learning, see http://udlguide lines.cast.org/.

10. George Barna, *The State of the Church: 2002* (Ventura, CA: Issachar Resources, 2002).

11. Michelle Obama, "Remarks by the First Lady at the "Let's Move!" Launch Anniversary Speech to Parents at North Point Community Church in Alpharetta, Georgia," American Presidency Project, February 9, 2011, http://bit.ly/APP-Obama.

12. Michelle Boorstein, "Church Donations Have Plunged Because of the Coronavirus. Some Churches Won't Survive," *Washington Post*, April 24, 2020, http://wapo.st/36ja4gy.

CHAPTER 6

1. David A. Joyner, Charles Isbell, Thad Starner, and Ashok Goel, "Five Years of Graduate CS Education Online and at Scale," in *Proceedings of the ACM Conference on Global Computing Education*, 16–22 (New York: ACM, 2019).

2. For a demonstration of this implementation, see https://vimeo.com/438671425.

3. For more on Thrun's prediction, see http://bit.ly/Forbes-Anders.

4. For more on how assessments in our program are evaluated, see Bobbie Eicher and David A. Joyner, "Components of Assessments and Grading at Scale," in *Proceedings of the Eighth Annual ACM Conference on Learning at Scale* (New York: ACM, 2021).

5. For more on the benefits of relatively novice teachers, see Jonathan Eckert, *The Novice Advantage: Fearless Practice for Every Teacher* (Corwin Press, 2016); and Megan Madigan Peercy, Tabitha Kidwell, Megan DeStefano Lawyer, Johanna Tigert, Daisy Fredricks, Karen Feagin, and Megan Stump, "Experts at Being Novices: What New Teachers Can Add to Practice-Based Teacher Education Efforts," *Action in Teacher Education* 42, no. 3 (2020): 212–233.

6. David A. Joyner, "Scaling Expert Feedback: Two Case Studies," in *Proceedings of the Fourth ACM Conference on Learning @ Scale*, 71–80 (New York: ACM, 2017).

7. Oliver Cameron, "How a Udacity Graduate Earns $11k a Month Reviewing Code," *Medium*, May 12, 2015, http://bit.ly/Medium-Cameron.

8. For more on the conditions under which peer assessment can be as reliable as expert assessment, see Nancy Falchikov and Judy Goldfinch, "Student Peer Assessment in Higher Education: A Meta-Analysis Comparing Peer and Teacher Marks," *Review of Educational Research* 70, no. 3 (2000): 287–322.

9. For efforts toward augmenting peer grading with artificial intelligence, see Chris Piech, Jonathan Huang, Zhenghao Chen, Chuong

Do, Andrew Ng, and Daphne Koller, "Tuned Models of Peer Assessment in MOOCs," in *Proceedings of the Sixth International Conference on Educational Data Mining* (Massachusetts: International Educational Data Mining Society, 2013); Pushkar Kolhe, Michael L. Littman, and Charles L. Isbell, "Peer Reviewing Short Answers using Comparative Judgment," in *Proceedings of the Third ACM Conference on Learning @ Scale*, 241–244 (New York: ACM, 2016); and Fei Mi and Dit Yan Yeung, "Probabilistic Graphical Models for Boosting Cardinal and Ordinal Peer Grading in MOOCs," in *Proceedings of the Twenty-Ninth AAAI Conference on Artificial Intelligence*, 454 (Palo Alto, CA: AAAI, 2015).

10. Joshua Goodman, Julia Melkers, and Amanda Pallais, "Can Online Delivery Increase Access to Education?" *Journal of Labor Economics* 37, no. 1 (2019): 1–34.

11. Drew DeSilver, "US Students' Academic Achievement Still Lags That of Their Peers in Many Other Countries," Pew Research Center, February 15, 2017, http://pewrsr.ch/2KXBcdC.

12. Gregory A. Strizek, Steve Tourkin, and Ebru Erberber, "Teaching and Learning International Survey (TALIS) 2013," US Technical Report NCES 2015–010, National Center for Education Statistics, 2014.

13. Benjamin S. Bloom, J. Thomas Hastings, and George F. Madaus, *Handbook on Formative and Summative Evaluation of Student Learning* (New York: McGraw-Hill, 1971).

14. For one such study, see https://www.iftf.org/realizing2030-future ofwork/.

CHAPTER 7

1. Joshua Goodman, Julia Melkers, and Amanda Pallais, "Can Online Delivery Increase Access to Education?" *Journal of Labor Economics* 37, no. 1 (2019): 1–34.

2. For one example, see K. Carey, "An Online Education Breakthrough? A Master's Degree for a Mere $7,000," *New York Times*, September 29, 2016, http://nyti.ms/2NHoZe6.

3. For more on the equality of learning outcomes between in-person and online sections of a class, see Ashok Goel and David A. Joyner, "An Experiment in Teaching Cognitive Systems Online," *International Journal for Scholarship of Technology-Enhanced Learning*, no. 1 (2016).

4. For more on the intersection of identity and experiences in computing and other STEM fields, especially among underrepresented groups, see Jane Margolis, Rachel Estrella, Joanna Goode, Jennifer Jellison Holme, and Kimberly Nao, *Stuck in the Shallow End: Education, Race, and Computing* (Cambridge, MA: MIT Press, 2017); Sapna Cheryan, Allison Master, and Andrew N. Meltzoff, "Cultural Stereotypes as Gatekeepers: Increasing Girls' Interest in Computer Science and Engineering by Diversifying Stereotypes," *Frontiers in Psychology* 6 (2015): 49; Joanna Goode, "The Digital Identity Divide: How Technology Knowledge Impacts College Students," *New Media & Society* 12, no. 3 (2010): 497–513; and LaVar J. Charleston, Ryan P. Adserias, Nicole M. Lang, and Jerlando F. L. Jackson, "Intersectionality and STEM: The Role of Race and Gender in the Academic Pursuits of African American Women in STEM," *Journal of Progressive Policy & Practice* 2, no. 3 (2014): 273–293.

5. David A. Joyner and Charles Isbell, "Master's at Scale: Five Years in a Scalable Online Graduate Degree," in *Proceedings of the Sixth ACM Conference on Learning @ Scale* (New York: ACM, 2019).

6. Amy S. Bruckman, "Gender Swapping on the Internet," in *High Noon on the Electronic Frontier: Conceptual Issues in Cyberspace*, ed. Peter Ludlow, 317–326 (Cambridge, MA: MIT Press, 1996); Tracie Farrell, Miriam Fernandez, Jakub Novotny, and Harith Alani, "Exploring Misogyny across the Manosphere in Reddit," in *Proceedings of the 10th ACM Conference on Web Science*, 87–96 (New York: ACM, 2019); Lindsey Wotanis and Laurie McMillan, "Performing Gender on YouTube: How Jenna Marbles Negotiates a Hostile Online Environment," *Feminist Media Studies* 14, no. 6 (2014): 912–928; and Jenny Preece and Diane Maloney-Krichmar, "Online Communities: Focusing on Sociability and Usability," in *Handbook of Human–Computer Interaction: Fundamentals, Evolving Technologies and Emerging Applications* (3rd ed.), ed. Andrew Sears and Julie A. Jacko, 596–620 (Mahwah, NJ: Lawrence Erlbaum Associates, 2003).

7. https://www.cs.washington.edu/academics/pmp/overview/tuition.

8. https://gradschool.princeton.edu/costs-funding/tuition-and-costs.

9. Kabir Abdulmajeed, David A. Joyner, and Christine McManus, "Challenges of Online Learning in Nigeria," in *Proceedings of the Seventh ACM Conference on Learning @ Scale*, 417–420 (New York: ACM, 2020).

10. David A. Joyner, Qiaosi Wang, Suyash Thakare, Shan Jing, Ashok Goel, and Blair MacIntyre, "The Synchronicity Paradox in Online Education," in *Proceedings of the Seventh ACM Conference on Learning @ Scale*, 15–24 (New York: ACM, 2020).

CHAPTER 8

1. Elissa Nadworny and Julie Depenbrock, "Today's College Students Aren't Who You Think They Are," *NPR: Changing Face of College* (2018).

2. For more, see Zachary Jason, "The Battle over Charter Schools," *Harvard Ed. Magazine*, 2017, http://bit.ly/2KUDEBv.

3. James W. Fonseca and Charles P. Bird, "Under the Radar: Branch Campuses Take Off," *University Business* 10, no. 10 (2007): 8–14.

4. One example of an organization already offering this is A Place Beyond; read about them at https://aplacebeyond.com.

CHAPTER 9

1. The higher ratio, one TA per fifty students, is used for our online graduate-level classes.

2. For more on Thrun's prediction, see http://bit.ly/Forbes-Anders.

3. Tobias Steiner, "Under the Macroscope: Convergence in the US Television Market between 2000 and 2014," *Image* 22 (2015): 4–21.

4. MasterClass, a MOOC provider specializing in recruiting celebrities such as Samuel L. Jackson and Gordon Ramsay to teach its classes, recently launched Outlier.org with this goal specifically in mind. Outlier.org offers foundational courses such as Calculus I and Intro to Psychology that qualify for credit from the University of Pittsburgh, which then may be transferred to other universities.

5. Richard A. DeMillo, *Revolution in Higher Education: How a Small Band of Innovators Will Make College Accessible and Affordable* (Cambridge, MA: MIT Press, 2015).

6. Justin Reich, *Failure to Disrupt: Why Technology Alone Can't Transform Education* (Cambridge, MA: Harvard University Press, 2020).

7. Nathan Kling, Denny McCorkle, Chip Miller, and James Reardon, "The Impact of Testing Frequency on Student Performance in a Marketing Course," *Journal of Education for Business* 81, no. 2 (2005):

67–72; and Daniel P. Murphy and Keith G. Stanga, "The Effects of Frequent Testing in an Income Tax Course: An Experiment," *Journal of Accounting Education* 12, no. 1 (1994): 27–41.

8. David Joyner and Alex Duncan, "Eroding Investment in Repeated Peer Review: A Reaction to Unrequited Aid?" in *Proceedings of the 18th Annual Hawaii International Conference on Education* (Honolulu: Hawaii International Conference on Education, 2020).

9. David A. Joyner and Charles Isbell, "Master's at Scale: Five Years in a Scalable Online Graduate Degree," in *Proceedings of the Sixth ACM Conference on Learning @ Scale* (New York: ACM, 2019).

10. Paloma Esquivel, Howard Blume, Ben Poston, and Julia Barajas, "A Generation Left Behind? Online Learning Cheats Poor Students, *Times* Survey Finds," *Los Angeles Times*, August 13, 2020, http://lat.ms /3cinHjV; and Dana Goldstein, Adam Popescu, and Nikole Hannah-Jones, "As School Moves Online, Many Students Stay Logged Out," *New York Times*, April 6, 2020, http://nyti.ms/2YyJrA9.

11. For more on Live2Coursera, see https://blog.coursera.org/live2 coursera-coming-soon-as-a-zoom-app/.

INDEX